THE ANNUAL YEARS

A Celebration of the World Distributor *Doctor Who* Annuals

Paul Magrs

THE ANNUAL YEARS

ISBN: 9781909031258

Published by Obverse Books, Edinburgh

Cover Design: Andrew-Mark Thompson

First published May 2014. This edition: November 2019

9 8 7 6 10 5 4 3 2

With special thanks to Stanley Freeman, Jason Elford, Mike Wild, Paul Scoones, John White, Adam Bullock, Keith Miller, Paul Castle, Steve Lyons, Clive Hopwood, Colin Brockhurst, Gareth Kavanagh, Nick Campbell, Jamie Griffiths, David Howe, Neil Perryman, Jeremy Hoad, Bernard Socks, Panda, Kenny Smith, Julie Douglas, George and Fiona Mann and Ian Phillip Snell.

Thanks to Mark Worgan for the 1972 Annual.

In this volume, the term 'Dr. Who' is used when referencing the character in the Annuals, and Doctor Who when referencing the character on television. The name of the TV show itself is always italicised. Otherwise usage has been left as is for interviews, story titles etc.

CONTENTS

Introduction

The usual story is that the Doctor Who Annuals published by World Distributors between 1965 and 1985 have basically nothing to do with the television show called *Doctor Who*. They were an example of shoddy, exploitative tie-in merchandise produced for the Christmas Market. They boasted poor art in both strips and text stories, featuring terrible likenesses of the TV stars. They contained bizarre and unreadable stories which bore very little resemblance to the Doctor's TV adventures. They were produced by writers and artists who seemed to know nothing about The Show and the work they created had very little merit at all.

However…

I never quite believed that. I read and re-read some of these books all through my childhood and recently I've been reading them again, and I've been chasing up the editions I never had and filling in the gaps. What I'm finding is that these extraordinary books are like weird, grotesque shadow-versions of the Show we recognise. They are mutations haunting the wilderness between the domed, protected cities of Canonicity. The world of the Annuals is odder, darker, madder, more psychedelic and surreal. These are adventures in a wilder, destabilised universe. The cosiness of what we recognise as *Doctor Who* has gone.

The received wisdom I'd like to turn on its head is that the Doctor Who Annuals are rubbish. I don't think that's at all true. I think that people – fans – have stopped reading them. We have, for a long time, been unable to see past our own assumptions about their contents and their worth.

I think that the Doctor Who Annuals from the Sixties, Seventies and Eighties are fabulously bizarre. They are an essential part of the patch-worked fabric of the Doctor's expanded universe of adventures. They are neglected and underexposed and unread, but to a certain class of *Doctor Who* fan, they are also terribly familiar. Several generations had them to puzzle and pore over. In the years before we had DVDs, videos, *Doctor Who* magazines, novels, and novelisations one of the few tangible *Doctor Who* souvenirs we had were the Annuals.

This was the stranger, wider, deeper galaxy that we could hold in our hands: the whole thing was squashed between pasteboard covers. These books were our Christmas Specials in those far-gone days and they have been neglected and given a rough deal, I think. Collectors want them still, I guess, but do they want them to read, or just to let them accrue monetary value?

I have discovered in myself a need to explore the perplexing, psychedelic, illogical world of *Doctor Who*'s Annuals. Or to re-explore a Neuronic Nightmare Zone that unnerved me more with its sheer strangeness than *Doctor Who* in any other medium ever did.

The Making of Doctor Who

On the 16th November 1964, Walter Tuckwell of Walter Tuckwell & Associates – a London-based merchandising agent – wrote to J. Hargreaves of BBC Publications on Marylebone High Street, with a brief outline of what a Doctor Who Annual for children might consist of, were it to be published the following year by one of the companies he represented, World Distributors of Manchester. He enclosed a rough cover image and breakdown of the possible contents and production details.

World Distributors, he wrote, would like to employ the actual script writers from the TV show. Right at the very start the Annual was going to reflect what *Doctor Who* was like on TV. Fidelity was the key. They'd pay William Hartnell fifty guineas to use his image on the cover, and 'interest' articles between the stories would fill the reader in on the background of the monsters – they might be called 'The Home of the Voord', 'The Home of the Daleks' and so on.

Evelyn M. Thomas from the BBC's publicity department wrote back on November 26th to say that the Head of Serials thought this preliminary work was 'splendid' and that it was hoped that 'the Corporation will get some financial benefit from the enormous sale(s) that will result.'

In the event, the very first Doctor Who Annual sold extremely well: over two hundred thousand copies when it was published, a year later.

Some of those responsible for TV scripts were contacted, though as things turned out, the Annual would be put together by a combination of non-TV writers: in-house World Distributor employees and freelancers. Peter Newman's agent wrote to World Distributors to inform them that, owing to a recent skull fracture, he wouldn't be able to contribute a story, even for a payment of fifty guineas (the agent seemed to think it would be some kind of adaptation or re-telling of his TV serial, 'The Sensorites.') At the same time, she wanted to know what kind of fee Newman could expect for the use of his alien creations in a story written by another author. This letter must be one of the earliest examples – outside of Terry Nation (whose Daleks were not covered by the BBC's agreement with World, and who had a separate agreement with Panther/Souvenir for publications such as *The Dalek Book*) – of an author asserting his copyright over elements of his creative contribution to the world of *Doctor Who*.

R. S. Hargreaves of BBC Publicity wrote to Tuckwell in February 1965 approving of draft versions of some of the stories, written by J. L Morrissey ('Our writer', as World Distributors refer in some of the correspondence to their staff scribe.) The BBC man then took the opportunity to remind Tuckwell that individual monster permissions must be sought from the various copyright holders. The Annual would be able to utilise the companion characters of Ian, Barbara, Susan or Vicki but further permissions and fees would have to be paid to the actors for the use of their likenesses.

Tuckwell was told by the BBC that he must make World Distributors in Manchester aware of the mongrelised nature of the Show's constituent elements. The individual elements that made up *Doctor Who* on TV were, then, from the very start, an imbroglio of tangled rights and separate credits. All that World actually used, in the event, were the Tardis itself and the very name and idea of *Doctor Who*.

And, for more than twenty years, that's all that World Distributors really needed. Famous monsters appeared in their stories early on, but the Annual writers (a faceless, numberless, unnamed, largely uncredited team) were happiest inventing their own, new ones. TV companions drifted through the hardbound pages and through the decades, but they often looked rather unlike their TV counterparts, depending on whether permissions for likenesses had been sought or paid for. As the Annual evolved as an entity in its own right, it seemed to need very little creative sustenance from the TV show. All it needed was the Tardis and the very idea of the Doctor. It didn't even really need to have the likeness of the current Doctor on TV. I would argue that its creative heights came when the Annual was actually furthest from its basis in the famous teatime serial on BBC TV.

Right from the start, what *Doctor Who* actually consisted of was quite hard for the BBC to pin down. Did it really boil down to just the Tardis and the idea of the Doctor himself? Even so, as early as March 1965 they were providing frowning editorial notes concerning these concepts.

On 17th March the Editorial Assistant from BBC Publicity – Ann Fitch – was giving bullet-pointed feedback to World Distributors.

"There are no weapons aboard the Tardis.
"The Dr. would never call himself Dr. Who. This title arose because no one knew his name.
"Dr. Who originally came from an unknown planet, not Earth.
"Page 22. Not true."

There is something very pleasing about this very fussy notational language trying to cope with the ambiguities and complexities of *Doctor Who*. In some ways this letter is the opening salvo in the very first of the Continuity Wars of *Doctor Who*, as Editorial Assistant Ann Fitch tries to lay down a little canon for the Mancunian anarchists (who had the Doctor introducing himself to everyone quite happily as Dr. Who, arming himself to the teeth and telling everyone that he comes from Planet Earth and left there some fifty years ago.)

Whatever Ann Fitch said in 1964, the World Distributors Annuals gleefully promulgated the wonderful myth that the Doctor is actually called Dr. Who (with or without a period after Dr) and the name is used interchangeably with the more proper soubriquet 'Doctor' (with or without a capital D) all the way until 1980 or so, when – presumably – John Nathan-Turner's BBC production office started to exert tighter control over merchandise.

I love the fact that Ann Fitch crossly types out a list of what is canonical and irrefutable in 1965, and World Distributors happily ignore it. Letters go back and forth between London and Manchester throughout the Sixties and Seventies about putting the 'Who' in 'Doctor Who.'

Ann passed the stories to then TV script editor Dennis Spooner for checking. He – presumably hugely busy with the Show – let them go by with nary a hitch in April. He did make one comment, though, to the effect that Doctor Who would never refer to himself as such. This is because Doctor Who 'does not know his own name.' This is a very intriguing factoid from the man who was currently in charge of all things canonical. Did he see Doctor Who as an amnesiac?

It was John Pemberton, Managing Director of World Distributors, who was held accountable for this bandying about of made-up names. Mr Hargreaves at BBC publicity wrote to him following Spooner's edict, informing the northerner that 'Doctor Who does not know his own name and is thus only referred to as 'Dr. Who.' He added: 'Perhaps you would be good enough to make the necessary amendments.'

It seems to me, from perusing these letters, to be a question of emphasis. Spooner is saying that when the Doctor is called Dr. Who it's always by other people, and not himself ('only *referred to* as 'Dr. Who.') When Hargreaves passes this message along verbatim, the stress is read differently. Spooner stresses 'referred to' but World Distributors reads the stress on 'only' ('*only* referred to as 'Dr. Who') – and henceforward the Doctor gets conscientiously referred to as 'Dr. Who' by just about everyone. Perhaps their adherence to the use of 'Who' as a surname wasn't so much anarchistic as it was a very slight misreading of memos?

Later in April BBC Publications was back on the case. Doctor (or Dr.) Who would never call himself Dr. Who. This name only cropped up because *no one* knew his name.

By now this was starting to feel less like an obsession than a neurosis. Did anyone ever know why he was called Dr. Who, and by whom?

The first Annual did extremely well, and everyone was pleased. A second Annual was commissioned and by October 1965 World Distributors were getting their next batch of editorial notes from BBC Publicity. Again, the comments and quibbles are very illuminating.

Violence seemed to be very much on the BBC's mind in 1965. They were keen to point out that, although Dr. Who carried a walking stick, he never used it as a weapon. It couldn't be utilised in a story as a 'sort of super ray gun,' for example. The Show's Story Editor Donald Tosh suggested that, instead of wielding death via his walking stick, Dr. Who might instead induce paralysis in his intended victims?

Our hero's apparent indestructibility was at issue, too, in 1965. (The Annuals were prepared with a lead time of at least twelve months and the convention was that each Annual was named for the year following publication. Hence, the Annual being written and edited in the latter half of 1965 and first half of 1966 is the one published in September 1966 and which we know of as the 1967 Annual.) The BBC informed World Distributors that Dr. Who was not indestructible. He would not be able to withstand death or such things as 'liquid fire or high-voltage electricity.' Indeed, such things would be dangerous to imply, since it might lead small children to think themselves impervious to such lethal forces, too.

Other points raised include details as to how the Tardis manifests itself in new surroundings. It does not 'gyrate like a spinning top', it materialises and dematerialises. The Tardis only spins around in the TV Comic strip because that is a different convention, and under separate licence. Also, the Tardis materialises of its own accord. The Doctor has absolutely no power over this whatsoever.

And there was a new variation on the business of being called 'Who': 'In descriptive passages you can say 'Dr. Who' but where he is addressed, it is only as 'Doctor.' The answer to the quandary in 1965 seemed to be that you can call him Dr. Who – only don't do it to his face.

These were established precepts for the Show and the character at that time: these fiddly details. If he carried an umbrella it wouldn't be one like James

Bond had. Dr. Who understands every language, but the Tardis helps translate foreign languages for his companions – and us. It's an absurd, impossible programme, that made up its own rules and messed with its own established continuity over decades of evolution, but here we have harried BBC employees such as Evelyn M. Thomas of the Publicity Department having to lay down the law on behalf of Donald Tosh. She has to tell World Distributors / Walter Tuckwell Associates that the Doctor has a 'super ring' which can nobble all kinds of locks and traps. And his trousers are not pin-stripe: they are 'sponge bag' type trousers. From such tiny incidentals is the fabric of a fictional universe woven and the level of detail observed is pleasing, if a little bizarre, given the wild and woolly nature of some of the stories themselves.

In December 1965 a story called 'The Terror Flash (of Cygnus)' came under extreme fire from BBC Publications. Not only was it 'abominably written', it 'horrified' the TV programme's Story Editor because the writer seemed to have no knowledge of the Doctor or how the Tardis worked. If it was published it would be liable to 'muddle' the young followers of the Show. The Story Editor wanted 'The Terror Flash' removed since it was well below the standard expected by the BBC.

A bigger crisis than finding replacement stories hit World Distributors just before Christmas 1965. M.D John Pemberton was concerned to hear that his Production Manager had read in the *Manchester Evening News* that William Hartnell was about to leave the series. World Distributors were going to be stuck with a whole lot of books poised to hit the market for Christmas 1966 with the face of a departed Doctor on their covers. They were going to look 'very old hat indeed', if the headlines had it right.

Pemberton wrote to his bosses at Walter Tuckwell, keen for them to find out more from the BBC. When was Hartnell leaving? Who would replace him, and how? It's interesting to note that there's no hesitation over the idea of the lead actor being simply replaced. This bookman simply wants to know which face should go on the cover of next year's Annual. It's our current received wisdom that the replacement of Hartnell with Troughton was, at the time, revolutionary in concept, and yet there wasn't even an eyebrow raised in Manchester in Christmas 1965. They didn't care about rejuvenation or regeneration particularly. They just wanted to know whether next year they were going to be flogging Annuals past their sell-by date.

Geoffrey Ward at Walter Tuckwell & Associates duly wrote to R. S Hargreaves at BBC Publications on the 21st of December, enclosing a Christmas gift of the text of what presumably was 'Doctor Who and the Invasion from Space', which World Distributors were publishing as a 'Colour Story Book' in 1966, separate from, but similar to, the Annuals. He also enclosed the clipping from the Manchester Evening News, seeking clarification about the Doctor's rumoured change of face. Was it actually going to happen? The article seemed rather ambiguous, but could it be that Hartnell was about to leave? The article contained a quote from Hartnell himself, saying that though the show had been scheduled to run for six weeks in the first instance, he still imagined it would go on for five years. In the quote he sounded confident that the show would go on without him in the role.

John Pemberton and others in Lever Street in Manchester were understandably concerned, that Christmas, about the possible retirement – or mysterious changes – in the offing for Doctor Who.

1966 began well. The Show's producer wrote to World Distributors, praising J. L. Morrissey's story, 'The Diagrams of Power', (later renamed 'Doctor Who and the Invasion from Space' and published as a single volume.) Story Editor Donald Tosh opined that he wanted it put on record that the story in question was of 'a writing standard higher than any of the various stories sent... for publication permission' during his time on the Show. This must have been pleasing for John Pemberton and the staff in Lever Street, Manchester, after a few sharp critiques and denied permissions of the previous year, and the Yuletide uncertainty over whose face should be on the cover of next year's Annual.

R.S Hargreaves passed on Tosh's compliments – making them slightly less fulsome in the process – and also said that he couldn't comment on the status of Mr Hartnell's contract with the Corporation.

Come April 1966, the increasingly severe-sounding Evelyn M. Thomas of BBC Publications was commenting on the artwork for 'Doctor Who and the Invasion from Space' and the forthcoming Annual. She found the illustrations 'rather weak' but 'acceptable', overall and left it to William Hartnell himself to approve of his own likeness. She sounded – perhaps unwittingly – somewhat exasperated with the whole thing.

It wasn't until October 1966 that John Pemberton and World Distributors got some clarification about *Doctor Who*'s future. By then it was established that Patrick Troughton would be taking over the title role ('Dr. Who' – though, as we know, he would be forbidden from calling *himself* that, and others must refer to him *only* by that name, but only *outside* his hearing...) By October Troughton himself had signed the necessary paperwork to allow his likeness to be used (or semi-likeness, if Evelyn M. Thomas knew anything about it, given the incompetence of the artists.) World Distributor's M.D still wanted details about the likely 'future direction' of the Show. What would the new Doctor be like? What 'costume will he be wearing'? Pemberton even suggested that the whole idea of the next Doctor Who Annual might have to be dropped if no more details of the elusive Second Doctor weren't made available soon.

In November 1966 M. Broadley (Mrs) BA – Children's Book Editor at World Distributors – sent another request for information to the BBC. Delightfully, she was struggling to quantify and describe the newly-minted concept of regeneration. The BBC weren't being at all helpful, it seems, and Mrs Broadley was theorizing as she typed her letter to R. S. Hargreaves of what it might actually mean, to substitute one actor for another and yet have them still play the very same character:

'We would be grateful for a directive from you on the new conception of the Doctor Who character. Is he, in fact, a reincarnation of the old man or is he a completely new character and if so what is his origin?'

She needed the information as soon as possible, so that she could instruct her authors 'accordingly.' I love the image of these authors in the wood-panelled offices above those busy Manchester streets, eagerly and impatiently waiting to hear whether Doctor Who was going to be reincarnated or reimagined or replaced entirely. Nothing seemed impossible, at this stage.

Hargreaves replied on behalf of the BBC, nine days later. It was late November and only now were World Distributors told what on Earth it actually meant when Dr. Who changed his face:

'I am told that the new Dr. Who character is a complete reincarnation of the original character, (who was about 900 years old!), and a hundred years or so younger. He was made into a younger version by some exceptional, unknown inner force and his character is likely to change as the programme develops.'

I would love to know what Mrs Broadley's reaction was to this curious, slightly mystical, explanation. It's hardly any clarification at all, and runs quite counter to *Doctor Who* lore established since then by the keen continuity-gatherers. He's younger, not older. He's the same, he's different. He's changed and he'll change even more. I imagine Mrs Broadley throwing up her hands in despair. She had to instruct her authors and they had to get these stories written and World Distributors had to get these books into the shops, but they knew as little as anyone did, about who and what Dr. Who had become.

1968 was all about liaison, it seems.

Even though their correspondence was being relayed through Charles R Leegood at BBC Publications, it feels – from reading their letters – that Mrs Mae Broadley of World Distributors' Children's Books and Ms. Evelyn M.

Thomas were writing directly to each other by now and managing to get things done a bit more efficiently, as they worked over certain points to do with the 1969 Annual. Evelyn's notes were properly (and somewhat irritably) nit-picking about characterization and continuity: why was Jamie able to pilot the Tardis and other space craft when he was established as a character with no technical ability whatsoever? Why was Victoria still featured in some of the stories and Zoe in others?

Mrs M Broadley was happy to respond, and to iron out these little inconsistencies and wrinkles. She also agreed quite happily with Ms Thomas that one of the stories, 'Dwellers Beyond Time' was quite unsuitable for the Annual, as it had little action and contained 'vast amounts of metaphysical speculation.' Mrs Broadley promptly scrapped it and replaced it with a tale about the Marie (sic) Celeste, which she hoped would be acceptable to the BBC. She took only a glance at the replacement herself before submitting it, but felt sure that Ms Thomas and her colleagues would find it had a level of excitement appropriate to a juvenile readership.

The two women seemed rather pleased with their flair for cooperation in these matters. Ms Thomas wondered why World Distributors hadn't asked for closer liaison with BBC Publications in the past. Mrs Broadley insisted that she had been trying to establish just such a rapport. In an internal BBC memo, however, Ms Thomas reflected that though the TV producer of *Doctor Who* felt disappointed at the Annual's lack of congruence with his show, he wouldn't actually want to have to work any closer with an organization outwith the BBC. His point was that the Corporation had given the licence out and they couldn't micro-manage – to use contemporary parlance – every aspect of it. Ms Thomas did try, however.

And she was right to, it turns out. The cover of the 1969 Annual – which was quite outside of Mrs Broadley's control – caused a certain amount of contention. An angry father from Shrewsbury wrote directly to BBC TV:

'On the front of this Annual is pictured several, I believe the term is "Cybermen." This surely is gross misrepresentation as when we open and read the Annual there is not one story containing this popular character (sic). Also, to cap it all, there is not one story or picture depicting my son's favourite robots, namely the Daleks.'

He goes on to lament the incongruity of the excellence of the BBC as compared to the shoddiness of the children's Annuals based on one of its most popular programmes. 'I really think you could have done better than this.' The BBC was very keen to point out in reply that they were not responsible for the contents of these books.

14

That same annual's back cover and title page also featured two very shabby drawings of Yeti, who also failed to appear in any of the stories. The poor representations of these famous monsters did nothing to deter their 'creators' Mervyn Haisman and Henry Lincoln from getting their agent to write in, complaining in the strongest terms that they hadn't been asked permission, nor paid for the use of their furry inventions.

These are testy and complicated negotiations that come to seem absurd, when images of the objects of contention are brought to mind. But lots of money had been made through the Daleks, and any writer would have been foolish not to protect their rights as cleverly as Terry Nation had done.

It does make you feel a bit bad for World Distributors, however. All they did was include a couple of cack-handed drawings of Yeti in their 1969 book and, by so doing, wandered foolishly into the no-man's land of contesting agents and lawyers. Parental disapproval and readerly disappointment wasn't all they had to worry about.

Following this, hardly any TV monsters appeared in the pages of the Annual. World Distributors' writers and artists were more than capable of dreaming up their own demons.

Minor crises came and went. Voyages were made into space, monsters were vanquished, villains were soundly beaten. 1972 was missed out because 1971 had sold so poorly. Pictures were drawn, likenesses were captured (or not), Doctors were re-cast, production teams left and new ones arrived. In Manchester, Dr. Who stories somehow got written.

When Patrick Troughton left there was more uncertainty, until it was revealed who his successor would be. World Distributors wrote to the BBC to congratulate them on their choice. The BBC sent colour transparencies of Jon Pertwee and new companion, Caroline John, along with details of the actors' agents. They sent rehearsal scripts for 'Spearhead from Space' and 'Doctor Who and the Silurians' so the creatives in Lever Street could see which direction the new series was taking. A vintage yellow roadster called Bessie was being introduced to replace the Tardis in the TV show, and would have to be used in a certain number of the Annual stories. A fee would have to be paid to use a likeness of the car. Jon Pertwee's agent was in touch on behalf of his client, fractious at the size of his nose in particular illustrations. Life went on for Dr. Who.

In the early Seventies TV Producer Barry Letts and Script Editor Terrance Dicks weren't especially impressed by the quality of the writing and artwork for the Annual, but they were perfect gentlemen in giving their opinions and trying to help. (In 1969 then-Producer Peter Bryant had been quite dismissive of World Distributors' work, declaring it was of a 'pretty poor standard.') In order to help them get a better hang on the Show, Barry Letts sent outlines of what kind of stories the Tenth season would involve. He and his colleague counselled on the removal of a story about a voodoo doll: not only did the story contain no science fiction elements whatsoever, they themselves had received terrible complaints when presenting a killer doll character on TV. Later, a story called 'The Killer Snails' was also squashed, due to content deemed too horrific by Letts and Dicks – surely the masters, if ever there were any, for deciding how far was too far in horror stories for kids in the Seventies.

Terrance Dicks made a few comments and suggestions about the quality of prose in the draft stories he was sent – and as a result Mrs Broadley was moved to announce that next year she would have them edited fully and properly before sending them down to the production office.

When Philip Hinchcliffe arrived in the Producer's role, and Tom Baker replaced Jon Pertwee, communications between offices became even smoother, with Hinchcliffe seeming keen that the Annual reflected the TV show effectively. He was at least as willing as Letts to help where he could, sending scripts for his first season, and also writing out a synopsis for the whole series of adventures for the benefit of Mrs Mae Broadley.

Hinchcliffe sounded very enthusiastic about the show he was involved in, as he demonstrated how one story linked seamlessly into the next... 'From the space station they travel by matter beam to uninhabited Earth only to encounter THE DESTRUCTORS who are the deadly Sontarans, an old adversary of the Doctor's. At the end of the story, leaving the Tardis behind them, the Doctor, Sarah and Harry are transported by Time Ring to the planet of Skaro and there witness the GENESIS OF THE DALEKS...'

I can only imagine Mae Broadley's expression as she sat at her hefty typewriter in her Lever Street office, reading this latest – rather extensive and rambling – news from the Omniverse of *Doctor Who*. I imagine her eating an apple in her lunch break, peering over her glasses, astonished by this strange memo. Hinchcliffe excitedly described the new Dr. Who himself:

'His companions don't always share the merriment... He is 748 years old... Bernard Shaw, Professor Challenger and Sherlock Holmes seem to flicker under the surface... and a mad, mischievous Harpo Marx beams through the face from time to time. It is a strongly idiosyncratic, chameleon-like characterization, difficult to summarise...'

16

Imagine Mae Broadley reading this, trying to make sense of it. A brand new, exciting Dr. Who was on his way, and Hinchcliffe was passing on the news, barely keeping the enthusiasm out of the properly sober tone of his letter. The Producer then went on to describe the Doctor's companions, and to provide a list of available monsters and their creators' agents – everything from Alpha Centauri to the spiders of Metebelis Three. Mac Hulke was put in the potentially very lucrative position of being credited as the inventor of the dinosaurs.

Mrs Broadley, poring over this list of monsters. Finishing her apple. Exxilons. Cybermen. Ogrons. What she really wanted, of course, was the Daleks. She couldn't understand why they'd never appeared in a Dr. Who Annual before. She made a mental note to look into this aberration, and perhaps get in touch with Terry Nation's agent…

Incoming Script Editor Robert Holmes sounded grumpier, just before Christmas 1974, when it came to the subject of the Annuals. He was 'sick' of reiterating that 'Doctor Who' was the name of the Show, not the character. This error – he sighed heavily, in a memo – presumably crept into the Show's lore as a result of careless secretaries, and its repercussions were everywhere, including the end titles of the Show. Doctor Who's name isn't known by anyone, Holmes declared. Also, he had no comment to make on the literary quality of the Annual stories.

It would be lovely to show Holmes the letter written almost ten years previously by one of his predecessors, Dennis Spooner, in which the stress accidentally fell on the wrong word. Holmes might have appreciated the irony of the famous misnomer being the result of a slightly clumsily expressed sentence.

Christmas 1974 was exciting, though. The Fourth Doctor was about to arrive on TV and, eventually, in the World Distributors' Annual. In my opinion, both would reach astonishing heights in terms of creativity, originality and sheer unforgettableness over the next few years.

By 1977 however, the BBC didn't really like what the Annuals were doing, at all. Incoming Producer Graham Williams noted that the artwork could be greatly improved if the artists showed the Doctor smiling a bit more ('He is, after all, a happy Doctor!') Head of Serials at the BBC, Graeme McDonald, was rather more damning about the work coming out of Manchester.

'[These stories] do not, of course, have anything to do with 'Doctor Who' as we know it, but they do not contain anything actually detrimental to the programme. We just are a little bewildered that these writers are able to get away with such poor material.'

By September 1978 Graham Williams was describing text sent from Lever Street in Manchester as 'the usual rubbish' that he expected from the Annuals. He deplored the gratuitously nasty nature of some of the stories, the poor likenesses and the inclusion now and then of pictures of 'sexy and attractive ladies.' Williams didn't seem very impressed by the Annuals at all. He complained about one story finishing with the Doctor killing his enemy with a 'hand-laser gun': 'I suppose it's all right but it bothered me slightly.'

With everyone under the pressure of deadlines each year, there seemed no real effort made on either side to bring the Annuals closer in line with what the BBC would prefer. There only ever seemed time to change 'Dr. Who' to 'Doctor' (not always successfully) or to swap the ex-companion's name for the new one. Because of the hastiness and, perhaps, genuine disinterest on both sides, a multitude of literary and artistic sins passed muster and got through to the printed page, and into the shops and then the hands of eager fans. And so we grew up reading *Doctor Who* stories of a most peculiar nature.

Thank goodness.

It amazes me that these BBC employees were decrying the Doctor Who Annual of 1979 which I – as you'll see – have come to view as one of the pinnacles of these books' achievements.

The Annuals were just associated 'willynilly' (as Hinchcliffe put it) with the TV show, and naturally the BBC would expect them to mirror it very closely. But the BBC weren't the fans and readers of those books at the time, and nor were they the people who would reread those books over the years: who'd take them down from the attic or track down faded replacement copies in second-hand book shops or car boot sales. They would never appreciate the weirdness of the Annuals' tonal distance from the TV show and come to admire it and wonder about it. They would never – naturally enough – think of the Annuals as belonging to a tangential shadow realm at the edges of the world of *Doctor Who*.

The people who made the Show didn't read the Annuals and the people who made the Annuals didn't watch the Show. It was a very ramshackle kind of franchising, years before the advent of aggressive brand management. In retrospect and, to this dilettante fanboy at least, the products are much more richly rewarding for all their oddity. Because of it.

The TV people wanted a yearly book that would advertise their show, in which pictures looked like the actors and the stories were a bit like the stories on TV and in no way contradicted or fell out of tune with them. They wanted disposable merchandise, in short. World Distributors wanted to pay fees to as few actors' agents as possible. They wanted to use artwork and text produced by their in-house creatives. They wanted just a few scripts in advance and a few character pointers and notes. They didn't want to have to watch every single episode of a kids' TV show to be able to bung a few stories together.

Somehow, in all of this very grown-up, professional chatter and politeness, books got produced and put out into the market place. The Annuals began reasonably well 'branded' as part of a TV format, and they certainly ended that way in the nineteen eighties, with a string of efforts that echoed the then current series' characters and situations pretty closely.

But somewhere in the mid to late Seventies things became rather peculiar. The writers and artists were doing their own thing. And, just for a while, the BBC let them get away with it.

I don't think there's been a wilder, stranger run of publications based on a pre-existing property in the whole history of TV tie-ins than the Dr. Who Annuals. And what's even more amazing is that this strangeness wasn't something anyone involved really intended to happen. It just did.

Dr. Who's most bizarre adventures all happened right here, on twenty one Boxing Days, between cardboard covers, in narrow columns of text on luridly colourful pages, somewhere in the dark, hulking warehouses and busy offices of Central Manchester.

POSTSCRIPT I

For World Distributors, the Doctor Who Annuals were merely the tip of the tie-in iceberg. Between the early fifties and the late eighties, it's been estimated that the company published well over one hundred different individual titles, many for multiple years (though *Doctor Who*'s twenty years run is unusual in its longevity)..

Additionally, they published non-Annual tie-in titles, such as the two *Doctor Who Puzzle Fun Books* (1966), the *Dr Who Travels in Space Painting Book* (1965), the *Doctor Who Colouring Book* (1973) and the *Doctor Who Press Out Book* (1978).

Of most interest to *Doctor Who* fans, however, are the Dalek Annuals, the first of which appeared in 1976. Previously, Souvenir Press had released three Dalek-related titles in the 1960s: *The Dalek Book* (1964), *The Dalek World* (1965) and *The Dalek Outer Space Book* (1966). Each of these early efforts to cash in on Dalekmania attempted to build a separate narrative and chronology from the parent show (though the final book did feature Sara Kingdom, from 'The Daleks Master Plan').

World Distributors' titles, however, were very obviously built using the model of the Doctor Who Annuals, though without being linked to the tv show in the way that the 'K9 and Company' Annual had been. Appearing from 1976 to 1979 – and more properly called 'Terry Nation's Dalek Annual' – each successive Annual utilised the same core cast of characters, members of the 'Anti-Dalek Force' such as Space Major Joel Shaw, and the android Mark Seven.

In the nineteen-nineties, Marvel published several new Doctor Who Annuals, while 2005 saw the advent of the updated version of the show, and the release of the first of a new run of Doctor Who Annuals and Storybooks.

POSTSCRIPT II

It has long been rumoured that script editor David Whitaker wrote the factual pieces in the first Annual. However, correspondence between World Distributors and the BBC shows these articles being mentioned with no allocation of authorship, which makes the rumour unlikely to be true.

It seems entirely possible however that World Distributors editor Mae Broadley BA (Mrs) actually wrote some of the stories in the Doctor Who Annual for a fair few number of years, at least until the start of the nineteen eighties. So it could be that while she was communicating with script editors and producers and stoutly weathering the often rude and dismissive things they said about the 'usual rubbish' from Lever Street, she herself was actually – secretly, modestly – the crazed mastermind behind those mind-bending and psychedelic text-based adventures for the various Drs Who and his supposedly interchangeable chums.

POSTSCRIPT III
The influence of the World Distributor Annuals is still felt today. In 2014, one fan published an unofficial but professional *Fannual,* featuring the Peter Cushing Dr Who, as seen in the nineteen-sixties' movies.

The 1966 Annual

This is our first Annual encounter with the enigmatic Dr. Who.

Even from the very beginning there is a complicated back-story, and we're visiting worlds where the Doctor already has history, and meeting aliens he has already met before. In this endless, ongoing story, there never is a starting point. We are always trying to catch up with the restless, inquisitive Dr. Who.

Here in a series of somewhat overlong stories, the old man has a number of bad-tempered encounters with alien creatures who are all keen to dissect him or to make use of his miraculous Tardis. He usually gets these alien beings to feed him, he escapes often by making lots of noise, and then decides who it is deserves to be soundly defeated and sent on their way. He isn't opposed to using a little judicious time trickery, or brute violence.

The Stories

THE LAIR OF ZARBI SUPREMO

Panting with excitement, Dr. Who lands the Tardis once more upon the planet Vortis. Through his radio comes a message in 'modern English', telling him to 'Beware Zarbi Supremo' and to 'Warn Earth.' He traces the voice to a spherical space craft, and inside he finds stranded humans: a half-dead Mr Hamilton and his son, Gordon. The rest of the crew of the Solar Queen has vanished and the boy is convinced the Zarbi are planning to invade the Earth. Dr. Who thinks he's talking nonsense.

However, it seems true that Vortis has moved unfathomable distances through space and, what's more, Menoptera are hiding themselves inside robotic Zarbi. The Doctor and Gordon themselves adopt a Zarbi disguise, and the Doctor gets them into terrible danger by switching his radio on as the pair are shepherded into the giant Zarbi termite hill. There they discover the colossal Zarbi Supremo, and some Menoptera, who are refusing to help in the subjugation of planet Earth. It looks as if war is on the cards for the Zarbi and the Menoptera.

The Doctor and Gordon de-hypnotise captured Earthmen and get them to fire ray-guns indiscriminately about the place, eventually killing the Supremo. The humans are terrible: once freed, they even want to shoot at the Menoptera, and enslave everybody in sight.

THE SONS OF THE CRAB

Far away in the Crab Nebula, the Tardis arrives in a 'normal street'. Dr. Who is frozen like a statue, while all about him throng hideous, flowing, egg-shaped monstrosities with multiple limbs. He's relieved when he's taken indoors by bald men in metallic outfits. Then he's horrified to find they think of him as a scientific specimen. The people here fear the 'changing death'. Their Chief Yend Fomal will want to dissect the Doctor himself, 'to see with own eyes into the glands of this creature.'

The Doctor opens up the Tardis to impress Chief Yend, but to no avail. Fomal himself succumbs to the weird metamorphoses, and is surprised that the Doctor doesn't. The Doctor says that, where he comes from, they don't really have mutants. Fomal says it's a star called Mortain that brings on all of his people's shape shifting woes, as well as their own foolish experiments. Will the Doctor take the Wengrol children to safety in his Tardis? Time is pressing, as Fomal says: 'I am degenerating as I speak…' The Doctor gazes at racks of test tube babies, unenthusiastically. He takes them with him into the Tardis and isn't surprised when the whole lot perishes in transit.

THE LOST ONES

The Doctor is back on Vortis – again! But this time, when the Menoptera flutter down to see him he doesn't appear to recognise them. They too, are unfamiliar with him, and are keen to dissect him. They suspect him of killing many of their kind. He hears a little of their history – and of the rise of a terrible Zarbi queen, and their developing of weapons. They pin him to an operating table, ready for his examination but he soon escapes their silken bonds.

He comes across what appears to be a red-headed superman in a 'close-fitting outfit', who greets him as a fool and a sluggard, but at least gets him away from the insects. The Doctor is livid when the humanoids strip him naked to get a better look. He impresses them with talk of his time travels, and is soon taken into their confidence. They are the people of the world-city Atlantis, and they're supposed to be colonizing the universe. Instead they are lost on this remote sphere with faulty locator instruments.

Aboard the impressive Atlantean space ship the Doctor has a synthetic supper and then cosmic, troublesome dreams. He toys with the idea of returning the Atlanteans to Earth – but in which time period? He's worried that they're a bit bloodthirsty. They turn on him: 'Blast this midget from existence.' He flees straight into a pitched battle between Zarbi and Menoptera. The Doctor nips into the Tardis and gladly leaves them all to it.

THE MONSTERS FROM EARTH

A little girl called Amy and her bulldog Butch hide in the Tardis while playing hide-and-seek with her brother, Tony. They are astonished by the interior and know at once that it's a space ship. When the Doctor arrives, unaware of their presence, he sets the ship travelling and winds up caught in a giant spider's web. He sprays prussic acid into the spider's face and, having escaped that peril, comes face to face with a gaggle of bald, naked spider-worshipping humanoids who claim to be Sensorites. He brandishes his syringe at them.

Meanwhile, the two Earth children and their dog wake up aboard the Tardis, to find it still swaying wildly in the giant web. They emerge into a dreadful-smelling cavern, and soon they find Dr. Who strapped to a circular dais. The old man hatches a plan to exploit the Sensorites' aversion to noise, and the children and their bulldog's ability to generate it. When he sees the Sensorites again he tells them that he has lots of poisons in his Tardis to help rid their world of the spidery Zilgans. They are appalled at the very idea of such blasphemy and are determined to sacrifice him. He starts yelling and makes everyone around him cringe. Then the human children and their dog join in, sending the Sensorites fleeing.

Our heroes make for the Tardis and are menaced by further Zilgans, but they manage to get inside and dematerialise. They take a broken-off spider leg along with them. 'A queer souvenir for you two to take back after your trip in Space-Time.'

PERIL IN MECHANISTRIA

The Doctor is amazed to emerge from the Tardis onto the planet Korad, which is apparently made all of metal. He is confronted by a Grukker – a robotic creature so large that it would make the 'dreaded Daleks' seem like 'children's toys.' A tentacle knocks him unconscious, but when he wakes he is relieved to find himself among humanoids. He feels like a prisoner but is mollified when given some food, even if it's only a mushy green porridge. The Doctor wants to meet the Wise Ones so that he can repair his damaged ship. He frets about these 'savages' and 'ignorant mechanics' getting their hands on the secrets of the Tardis.

Next day the Doctor is astonished to hear that the 'wise ones' and the masters of these people are the machines. The humanoids have forgotten creating them and have let them take over. Drako, who has been communicating with the Doctor, wonders if our hero might help his people escape this world.

Beran of the 'Wise Ones of Haven One' turns up with a gun and threatens to destroy the Tardis. The Mechanistrians don't allow imported goods. Drako facilitates an escape for them from Beran, but he himself turns nasty then, threatening Dr. Who at gun-point and demanding that he take him into the Tardis. He wants to return to the past and stop the deadly mechanisation of the planet Korad. The Doctor seems to think this is a very civilised plan, and goes some way to prove his new colleague's trustworthiness. This is odd, given Dr. Who's usual feelings about changes to history.

They are interrupted, however, by a horde of mechanical beings of all shapes and sizes advancing on them across the metal plain. The Doctor takes the Tardis back in time and Drako steps out onto the grass of a younger world. The Doctor is thanked for saving a world, but surely he has a lingering fear that he has unleashed untold paradoxical harm upon the universe..? He has a bit of a ponder as he stoops over the console, about the mighty forces of Destiny shaping the universe. Then he decides he's not that bothered.

THE FISHMEN OF KANDALINGA

At first he laughs at the clownishly ugly creatures of Kandalinga, but when they start chewing the Tardis with their needle-like teeth Dr. Who isn't quite so amused. He has materialised his ship underwater, which is bothersome, but not life-threatening. He relocates to the surface of the planet and discovers fishmen lying about in water-filled pits. They drag themselves out and hop into the ocean, just as a barge passes by. He is appalled to recognise the occupants as the Voord, who he last saw in that terrible to-do on Marinus. They take him prisoner and he's discomfited to realise that they seem to remember their last meeting, millions of years ago on Marinus. He laughs all this continuity stuff away.

He refuses to eat the hideous raw fish they provide for him and soon they arrive on an artificial island and he is taken underground, where it smells of fish. The Doctor hears how the Voord are trying to make this world habitable by reclaiming land from the sea and enslaving the poor fishpeople. He decides that the Voord are absolutely horrible. Their leader wants to take possession of the Tardis in order to expedite his plans. The Doctor is careful not to mention that the ship travels in time, mindful of the fact that the Voord might want to go back and change history on Marinus.

They use the remaining Keys of Marinus to take them back to the causeway where the Tardis is situated. The Doctor whirls into action, grabbing hold and snapping off the Voord leader's telepathic forehead aerial. 'The organ broke off in Dr. Who's hands and the fishmen rushed in.' With revolution in the offing, the Kandalingans cease at once to be 'limp and flaccid, like walking fishes.' The injured Voord staggers about, rather disturbingly 'mewing like a cat.'

The Doctor is sure that the fishpeople will be able to overpower the remaining Voord, and so reclaim their world from their invaders. What an amazing world! The Doctor thinks. He might have learned a great deal from the technology of the Voord. He didn't, but never mind. He's off on further adventures.

24

Other Content

WHO IS DR WHO?

'After Sir Isaac Newton came Dr Albert Einstein. After Einstein came Dr Who.' An in-universe introduction to Dr Who and his Tardis.

JOURNEY BACK TO EARTH

A board game for two players or more, in which the aim is to guide the Tardis back to Earth. The route back is obviously a convoluted one, as you land on Mars at position 8, then spend most of the 30s and 40s on Vortis, before landing on the Moon at 52, and then moving onto Venus at 55!

THE EQUATIONS OF DR WHO

'The equations of Dr Who embrace all of Space and all of Time, both tightly locked together in one Idea, the Idea of Living Matter.'

A rather trippy and way out attempt to explain the science of the Tardis, via the medium of hippy technobabble.

Doctor Who Himself

The old gent is 'tantalised' by mystery. When he arrives on Vortis at the start of the first Doctor Who Annual he is almost 'dancing with impatience' at the prospect of adventure. He thinks of himself as a 'feeble, weaponless Earthman,' unnecessarily doing himself down. Fascinating to see him referred to as 'the doctor' in lower case. It's almost as if he isn't quite himself yet. A proto-Doctor, slightly human... one who can't think of a time when he's been in as much 'hideous danger' as this. However, he has a compulsion to help people in danger: he is honour-bound to rescue them, even if he spends a lot of time feeling exasperated and irritated. The game old bird 'writhes' in 'excitement' when the story gets going.

The feature article 'Who is Doctor Who?' focuses on the Doctor's purpose in life:

'Where is he going? What is his objective? What goal draws him on through the endless spheres, the millions of ages? No one knows. Perhaps he himself has long forgotten, so distant, in our years, is the time when he first set out on his odyssey. Are his voyages haphazard and merely satisfying the urge to travel everywhere and see everything, or is he seeking something definite? Again, no one knows.'

Haphazard, I think, is what we discover, eventually. Just kind of pottering about and getting into bother. That's his thing. But these are the years before we knew very much about him. He is a fussy old gadabout, on a cosmic scale.

There is a feature called 'The Equations of Doctor Who' which is mostly goobledegook about dimensions, but it finishes with the memorable lines:

'He is human curiosity personified. He must see for himself; he must go there; he must learn all there is to know. Are we not all a little possessed of the spirit of Doctor Who?'

A great deal is made of his endless scientific curiosity, which is odd because, whenever he arrives in some intriguing new place, he is often heard querulously shouting things like: 'I say… I've had enough of this place!' Also, his sense of time and history is appalling. His adventure on Marinus took place 'millions of years either in the past or the future, he had never… found out.' At this stage in his life he isn't much of a Time Lord in more ways than one.

He is furious when the bald scientists of Wengrol treat him like a guinea pig. He tells them he's as human as they are, which is literally true, but not in the way he means. He stares angrily at people through his monocle and, when on Earth in 1966, is wary that some 'yokel' doesn't go wandering into his Tardis.

Dr. Who isn't as liberal here as he'll eventually claim to be. Confronted with giant spiders or insects, his first instinct is to recoil in horror and then kill them. Anything without a humanoid shape is suspect. When he first sees the creatures of Kandalinga on his viewing screen he bursts out laughing at their ugliness. He is far from respecting all alien life forms just yet. He also keeps claiming to know very little about insects and spiders. Given the kinds of adventures he's coming up against, you'd think he'd read up a bit.

He couldn't care less about creating time paradoxes and messing about with history. Who gives a hoot? Also, he can't remember – and doesn't even care – how many Keys of Marinus there were. At the very end of the Annual we are told that it's 'rare' for him to interfere with the 'affairs of any of the strange worlds he had visited in his time', but we know by now that this is just nonsense. Try telling that to the Mechanistrians! The truth is, if Dr. Who takes against a certain people or planet, he will have no compunction in dabbling in their history.

Monsters and Villains

The Zarbi are back! Like giant termites scuttling around their hundred-feet-high mounds. These loathsome beasts could tear the limbs from a man, 'just as a man might tear apart a roasted chicken.' We even meet a bloated Zarbi queen, being stroked by Zarbi drones and having all her wants attended to.

The people of Wengrol turned themselves into hideous mutants by messing around with biology. The Doctor thinks they brought it all on themselves. He's quite unforgiving about this, and isn't too fussed when all their test tube babies die in the vortex.

The Doctor would like to explain to the Menoptera how life in all its infinite variety works throughout the universe, but he hasn't got time just now. For the first time in the Annuals' history we hear him say, 'Some time I will explain to you about the universe…' Dr. Who will make a fine art out of such lofty prevarications.

The Sensorites are back! But they aren't so much monsters and villains in 'The Monsters from Earth' as just silly dupes, given to worshipping giant spiders and determined to sacrifice Dr. Who. Also, they are running about in the nude.

The Mechanistrians are the robotic 'Wise Ones' of the planet Korad, with human brains built into their metallic forms. They subjugate the original, humanoid inhabitants of their world. Immortality is their aim. Dr. Who is not impressed.

The Voord are back! And they are trying to colonise Kandalinga. They are quite ruthless: 'It is the survival of the fittest and we can only go on trying.' They are making slaves – and revolting meals – of the local fish people.

Curious Companions?

Gordon Hamilton the spaceman's son is a character in the mould of many from schoolboy adventure stories: 'I say, this is a bit of fun, isn't it?' It's a wonder the famously tetchy First Doctor doesn't brain him.

In 'The Monsters from Earth' two human children, Amy and Tony, plus their dog Butch, are mistakenly dragged along into an adventure with the Sensorites. Their ability to make lots of noise proves to be helpful and the Doctor is keen to dump them back on Earth, giving them a snapped-off giant spider leg as a grisly keepsake. It might be a nice idea if he gave all his departing companions mementoes hacked from the bodies of dead enemies: a maggot for Jo Grant, perhaps. A hank of Yeti fur for Jamie.

Fiendish Wheezes

The Zarbi have become extra cruel and destructive, and intend to invade the Planet Earth. They have somehow piloted the whole of Vortis to our world's vicinity. Elsewhere, the Mechanistrians have enslaved their own organic creators and the Voord are intent on terra-forming Kandalinga and eating all the fishpeople. Back in 1966 fiendish wheezes were big and bold and quite straightforward.

TV Feedback

'The Lair of the Zarbi Supremo's' selling point is that it returns us to Vortis, as seen in 'The Web Planet.' But Dr. Who has come to a part of the planet devoid of that strangely blurry mist and needle-like spires.

It seems to be a fixed trope in *Doctor Who* already that, having arrived on a planet of monsters, you find yourself a dormant one, empty it of its organic contents, and use the robotic shell as a Trojan Horse. There must be a folk tale origin for this, perhaps? A story about dressing in the skin or pelt of the enemy in order to go unnoticed, or to adopt its powers…

The bald, naked people that the Doctor meets after killing the giant spider in 'The Monsters from Earth' claim to be Sensorites, just like off the telly. Also, there are nice little mentions of how escaping from the Daleks ruined the Tardis' navigation systems, and what the Voord were up to on the planet Marinus.

Anticipating the Future

The hideous creatures of 'The Sons of the Crab' sound a little like the poached egg monsters that the Doctor and Jo discover in the Australian desert in the 1973 Annual. Scientists messing with nature and producing monsters will be a great stock-in-trade for the TV show. Fomal of the Wengrol laments his people's dabbling, when they tried to create 'new men with organs and powers we only dreamed of.' Shades of the Cybermen here, perhaps, and also Davros's shenanigans. Lots of shady characters in Dr. Who's future will spend time dreaming of outlandish organs.

This Doctor is always asking for refreshments, wherever he visits in time and space. Even if it's horrid green porridge, he's keen to eat something to keep his strength up. This anticipates his arrival aboard the Fifth Doctor's Tardis in 'The Five Doctors', when the first thing he does is demand refreshments and nibbles fastidiously at a pineapple slice.

Egregious errors

Dr. Who isn't an Earthman. He keeps claiming to come from Earth throughout this first Annual. His being completely au fait with the inhabitants of the planet Vortis at the start of the book and then, two stories later, confessing complete ignorance of the Zarbi and Menoptera is infuriating to the reader.

Classic moments

The Menoptera pick up Dr. Who with their 'tiny, furry, clawlike hands' and fly him gently back to his Tardis. 'We know we have nothing to fear from you, strange immortal human who can flit in and out of all the ages.' The Doctor taking the boxload of test tube babies into the Tardis, and his casual acceptance that the people of Wengrol are doomed by their own hubris is a fascinating moment.

The flame-haired Atlanteans chasing Dr. Who through a horde of battling Zarbi and Menoptera on the misty surface of Vortis is a lovely image at the end of 'The Lost Ones.' As is the spectacle of the massed hordes of Mechanistrians scooting along the metal floor of their world towards Dr. Who.

Dr. Who snapping off a Voord leader's organ, leaving him 'mewing like a cat', and exhorting the fish people of Kandalinga to revolt is a marvellous – if disturbing – moment.

What I learned from the Doctor Who Annual 1966

While the webs of giant spiders are 'malodorous' and the Menoptera smell of musk, it absolutely stinks inside the Zarbi lair. The Tardis' interior has the scent of a dentist's surgery or a hospital but the artificial island of the Voord smells of fish.

Monsters are mostly mindless. It's only when they have some kind of supreme being with a nefarious purpose in mind that the bad stuff starts to happen. This is a lesson Dr. Who learns here that will stand him in extremely good stead throughout all of his future lives and adventures. Beware all so-called Supremos, I'd say.

Don't mess about with genetics and watch out for the 'mighty and everlasting fingers of nature.' Humanoids in close-fitting silver coveralls might seem as if they're sophisticated, but often they'll be a let-down.

You can use the Tardis to solve your problems by going back in time and changing history. It's quite all right. No one minds.

Illustrations

Artwork for the Annuals between 1966 and 1969 was handled by Walter Howarth and David Brian (but see 'Interviews' for a new claim regarding the front cover artwork!)

The drawings in the early Annuals are rather cheery, I always think. They mostly consist of extremely sketchy pen and inks, with washes of two or three bright colours. There are lots of floppy-armed, rather helpless, wide-eyed aliens scattered through these pages, borne about the place in clumsy-looking spacecraft. There's something pleasingly rudimentary about the look of the whole thing. Children must have felt quite keen to draw their own versions of these cartoony Voord and Menoptera: this is the cleverly simplistic sort of illustration that invites imitation.

Doctor Who and the Invasion from Space

In the beginning there were certain things World Distributors hadn't quite worked out about producing the Doctor Who Annual, and the first of those things was that they should only publish one a year. 'Doctor Who and the Invasion from Space' is an extra volume. A curiosity. A sought-after novelty.

It's also a kind of prequel to the whole thing. It's the first story in the on-going tales of the Annual Dr. Who. If we see him as a character quite distinct from his TV self, and having his own continuity, development, story arc and themes, then this present volume might be seen as the one in which these notes are struck and announced for the first time. It is, in effect, our Doctor's origin story.

It begins with him saving a whole family of 'peasants' from the Great Fire of London. Accidentally he brings the Mortimers aboard the Tardis and pretty soon they are all caught up in a terrifying adventure upon the futuristic world-ship of the One and the cloned race of Aalas who come from Andromeda.

While the humans are off being examined by the impossibly handsome Aalas, the Doctor contends with the disembodied group-mind of the One. In this – it has to be said – rather wordy and cerebral space adventure story, Dr. Who hears all about how the super-mind evolved from all the minds of its own galaxy, and now it intends to invade the Milky Way. Hearing of the Doctor's Tardis, it tries to steal the miraculous Ship for itself. It also reveals that its plan is to invade our galaxy very gradually, so that we the inhabitants hardly even notice it happening.

The furious and incredulous Dr. Who makes up his mind to defeat the alien intelligence and pits his wits against it. However, in the end, it is the children of Earth he has ineluctably brought with him who wind up providing a surprising solution to this cosmic dilemma.

Doctor Who Himself

He's a wretched, cross old man in this. He never intended to save the Mortimers from the Great Fire. He just opened the doors of Tardis and in they hurried. When he loses track of them later and realises that he has left them behind he gives a kind of shrug.

He's at the stage where he's only just becoming the Doctor we will know in the Doctor Who Annuals. He's sceptical about the kinds of things he is finding in space and time, dismissing a lot of it as 'moonshine':

'Androids indeed! Thinking machines and invasions of galaxies! What utter rubbish!'

Little does he know just now but this kind of thing is going to be his bread and butter from now on.

It's tempting to think of this single-story Annual as his very first adventure. It's the first time he comes up against a vast, alien, antagonistic intelligence. He wants to face it man to man. He pits his own 'puny mind' against its 'deathless intellect.' When the One tries to command him he flatly refuses. When he learns that there are millions of world-ships poised to invade Earth's native galaxy it galvanises him. He is learning to stand up for what he believes in.

'Why should he consider the fate of the galaxy?'

As the brilliant scientist in possession of the universe's only Tardis, Dr Who comes to realise in this story that considering the fate of the galaxy is going to be something he must get used to.

Monsters and Villains

The One of Andromeda and his golden-haired minions is a kind of blueprint for every non-human group-mind and Great Intelligence that Dr. Who will ever have to face. Eventually the day will come when he'll be quite used to invisible gestalt entities with delusions of grandeur. Right now, though, it's all very novel. Their implacable sense of purpose and cosmic schemes cause outrage in Dr. Who.

Curious Companions?

Dr Who is very unimpressed by the Mortimer family – George and Helen and their children Alan and Ada. He keeps referring to them as 'medieval oafs' or peasants and there is nothing ironic in his utter contempt. We might see this as the first time Dr. Who has any kind of travelling companion aboard his Tardis, and the experience is not a happy one. He tries to abandon them to their fates, but can't help himself having qualms. Unconsciously, it seems, he guides the Ship back to save them.

But, as always in *Doctor Who* stories, it is a piece of hapless human behaviour that saves the day and astonishes our hero. Ada Mortimer – the youngest member of the family – unwittingly puts an end to the Invasion from Space.

Fiendish Wheezes

Invading the galaxy by doing it very slowly, so that no one notices is very fiendish.

TV Feedback

The Doctor's characterization is very faithful to the first Doctor as we first knew him on TV. He's selfish and snobby and wants to be fed.

Anticipating the Future

Many stories in which the Doctor faces up to an artificial intelligence or a demented group-mind are anticipated. But also, by presenting a Doctor who owns the only Tardis in the universe, right at the edge of the galaxy, face to face with unfathomable beings and finding himself charged with the responsibility of defending us all, this story anticipates the more epic and mythological aspects of 21st Century *Doctor Who*.

Classic moments

The very fact that the Andromedans go to the trouble of putting on a kind of buffet spread for the kidnapped Mortimers and the Doctor is amazing enough, but their making jelly as well is just genius. The best moment in the whole story comes when the piqued Ada Mortimer attacks the One with a bowl of jelly and manages to drive it completely barmy.

What I learned from Doctor Who and the Invasion from Space

Defeat your enemies by keeping them talking. This gives you time to think up a brilliant escape plan. Or you may learn enough from their boastful loquaciousness to discover a way to defeat them. Alternatively, someone might come along with a deadly bowl of jelly, just in the nick of time.

Illustrations

Very rudimentary swirling acrylics. The Doctor does, on occasion, look like Hartnell, but the illustrations add only a very little lustre to this story.

The 1967 Annual

Suddenly Dr. Who is involved in rebellions and revolts and all kinds of excitement. He helps the vaporised Ethereals regain their world from upstart automatons and he exhorts cockroaches and butterflies to rise up against the ruthless Sons of Grekk. All of a sudden he's dashing about like an action hero – falling into pits and hurling himself at the Tardis as it teeters off a window ledge. He's in deadly skirmishes with Devil-birds and generally dashing about in a terrifically adventurous manner.

A novel feature of this Annual is that some – if not all of the stories – happen one after the next, with inter-story continuity cropping up here and there, almost as if there's some editorial control going on this year! This does, however, conjure up the idea that poor old Dr. Who is hurtling pell-mell into one exhausting escapade after the next with nary a sit down. Just where is all this energy coming from?

The Stories

THE CLOUD EXILES

Emerging from the Tardis in his atmospheric waistcoat Dr. Who finds himself walking on 'spongeous 'grass'.' His attention is attracted at once by the impossibly incandescent clouds. When he tries to take a sample of the seemingly-living miasma, he is rendered unconscious. He wakes upon a metal slab in some kind of hall, where the clouds are threatening to use something called 'the epitomiser' on him. They are the Ethereals, and they believe the Doctor is the key to their salvation.

They explain their history. Once humanoid like him, they created the Baggolts: sophisticated robots who eventually turned against them. They vaporised their masters into their present form, but have no idea the Ethereals still survive, biding their time. They've been waiting for a solid humanoid to one day visit. They will place the Doctor in their epitomiser and use him as a 'mould' to provide them with solid bodies once more.

Making a great hullaballoo and whirling like a Dervish, he manages to prevent their reducing him to a mere shell. Even so, he promises to help them defeat their mechanical enemies. He adapts the epitomiser and is suitably awed by the Ethereals returned to human form. They are rather haughty-looking, and wearing evening gowns. He offers his help to their leader Mitzog to rid their crystal Droog city of robots. Nalog of the Baggolts sits atop their steel

35

brain annexe, with the buttons of his control panel set permanently to 'rebellion.'

The Doctor brings out one of his classic, favourite plans: shall we dress up as the enemy in order to get into the city? They manage to cause a counter revolution, with laser guns going off and robot policemen exploding all over the place. Once inside the leader Nalog's control room, Mitzog jumps onto his back and the Doctor switches the crucial dial from 'Rebellion' to 'Peace.'

THE SONS OF GREKK

A mechanical manservant in a medieval castle? The sight of a pig's head on a platter and the wafting smells of a banquet draw the Doctor to a minstrel gallery, where he arrives just in time to prevent an assassination attempt. He is captured by robot servants and accused of being a Crustian spy by the Sons of Grekk, who fall about laughing when he tells them the Tardis is his spaceship. They take him to their Pit, intent on chucking him in, along with all the other varied grotesque life forms they have banished there. It seems that the Sons of Grekk want to rule this world alone.

Down in the Pit the Doctor receives a reasonably warm welcome from the cockroaches, butterflies and turtles. The Doctor adapts their 'sustenance unit' into a transmitter, sending a signal to the Crustians to come to their rescue. With 'deadly weapons ready to spew death' the Sons of Grekk prepare to murder the creatures in the pit. Soon there are all kinds of battles going off between Mechanislaves, butterflies and the like. In the control room the Doctor faces Deemon the assassin, who's been the one stirring up all the bother. The Mechanislaves throw the Tardis out of a castle window – but the Doctor manages to fling himself aboard and dematerialise before any permanent damage is done.

TERROR ON TIRO

Returning to the planet Tiro – with its Alloy Mountain and mobile trees – Dr. Who hopes to meet his old friend Argon and his fellows, the amphibious Staggs. Last time the Doctor was here he saved them from invading Outerfringe forces. The Tardis is in dire need of Magnatite for its valves and so the Doctor sets off through a jungle of 'gyrating tentacles' and vines, looking for help. En route he is attacked by carnivorous birds and flowers. When he pauses by a pool to eat a fish-flavoured food tablet, he sees his friend Argon under the water, but can't attract his attention, which depresses him.

Night falls and he makes himself comfortable inside a giant cabbage. His troubled dreams wake him and he finds that his vegetable sanctuary is rolling downhill. It's being pushed into an ant city by one of the Zarbi-like drones. Soon, however, he is reunited with friendly Staggs. One of them gives an 'eager gurgle' of recognition: 'Doctor Who!' But they are in trouble. Argon promises to show his friend horror of the like he has never encountered,

36

during any of his travels. Their old enemy Klarimo is poisoning the water supplies.

The Doctor proposes another of his favourite plans: setting explosives to make a volcano erupt, which works beautifully.

MISSION FOR DUH (Picture strip)

Another return visit sees the Doctor finding the planet Birr looking lifeless and grim, and lacking his friends the Verdants. The bald humanoid Rostrows kidnap him easily, seize his walking stick, and drag him back to their rather rudimentary space craft. But he soon discovers that the Rostrows are holding Verdants prisoner on board.

The Rostrow Duh is astonished to hear that the Verdants are sentient. It appears that, upon arrival, samples were taken, and all of Birr's Verdants retreated underground to safety. Dr. Who will lead Duh on a mission to make peace.

Once inside the underworld Dr. Who and Duh are seized by tendrils and almost executed by a giant flower. Only by making lots of noise can they save their own lives. They dodge barbs (Duh gets hit) and meet Phlege, leader of the Verdants, who looks like a flowering thistle, and who recognises the Doctor. Soon, everything is explained and Phlege is relieved to learn that there has been a mistake and the Rostrows didn't realise his people weren't just ordinary plants.

THE DEVIL-BIRDS OF CORBO

Landing in a fetid swamp, the Doctor is impressed by crystalline cliff formations. He's even more impressed by the sight of birds twice the size of the Tardis itself and is horrified to find the island he has landed on consists entirely of the bleached bones of human beings. Undeterred, he sets sail in a 'deflatable cushion-craft of his own invention.'

Soon he finds a gigantic footprint, and a piece of sword, which communicates with him telepathically – or 'astrobolically.' The voice wants to know the whereabouts of Lohk and his army. The Doctor hotly denies being Ulla, controller of the devil-birds. He flings down the shard of sword, and has a nasty encounter with one of the vicious birds. Following that he meets humanoid children, Dot and Jack – offspring of the top Earth scientist Harroll Strong. Their tale of being colonists on this world of Corbo is a terrifying one, culminating in a battle between giant green-skinned people and the devil-birds. The children are the only living survivors.

Together they climb the cliffs to get a closer look at the giant devil-birds, discovering that they are actually robots! Ulla the bird king is in the cavern, perched on an armchair and gazing with 'spiteful eyes' at four Earthmen, among them the twins' father. 'Look upon my devil-birds – and then die!' squawks the wicked Ulla.

The Doctor steps in to prevent a nasty and brutal execution, wielding his walking stick against gleaming swords. There is an outbreak of violence and a 'flurry of feathers.' The green-skinned aliens have landed again, so Ulla sends his robot birds out to do battle. Harroll Strong is reunited with his children and everyone hurries to escape aboard Dr. Who's homemade cushion-craft, which zips them back to the island of bleached bones.

Having urged his friends aboard the Tardis, the Doctor comes under attack from Ulla himself, who swoops out of the 'brazen skies.' Dr. Who gives the bird king a well-deserved thwacking with his walking stick. 'I feel all the better for giving that bully of a bird king a taste of my cane!'

A black feather is lodged in his silvery mane, and the Doctor gives it to the Earth boy Jack as a souvenir, just as he gave the Earth children in last year's Annual a hacked-off spider's leg. Another touching memento of a space adventure shared with Dr. Who.

THE PLAYTHINGS OF FO

Jack and Dot and their space captain father are still aboard the Tardis! When the new story opens Dr. Who is still lumbered with the task of getting them home. He seems quite irked. There are also some other spacemen left over from the previous adventure and it is they who accompany the Doctor into a jungle. He suggests they all don contra-gravity suits so they can gain a wider perspective on where they have fetched up. It turns out they've landed in the palm of a gigantic sleeping Cyclops.

The Doctor and his spacemen chums are drawn into a newly-arrived spaceship by beings who speak an unfamiliar, gobbling tongue. The hen-like beings observe that the giant Fo has woken up and made off with Dr. Who's Tardis. As the space craft flies off the Doctor is in an 'agony of mind' for a good half hour. They zoom into a cavern in the side of a mountain, and discover an underground city, filled with hen people who want to get a good look at them. They are the Kaarks of the planet Rhoos, and the Doctor and his friends are taken before their friendly Kaark Supremo.

While the humans are invited to feed themselves buffet-style the Kaarks tell all about the giant Fo, who drifted through space from the Black Galaxy, and who has made their lives a misery. Dr. Who and his friends soon find themselves captives – and playthings – of the terrifying Fo, who appears to have built a kind of model village, alien zoo and combat arena. Even when he finds Tardis, Harroll Strong and the twins safely intact, the Doctor cannot simply 'dissolve' away out of this place. He feels he must help his new friends the Kaarks. He dashes out of the Tardis, scares a leopard with his walking stick, and flings a bomb at Fo, killing the giant stone dead. It's as if he gets tired of all the faffing about, and decides to finish the story quickly, and so liberates the planet Rhoos in a violent rush of action.

JUSTICE OF THE GLACIANS

Suddenly free of companions, the Doctor arrives somewhere chilly beyond the G-Star of Ambivalence 5. He observes a short, hairy fellow escaping on his ski-like feet down a glacier, fleeing from a group of similar-looking creatures who are firing Ultra-Beam guns at him. Donning Zero Boots, the Doctor wades in to help. From a deadly crevasse he manages to rescue a smooth-faced, furry and very grateful creature: Grahm the Glacian from the planet Bruhl. Accused of stealing a thought-cube, Grahm is on the run. There is no justice on this world since Rraprro became Wise One in the City Under the Ice.

The police catch up with them before they can make it to the Tardis. They are dragged before thin-faced Rraprro, who without hesitation condemns Grahm to 'death by icicles.' He dismisses the Doctor as a 'weird creature', making the Doctor bridle furiously. With a bit of probing, Dr. Who learns from Grahm that Rraprro came to power after the disappearance of the Zilgors – a peaceful alien race who brought their telepathic cubes of knowledge for the benefit of the Glacians.

Soon they are rescued by the scientist Ffreuf in his spherical car. He explains that it was he who stole the thought cube because he and his companions believe it contains a clue as to why the Zilgors left, and how to overthrow Rraprro. Dr. Who is flattered that the Glacian rebels are seeking his help in trying to read the thought cube. Mystifyingly, he wants to know if the Zilgors left an old couch behind. The Glacians rather embarrassedly explain that they threw it out. Ffreuf and the others go out to hunt for this important settee – and as luck would have it, they succeed.

While he looks as if he's taking a nap, the Doctor is actually communing with the Zilgors – who, it turns out, are still here! They are frozen into a block of ice in a cavern known as Mura Six. The Glacians are both pleased and furious, setting off at once to liberate their alien friends. As the Doctor makes his way back to the Tardis, he struggles through a heated battle between rebels and Rraprro's men, mulling over the possibility of one day inventing a device that will give him fair warning of how dangerous and strenuous an adventure is likely to be.

TEN FATHOM PIRATES

The Doctor is resigned to the inevitability of the Tardis materializing deep underwater, reminding himself of his tangle last year with the Fish-men of Kandalinga. Men in multi-coloured rubber suits swim into view brandishing their vibratory rifles. They are pirates! And they drag the Doctor and his ship into their underwater dome. He meets some flamboyantly dressed men, one of which displays physical grace, a cruel expression and a half-missing ear. The Doctor deduces he must be the pirate chief. The Tardis seems to them to be like a treasure chest, but it won't yield its secrets to axe-blows or any other kind of force.

The Doctor blags it. He needs a Renticular Celluprime Number 2 to fix the Tardis lock, he says. He is to be sent on a piratical mission against his will, but finds himself exhilarated by the journey anyway. In the Secretariat building Dr. Who's special tool proves to be non-existent, and the pirates' attack goes badly awry. The Doctor nips aboard the sea-scooter and races underwater once more to the undersea citadel, where he soon eludes the guards and gets back aboard his precious Tardis – wily old twister that he is.

Other Content

ESCAPE FROM PLANET X

A board game for two or more players, in which the aim is to journey across the hazardous Planet X, in order to reach the Tardis and escape! Among the hazards are a prehistoric monster, robots, enemy flying saucers and, more prosaically, bad weather.

Doctor Who Himself

He is 'inured' by now to 'many unbelievable wonders.' He carries with him a 'super ring' which carries out many of the functions his sonic screwdriver one day will. He is very averse to the idea of organic peoples allowing robots to take over the running of everything. Dr. Who is wonderfully and deceptively insouciant in the face of deadly danger. 'Tut tut!' he scolds the wicked lackeys of the bird king of Corbo, just as they are about to behead some Earthmen.

Dr. Who doesn't think of himself as especially brave, and he thinks Fate has a hand in directing his travels in time and space. He is wonderfully indignant wherever he goes: rapping his cane upon the floor at the outrageous things aliens say. Not one for subterfuge, he announces to anyone who'll listen that he is a traveller in space and time. He keeps microfilm records of his past adventures on shelves in the Tardis, ready for consulting when he returns and needs to remember the names of his friends, erstwhile enemies, etc. However, when asked where he originated from, he has no answer. It was so long ago, and so much has happened to him, his beginning has 'long since' been forgotten – perhaps, even by Dr. Who himself.

'You are all friends now. That is my reward!' These are the final words of the Doctor to Duh and everyone he has met during his return journey to Birr. It's a succinct and pleasing mission statement. All the old man wants is to see

40

everyone happy and at peace. However, I have the sneaking suspicion that he likes just as much – if not more – those occasions when he has to cause a massive brouhaha and a revolution, destroy all the robots, trounce the villain in a battle of mind powers and finally blow the whole shebang into smithereens.

Monsters and Villains

The vaporous Ethereals are victims of a robot revolt. They intend to use Dr. Who rather like the rubber mould in a 'Shaker Maker' to provide themselves with new humanoid forms. The Baggolts with their shiny heads and bell-shaped feet are their robots who revolted and seized control of Droog City.

The 'evil genius' Deemon wears tight-fitting black costumes and stirs up trouble between the Sons of Grekk and the insects with which they share their world. Ulla, the masked bird king of Corbo, wears even more black, and is even more tiresome in his determination to make the Doctor suffer for interference in his plans. The giant Cyclops Fo has floated from the Black Dimension to the planet Rhoos, much to the consternation of the local hen people. He delights in creating miniature zoos and forcing aliens to take part in gladiatorial contests, of which we see very little before Dr. Who blows him to smithereens. Rraprro in his frozen city and the pirate captain, dressed in tight-fitting gold in his subaqueous citadel, are both intriguing villains, but we don't see them actually do very much.

Villains are fond of tight-fitting outfits.

Curious Companions?

Halfway through the 1967 Annual the Doctor meets the space astronaut Harroll Strong, his flame-haired children and three assorted spacemen. Having rescued them from the devil birds of Corbo, the Doctor makes the rash promise of getting them back to Earth.

Fiendish Wheezes

They aren't particularly clever, but they're fiendish enough, throughout the 1967 Annual. Mostly, subjugation is the order of the day: robot uprisings and giant birds attacking human beings. There are a few black-robed super villains – Deemon and Ulla, for example – slinking about their control rooms and sitting on thrones and plotting the downfall of everyone else. Mostly, the plans are not terribly sophisticated.

TV Feedback

Before colour TV the mysterious region that the Tardis flew through was grey, and it was called 'the transdimensional flux', which sounds even less inviting than 'the vortex.'

Anticipating the Future

When the Ethereals explain that, during the revolt of the robotic Baggolts, the first up against the wall and shot was the creator who gave them the power of independent thought, we think straight away of Davros.

Classic moments

The Sons of Grekk laughing at the Tardis, and the Doctor being pop-eyed with fury at their lack of respect. Later, when their robot slaves push the Tardis out of a castle window, the Doctor reacts like an action hero in order to save his beloved ship.

The giant thistle creature Phlege of the Verdants on Birr recognises our hero: 'Why..! You… you are Doctor Who!' This is a moment that gives me a warm glow. It feels like living in a very reassuring universe, that prickly kings of vengeful species can suddenly cheer up like this. I love the way that Duh and the Doctor sit either side of his throne as he gives an elaborate shrug at the thought of the entire conflict simply being an enormous mistake. 'I am glad!' he says.

The Doctor giving Ulla the bird king a thrashing with his walking cane is a perfect moment of mid-Sixties Who. Later, he takes up the same silver-topped can to threaten an alien leopard, which soon slinks away from him.

Faced by deadly and flamboyant underwater pirates Dr. Who bamboozles them by instantly concocting ripe technobabble and sending them on a wild goose chase.

What I learned from the Doctor Who Annual 1967

The Doctor has a number of favourite plans which he proposes whenever the going gets tough and an urgent solution is required. Often the enemy's city or base needs to be infiltrated. Dr. Who and the rebels will capture some guards and wear their uniforms, their armour or even their very skins in order to bluff their way inside the base. Once there, the Doctor will seek out the control room and the evil genius villain, who will be stooped over a control panel, monitoring progress of his fiendish plan and / or the battle between his forces and the revolutionaries. Often the Doctor will engage the villain in some kind of contest. A battle of wits or wills or – more likely – a mind duel. If all else fails, the Doctor will suggest blowing up a handy volcano, in order to cause an almighty eruption.

Also, if an adventure is going badly wrong, we learn from Dr. Who that all we have to do is just stop – nick a vehicle of some kind – and peg it back to the Tardis as fast as we can. Just drop everything and get out of there.

Most alien monsters – whether vaporised and disembodied intelligences or murderous flowers – are extremely sensitive to loud noises. Be prepared to scream your lungs out.

Illustrations

Hartnell is more recognizable in this year's illustrations. The style is, on the whole, much the same as the first annual's – simplistic and cartoony at times, but it's not without a rudimentary charm, especially in depicting outlandish aliens such as the king of the Verdants, Ulla the bird king, or Duh the Rostrow.

The 1968 Annual

With the Doctor's regeneration, the universe he lives in has become a more deadly place. He and his friends watch horrified as the brains of their enemies burst, sending out plumes of smoke. The Tardis crew are brainwashed, recruited to murder alien overlords, and menaced by metal grasshoppers as soon as they step out of the Tardis. This is a new, young, energetic crew led by a reinvigorated Doctor, and it seems they will need every bit of their courage and zest.

The cosmos is infinite, the Doctor keeps telling his companions. Destiny guides him, and there are many more dimensions than even he thought possible. This is a young Doctor, getting used to the idea of a bigger, richer and even more exciting universe.

Sometimes he can be a bit snappish.

The Stories

THE SOUR NOTE

Polly and the Doctor go chasing after Ben, who is off jogging on a new, inhospitable planet. When they encounter a giant robotic grasshopper their first thought is that it must have eaten the young sailor. The Doctor entices the monster back to the Tardis by imitating its chirrups with his 'musical pipe.' Back at the Tardis they discover Ben himself, and have to dash to escape the robot insect.

THE DREAM MASTERS

Dr. Who is a prisoner in a kind of factory where he turns dials and works on a vast machine, then sleeps in a nearby bed and has the most wonderful dreams of being a hero. Two nice young people called Ben and Polly both work close by, but he can't chat with them, because he receives an electric shock every time he pauses in his labours. The three friends realise that they are being brainwashed, and still they don't remember what the blue box in the corner is for.

   A blank-faced man liberates them and gives them a mission: to kill the beings who keep the populace working like drones. They are shown to a room filled with a hundred once-human brains: the Dream Masters! Will the Doctor comply and actually murder living beings?

THE TESTS OF TREFUS *(Picture strip)*

On a less hostile world than usual, a gaggle of long-haired aliens greet the Doctor with great reverence, and assume Ben and Polly are his servants simply because they have fair hair. Tonga tells them that people with black hair rule this world. The Doctor speaks up for Tonga and his blond folk when he meets the king of the black-haired people. The king responds that the blonds will only be treated like actual people if they can pass the Tests of Trefus.

The tests include swimming with deadly crocodiles and a tug-of-war. The Doctor helps out by stunning the crocodiles and rigging the tug-of-war by using a magnetised belt. Thus Dr. Who ends slavery on this strange world.

THE WORD OF ASIRIES

On a rainy world Dr. Who receives an abrupt visit by amber-eyed, green-cloaked aliens whose leader, Qar, is apparently waiting impatiently for him. He is taken to observe live Tryods in the wild: strange, golden-haired creatures with organs that secrete a healing balm. Qar offers money for their hides, which doesn't impress the Doctor. It turns out that the 'frigid-featured' Qar is mistakenly expecting the Doctor to bring permission for her to massacre the Tryods. The Doctor has been mistaken for a messenger from the leader of the galaxy! Qar starts to doubt him: his hair is too straggly, his teeth uneven, and he grimaces so queerly.

Far from succeeding in saving the Tryods, it looks as if the Doctor is going to be fed to them instead. The true messenger Asiries burns him free of the sticky lichen that traps him, but when they are attacked by a savage Tryod everything looks hopeless. Only his 'superior agility' can save the life of Dr. Who. And only his highly-developed sense of moral responsibility can make Asiries see that the Tryods must be saved.

ONLY A MATTER OF TIME

The Tardis is like a speck of dust in the midst of a fleet of Arcturan warships on their way to Earth. The Doctor believes they have been drawn here by Destiny. Soon they are taken aboard a ship and are confronted by the small, birdlike Arcturans themselves. They left their world many generations ago because its atmosphere was leaking out into space, and they are on a hunt for a new home. The Doctor frets for the safety of their eggs on Earth, and leads them into the Ninth Dimension.

PLANET OF BONES

They've landed in what Polly describes as heaven, but even so, Dr. Who and Ben are still peevish and sarcastic with each other. The Doctor even threatens to abandon him on a world of 'loathsome monsters' because of his 'youthful cynicism.' They decide to call this world 'Arcady', and Polly muses that perhaps they'll find colours here that Earth people – lumbered with just 'seven stodgy' hues – don't even know about.

The locals sing their language at them. 'Lead me to the eats,' says Ben. They discover a neo-classical civilization where all seems peaceful. They gobble up fruit and cakes 'to repletion.' Ben is very approving of 'space grub', but the Doctor is suspicious. Soon enough he finds a room filled with macabre heads and he overhears what the locals intend for him and his companions. He almost faints with horror. 'Frightful discords' from his recorder scare away the flesh-eating aggressors long enough for the Tardis team to make good their escape.

WHEN STARLIGHT GROWS COLD

'My biological probe is completely cold and neutral,' announces Dr. Who, startling his two young friends. By this he means he can discover nothing about the blank portion of space they have arrived in. The Doctor and Ben wear spacesuits to explore the cold, dark expanses between the universes. Signs of life are detected and the sceptical Doctor is confronted by something that looks like a giant erector-set.

Inside, they find giant cocoons which have at some point burst open, revealing a dozen creatures lying in suspended animation and extruding masses of hair. Polly manages to shift the Tardis – against all the odds – and rescue her friends before the hideous beings from another universe can wake up.

WORLD WITHOUT NIGHT (Picture Strip)

All three travellers are impressed by the acrobatic men flying about in a stadium the Tardis lands in. This is the Planet of Light, where our friends find that they are expected by Igor and the elders, who study the heavens. They are living in fear of a coming eclipse, when they think everyone will go crazy.

It happens every three hundred years and it seems that, aside from sending the youngsters into hibernation, there is nothing to be done to prevent the coming disaster.

H.M.S TARDIS

'Golly!' Ben is delighted that Tardis has materialised upon a ship in Earth's past. Emerging into the chaos of a sea battle, the travellers learn they are aboard HMS *Victory*, just before they are arrested as French spies. The young seaman's eyes bulge almost out of his head when they are brought face to face with Admiral Nelson. Ben is almost flogged as a deserter, Polly is sick over the side, and the Doctor decides to alter the outcome of the Battle of Trafalgar and change history.

Posing as a wizard and an astrologer, the Doctor tells Nelson that he will be triumphant. But Nelson won't heed the Doctor's warnings to go below decks. Ben tells the Doctor philosophically: you can't beat fate. Nelson dies as

46

history decrees and, mystifyingly, the Doctor comments: 'One has to try, hasn't one?' This is, of course, quite out of character for Dr. Who. (So is having green hair, like the thatch he's sporting in the accompanying illustration.)

THE KING OF GOLDEN DEATH

Ben, Polly and the Doctor land in a Pharaoh's tomb in Ancient Egypt and the mummies are still fresh. While the Doctor reasons that this must be the burial place of 'Tut-Ankh-Amen' himself, Ben and Polly are more interested in stuffing the Tardis with all the loot that's lying about. 'You two make me sick,' snaps Dr. Who. Clearly the events of 1968's Annual have left him cheesed off with his travelling companions. I wouldn't be very surprised if they don't make it into 1969's.

There are other tomb-robbers at work here, and they can be heard digging their way toward the treasure. The Doctor hits upon a spooky plan to chase them away. It is Ben who carries it out, scaring the robbers by wearing a golden mask. They flee, causing a rock fall and the tomb of King Tut can stay undisturbed until the twentieth century. Ben has seen the sense in not stealing anything and he's keen to continue travelling with the Doctor and Polly: 'Let's get where the stars are!'

Other Content

AIMING FOR THE MOON

A factual article by Kevin McGarry on the then current race to land on the Moon. The writer mainly concerns himself with a description of the training US astronauts undergo, which is perhaps fortunate, as his one prediction – that 'there should be an Earth Colony on the Moon before the year 2000' – proved sadly optimistic.

PHOENIX IN THE TARDIS

A description and explanation of Dr Who's recent rejuvenation into a younger, more 'with it' 900-year-old man.

TRAVELS OF THE TARDIS

A board game for a very precise '2,3 or 4 players'. Split over two very colourful pages, the aim of the game is (for unexplained reasons) to move the Tardis from London in 1993 to Trafalgar Square in 1967, via 11 different locations in space and time.

Visits to Scotland in 1745 and Rome in 33 A.D presumably refer to the TV stories 'The Highlanders' and 'The Romans', but it seems that the Tardis has had plenty of unseen adventures.

THE LOST CONTINENT OF ATLANTIS

An extremely peculiar two-page piece on the mythical kingdom of Atlantis (possibly prompted by the TV story 'The Underwater Menace') which states that 'there can be no doubt that Atlantis was the fountainhead of Eastern and Western civilisation'. It's a bit like finding a serious article on the reality of a Flat Earth in the latest Jodie Whittaker Annual.

- THE PASSENGERS – Brief character portraits of Polly and Ben.
- SPACE DICTIONARY – Basic definitions of common space terms.
- MEN WHO MADE HISTORY – Articles on Galileo and Yuri Gagarin.
- PEEPHOLE AT SPACE: TARGET ONE – Article on the Moon: why does Man want to go there, and what can he expect to find.
- A SKYFUL OF SAUCERS – A potted history of UFO sightings.
- THE SKY AT NIGHT – A guide to the Zodiac and the constellations which comprise it.
- TEST FROM TARDIS – Crossword.
- THE SOLAR SYSTEM – A guide to the planets of the Solar System.
- LOST DR WHO – A maze puzzle, in which the reader must help Dt Who find his way on the planet Zarba.
- TIME AND TIME AGAIN – A short article on the history of calendars.
- DR WHO 'BACK TO THE TARDIS' – A board game, based on Ludo.
- STAR FACTS – Facts about astronomers.
- ALL SET FOR TAKEOFF – A multiple choice space quiz.

Doctor Who Himself

This early after his first regeneration he isn't quite himself. He says things like 'My dear boy!' and wears a 'tall, furry hat'. Polly finds him full of 'sardonic ways' and 'whimsical fancies.' Since his 'reincarnation', as he puts it, he finds himself with an altogether more youthful cast of mind. A feature article describes him as 'the Phoenix in the Tardis', made young again after 900 years in his first incarnation. This Doctor is much more 'with it' and 'switched on' to 'our' modern world.

His new self has invented a few devices that his previous one wouldn't have bothered with, including a machine that tells him all about each new locality and its inhabitants without him even having to set foot outside. Nowadays he knows that there is nothing chancy and random about his travels. Destiny directs him to where he needs to be.

He is Pan-like and, like that capricious god, he tootles away on his pipe. He's more impulsive and geared to action than the old Doctor was. He *fidgets* – and that he can 'never settle down to our mundane existence' is an interesting observation. One day, not too far distant, he will have to contend with that very inconceivable thing.

In the meantime he is becoming a brave hero, rather than the dabbling scientist and thrill-seeker of previous years. When Asiries gives him the chance to return to the Tardis, he elects to stay and to try his level best to prevent the massacre of the Tryods.

He is just a bit patronizing, casting superior looks at his companions, and calling them 'my children.' This is a Second Doctor who does a lot more sneering than he did on TV. 'Weren't you exposed to any sort of culture in your education?' he chides his poor friends.

Monsters and Villains

Robot grasshoppers and disembodied brains that control people's dreams abound in the world of this Doctor. Queen Qar – keen to massacre the Tryods that infest her world – is openly contemptuous when the Doctor stammeringly explains how little control he has over his path through time and space. The seemingly peaceful, toga-wearers of Harmony turn out to be human flesh-eating fiends. But apart from these few, there aren't many out-and-out fiendish villains in this year's Annual.

Curious Companions?

The Annual begins with Ben Jackson pummelling his own midriff. He feels cooped up and restless aboard the Tardis and decides that wherever they materialise next, he's going out for a run. All the talk of time, space, destiny and dimensions makes Ben's 'nut ache', and he's always asking Polly to pass the aspirins. The Doctor loves to wind him up.

Polly 'being a girl' has a much better grasp on the idea of time travel and paradoxes than Ben. She also has a greater implicit faith in the Doctor. And in turn he thinks she has 'a good head on those pretty shoulders.' Even so, when danger is near, both the Doctor and Ben grow impatient with her girly 'snivelling' and 'grizzling.' Polly does, however, impress the Doctor by being

49

able – through sheer mischance – to pilot the Tardis through space without altering the time factor: something he has longed to be able to do.

Fiendish Wheezes

Below ground the enslaved Doradans do all the work, pushing buttons and turning levers, while above-ground their alien Dream Masters have taken over their world completely, using the power of dreams and nightmares to keep everyone controlled. The rulers of the unknown planet divided by hair colour keep their underlings servile by being better at tug-of-war and swimming. The people of Harmony have a fairly straightforward plan: feed their visitors from space with cakes and sweets until they themselves are good enough to eat.

Egregious errors

Is it an error to claim that the First Doctor was 900 years old when he regenerated into the Second? 900 is often used in all kinds of *Doctor Who* stories as a term simply to mean 'very old.' The Sixth claimed to be that old, as did the Tenth. The Second was sometimes 450 and the Fourth about 740.

'We'll defy Fate, Ben. We'll change history!' A queer mood overtakes the Doctor when he visits HMS *Victory* during the Battle of Trafalgar. He becomes determined to see that Admiral Nelson doesn't die. Surely this is the most egregious error ever? When was the Doctor ever so heedless of messing about with what he will later call 'the web of time'?

Already in this Annual he has talked about his travels being guided by Destiny. Is he perhaps rebelling against his role in the universe? He is trying to do the very thing that the Time Lords will eventually punish him for.

Classic moments

The Doctor detonating crocodiles is a startling moment. It's a relief to hear that the reptiles soon recover. Suspicious at the paradise that has welcomed him and his companions, Dr. Who has a shufti around the 'Planet of Bones' and discovers a roomful of severed heads! Ben and the Doctor are excited to be aboard *Victory* during the Battle of Trafalgar. Polly vomits.

What I learned from the Doctor Who Annual 1968

Jogging is bad for you. Boring jobs are not to be trusted: somewhere there is a crazed living brain controlling all your thoughts and actions. Hair colour is no reflection of a person's worth. If you're going to invade Earth, you're going to need some proper weapons. History cannot be rewritten, it turns out. You can argue with everyone involved in a historical turning point, but they won't take a blind bit of notice.

There are many more dimensions than even Dr. Who knows about. And gaps and strange bits between universes.

Illustrations

The style is very much like the first two Annuals, with its sketchy aliens and rudimentary space craft. The artists seem to find it harder to capture the likeness of Patrick Troughton than they did William Hartnell.

The 1969 Annual

These Sixties Annuals have a strapline on their covers: 'Fascinating stories of the unknown based on the famous television series.' It's a charming slogan for these books to adopt, promising in one breath familiarity and cosiness, as well as novelty and strangeness. The relationship between the cover and the contents of the 1969 Annual is a kind of embodiment of this tension between the familiar and the new. The cover illustration depicts a highly dramatic moment in which the Doctor is apparently saving the life of brawny young Scots companion, Jamie, from a marauding Cyberman. Very excitingly, it seems as if the steel monsters are about to gain access to the interior of the Tardis itself. The roundels have turned blood red as if in dismay. Jamie is brandishing what appears to be a Dalek pincer-arm in self-defence and the Doctor is managing to give his brawny companion – even in the midst of all these goings-on – a crafty little cuddle.

But the fact is nothing remotely like this stuff happens anywhere in the whole book. No Cybermen, no Yeti (one can be seen giving a despairing shrug on the back cover) nor any villain even remotely familiar from TV series graces the stories inside.

This should make the 1969 Annual disappointing, but it's nothing of the sort. There's plenty to keep us entertained here.

The Stories

LORDS OF THE GALAXY

The Tardis has brought Dr. Who, Jamie and Victoria to a No Man's Land in the midst of an interstellar war. A lilac beam lifts them through the cosmic conflict into a space craft belonging to revolting, tusked, musky-smelling alien beings. They are Saurians, like the ancient Earth reptiles, but ones who have a spaceship. Taken before the ten-feet tall Supreme Lizard Haxtl, our heroes are treated as quite a prise. The lizards are very keen on learning more about Earth people and their apparent ability to turn invisible. In this version of the future, Earth pilots its way round the galaxy like a colossal pirate ship..! The Doctor seems very impressed by the idea of the people of Earth becoming 'Lords of the Galaxy,' and he tricks the Saurian leader by pretending to become a traitor.

FOLLOW THE PHANTOMS

In a curious instance of intra-Annual continuity Jamie glares at the detector device that the Doctor invented in the 1968 book. This 'pet invention' is supposed to deliver the low-down on each new environment the Tardis lands in, and also on the local population. It's not saying much and neither is the Doctor. All they can see on the scanner screen is a parade of oddly handsome humanoids and a very strange cloud.

They travel in the Doctor's homemade plane (a 'Floater') after the column of marching men but they can't attract their attention. And then they witness those men marching into the cloud, and the mirage of a city from long-ago…

Jamie ends up being whisked into the past, where the natives believe that he has been sent by Otinogg, their god of war. It is prophesied that one such as the young Scot will come to lead the battle against the Scythias. Monstrous slugs, these turn out to be, and Jamie isn't keen on the prospect of tangling with them. The Doctor pops up in the mysterious cloud just in time to rescue his friend and, when they are safe once more, he pretends to be cross with the brawny young man. But you can tell he isn't really.

MASTERMIND OF SPACE

Our friends from the Tardis find themselves captured by the Masters of Space and Time, who want to leach all the knowledge from their brains. The Doctor fills up his own mind-screen with everything he has ever known and seen, including all the galactic horrors he has encountered – most notably, parrot-men. What his captors are most interested in, however, is his ability to think of absolutely nothing and to still his mind completely.

Victoria pities their non-corporeal hosts, who – it turns out – want to find their way back to being flesh and blood creatures again. It's such a long time since they had 'organs of living.' The Doctor is left to consider a whole new universe populated by Victorias and Jamies.

FREEDOM BY FIRE *(Picture Strip)*

On an alien world the Kraals are mountain-dwelling plants that have developed a taste for human flesh. The Doctor realises that the local inhabitants haven't yet discovered fire since their world doesn't have seasons and they never get cold (the natives all seem to go about naked but for ragged-hemmed skirts.) Dr. Who invents fire for them and they set about destroying every single one of their enemies.

THE CELESTIAL TOYSHOP

When they arrive in a place filled with gigantic toys the Doctor declares that he's 'in the mood for magic.' Amongst the bears and trains and soldiers the Doctor gets caught up in an infinitely recursive dolls' house, and soon the faces of the toys around him start to seem subtly wrong… Things get very trippy indeed before he realises he's caught in an 'intra-dimensional flux' and he feels compelled to make a 'frantic search for reality.'

When he gets back to the Tardis he sleeps but doesn't dream and will always be left with a sense of regret about the wonders he didn't quite manage to see that day…

VALLEY OF DRAGONS

They've landed in the 'deep galactic environs', and apparently on the back of a giant reptile..! When the Doctor suggests they all wear contra-gravity belts in order to fly about the place, am I the only one wondering what's become of his much-vaunted Floater?

They spy on bird people fighting a giant crocodile, and pretty soon wind up having a conversation with one of the creatures (who are really very reminiscent of the hen-like fellows in the 1967 Annual.) The Manti rule over all, however, and it is they who try to feed the Doctor to the dragon. The Doctor pacifies the beast with his pipe-playing, claiming that it is enthralled by the marvellous music he's making.

PLANET FROM NOWHERE

Dr. Who and his friends have found a weird, cathedral-like place filled to the brim with dormant humanoids in glass coffins. Picking out the right lever, the Doctor rashly decides to bring them all back to life. As soon as they revive, they start to worship the Tardis trio which, as the Doctor muses, really won't do at all. 'You are the gods we never believed in,' one man in a metallic outfit tells them. They are Salonians, and put themselves to sleep in order to suffer penance for their warlike ways.

The Doctor is quite curt with them, accusing them of 'sleeping (their) cowardly sleep of unconsciousness.' They are appalled to see everything on their world destroyed, but for the temple where they have been sleeping. Suddenly the Salonians are intent on launching revenge against the Colonians and the Doctor's feeling a bit silly and guilty for waking them up. 'How dare they come and obliterate our lovely hemisphere?' moan the Salonians.

The Doctor can't explain to them that time and erosion have taken away their home. He even weeps with frustration. He feels he is 'lost': the 'most wicked man in the universe.' He begins to suspect that they are seeing the far future of Earth itself, in which mankind is in the process of wiping itself out.

HAPPY AS QUEEG

The working class of the planet Krill like to go about in rainbow-coloured tights and cloaks, we are reliably informed. Dr. Who has been brainwashed and is quite happy working for his robot masters. He doesn't even recognise Jamie and Victoria when they come to rescue him! 'Poor old Doctor Who!' cries Jamie, slapping a ray-foil helmet over his head.

54

Back in his right mind, the Doctor is determined to 'smash the rule of the robots' and free the slaves. At last he finds Queeg – whose happiness everyone in this Dystopia tries to emulate. Of course he is just a lump of disembodied brain who foolishly challenges the Doctor to a mind duel... which our hero wins, but is left feeling giddier than his favourite Aunt.

ATOMS INFINITE (Picture Strip.)

Dr. Who has worked out a way to shrink the Tardis in such a way that will allow him to explore inner space, as a change from outer space. He and his friends soon discover that it is a 'sad time' to visit the nucleus of an atom. A face inside a tree starts telling them all about the history of this world inside the Uranium atom. 'Quickly!' shouts the Doctor. He has a shrewd idea that the whole planet could explode at any moment, which it does. By the end of the story he's imagining huge galaxies in which our Earth is just the size of an atom.

WORLD OF ICE

The Doctor has always wanted to explore the snowy world of Pendant. When the Doctor and Jamie return from exploring, Victoria is horrified to find that they have been replaced by lookalike robots. There's a fracas involving an elongated furry monster, a bottle of perfume, Victoria and the robots: the whole thing observed by badger-like aliens clutching 'strange, tubular weapons.' These are the Morogs, who are forced to live underground by the aggressive and robotic Cogwens. Clever Victoria proposes using the Tardis as a Trojan horse to get the Morogs into the Citadel. Once the revolution is in progress, she is able to set about rescuing her friends.

THE MICROTRON MEN

Arriving somewhere rather pleasant, the Tardis crew are dismayed to find themselves rapidly shrinking to the point that a nearby ant becomes the size of an elephant. They meet some tiny, gloomy people who tell them that life is too short here in their miniature world for 'long-term problems.' It is given to the Doctor to solve the riddle of their miserable existence, so he lies in the grass on his stomach, thinking of impossible things. Eventually he figures out the amazing truth – that they have landed upon the nucleus of a Uranium atom. The revelation would be a lot more impressive had it not come after 'Atoms Infinite' in which precisely the same thing occurred.

Oddly, some of these stories seem to have actual science in them.

DEATH TO MUFL

We don't hear much about their disturbing adventure in Galaxy G, but the Tardis crew are still recovering from it. Out exploring by himself, the Doctor is so distracted by the three moons that he falls down a hole. Below he meets men with antennae and terrier-like guards who accuse him of coming to kill Mufl.

The Doctor finds that this planet of Vegan is home to two races, and one race of rebels are forever trying to assassinate the ruler of the other. During his audience with Mufl, Dr. Who realises that he has been hypnotised by a traitor in the camp and is under instructions to kill the gentle ruler himself! The Doctor's 'musical pipe' proves essential to making sure that everything turns out well.

Other Content

There seems to be no need to describe the contents of this year's features in any detail. Everything anyone needs to know is contained in the title!

- STAR FACTS
- ABOUT THE MOON
- THE UNKNOWN WORLD UNDER THE SEA
- SPACE DICTIONARY
- OUR SOLAR SYSTEM
- SPACE PANORAMA
- MEN IN SPACE
- LOOKING BACK
- PIONEERS OF FLIGHT
- SPACE QUIZ
- RETURN FROM HADES
- SPACE SPECIAL
- DR. WHO'S PLANET QUIZ
- THE MYSTERIES OF SPACE

Doctor Who Himself

'This, children, is where the action is,' Dr. Who announces to Jamie and Victoria as they arrive somewhere terrifying at the start of this Annual. His two new companions are ribbing him about never being able to pilot the ship properly. The truth as we know it from the Annuals is that Dr. Who simply can't control the Tardis. His machine is complicit with the mysterious workings of Destiny. Is this why he says, so heavily: 'It's all happening here'? Perhaps he is speaking with the gravitas of one who knows that his existential struggle is essentially meaningless and he is, ineluctably and already, 'Time's Champion'?

He assumes he stands on a pedestal of greatness in relation to ordinary mortal beings. This isn't the shabbily unassuming Second Doctor that we know from TV. Apparently he's always been sure that his is the greatest scientific mind of any century..!

He's indignant and brave when it comes to dealing with wrong-doers: 'Wait till I come face to face with them, I'll tell them!' He describes their captors in 'Mastermind of Space' as 'someone or some*thing*', which is exactly what his TV counterpart would say.

Even his 'strong spirit' isn't enough to withstand the 'ineffable light' that lies behind the complex dimensions of the Celestial Toyshop. That place really does his head in. He's torn between infinite wonders and getting back to familiar reality.

He's given to crying out things like, 'Great galaxies!'

Monsters and Villains

The Supreme Lizard Haxtl, slithering across his throne room, is a lovely, silvery, ferocious beast, determined to dissect the Tardis trio. He's quite used to 'raying out' his deadly beams, softening up the galaxy's more 'decadent' races. The Doctor says his scaly people are 'filthy monsters.' The Scythias, meanwhile, are hideous sluglike beings which 'wriggle' towards the appalled Jamie at a 'tremendous rate.' Elsewhere Doctor Who meets life-sized dollies, praying mantises who wear multi-coloured cloaks, flesh-eating jungle plants, robots who rule worlds of ice and the self-proclaimed Masters of Space and Time, who are a non-corporeal gestalt entity who capture other life forms in order to study them.

It seems that just as *Doctor Who* on TV is rejoicing in a Golden Age for heterogeneous monsters, the Annual is doing likewise, and all the poor Tardis travellers can do is run for their lives.

Curious Companions?

Victoria screams at the feel of alien claws running over her body, while Jamie stiffens angrily. Both are easily discombobulated by encounters in space. Victoria says and does everything 'a trifle anxiously.' She sticks up for the Doctor and his eccentric whims in the face of Jamie's aggression and bluster. The dynamics – it has to be said – are rather similar to those between Ben, Polly and the Doctor last year.

It is Victoria's selfless compassion that allows the Masters of Space and Time to call into existence a whole new universe for themselves. The Doctor is very impressed with her as she philosophises about love and the idea of the soul in a quite un-Victorian way.

Jamie wears a raffish Ascot as well as a kilt in this reality. He has a camera and wants to take snaps of the exotic places they visit and he impetuously gets himself into dangerous scrapes. In 'Follow the Phantoms' no one's heart can fail to be warmed by Jamie's excited shout of 'Doctor Who!' when his friend comes to rescue him. Nor, surely, can they fail to smile when the Doctor cries: 'Quick, my boy! Into the cloud! Hold my hand and don't let go!' This is the stuff that legendary cosmic friendships are made of.

Fiendish Wheezes

The Masters of Space and Time are kidnapping beings and draining minds of all knowledge. So advanced are these non-corporeal geniuses that they have discovered that the universe goes in circles and so they must return to the start and reincarnate as physical beings once more in order to evolve. The Doctor is not impressed by their asseverations 'All this,' he says gruffly, 'is of course nonsense.'

Captain J'nk is a traitor of the Planet Vegan. He uses the Doctor as the means to assassinate his leader Mufl, hypnotizing our hero when he should have been reading his mind, and slipping a ray gun into his coat pocket.

TV Feedback

As a weird dimension of space / time dressed up with monstrous playthings 'The Celestial Toyshop' seems to hark back to the TV adventure to do with a similarly cosmic Toymaker.

Anticipating the Future

Saurians with advanced space-faring technology anticipate the Silurian storyline running through TV *Doctor Who*, beginning with 'Doctor Who and the Silurians' in 1970 and continuing all the way until 2012's 'Dinosaurs on a Spaceship.'

The mind-bending shenanigans in 'The Celestial Toyshop' anticipate the infinitely recurring TARDISes of 'Logopolis', but also moments from the Annuals ('The House that Jack Built' from 1975, and 'Conundrum' from 1982.)

Egregious errors

Is it so out of kilter with the TV show that Dr. Who has a Floater? He has designed and built a flying machine for use on alien planets. I don't think it's an error as such. It's the kind of invention that would have worked marvellously for the Second Doctor as seen on TV, had the budget ran to such airborne fripperies.

Dr. Who claims to have constructed the Tardis himself...! The materials he used were intended to minimise all kinds of shock. It's a shock to the reader to hear him taking responsibility for the ship's existence like this. Surely he's got it wrong?

Not only has he built Tardises and Floaters, according to 'World of Ice' he has designed his own range of fleecy Arctic wear.

Victoria is called Polly at one point in 'Freedom by Fire'.

Classic moments

The Floater makes its Doctor Who Annual debut. It turns out that our hero has invented a portable flying craft that he keeps in a store cupboard. This easily outclasses the First Doctor's floating cushion of 1967. The Doctor lying in the long grass, figuring out the complexities of nuclear physics in a micro-universe is a lovely image, as is that of the Doctor falling down a hole in the planet Vegan, imagining he's Alice in Wonderland.

What I learned from the Doctor Who Annual 1969

Fate guides the Tardis to where it needs Dr. Who to be. In the future mankind will learn the secret of invisibility and every last person on the planet will become a pirate. Don't go chasing mirages. You will wind up being part of a hideous prophecy and have to fight gigantic slugs.

There's room for magic in an infinite universe. The Doctor states it quite plainly, when they arrive in a shop filled with marvellous, over-sized toys.

Dystopias are always ruled over by bodiless brains and maintained by bullyboy robots. Dr. Who will always, always overcome brainwashing, and whatever else they can fling at him, cause a revolution and win the day.

Stuff about the nuclei of atoms.

Illustrations

A change of artists this year brings us a more Doctorish Doctor, but also some rather generically pretty companions. The Doctor has a look of Ken Dodd about him at times.

The 1970 Annual

The Second Doctor's adventures often involve scientific facts about such things as prehistoric Earth, the structure of the atom, or the make-up of crystals. None of this stuff gets in the way of the more exciting business of ape men lopping the heads off plesiosaurs or Zoe getting kidnapped by blobby monsters. In these stories Dr. Who is kind of a fussy, grumpy, badly-dressed, unheroic-looking Flash Gordon.

The Stories

THE DRAGONS OF KEKOKRO

The Tardis has brought Dr. Who, Jamie and Zoe to what appears to be Earth in the time of the dinosaurs. Complicating matters is the appearance of gruff, armed ape men on a boat, who kidnap the time travellers. Our friends are astonished to find this erroneous civilization. 'You know, I wouldn't have missed this for worlds,' exclaims the Doctor in the midst of a skirmish. He's keen to study this world, but it's too dangerous. Zoe and Jamie drag him onto the back of a Stegosaurus, which carries them home to their ship.

THE SINGING CRYSTALS

A worrying opening sees the Tardis trio trapped in an ice cave and in imminent danger of being rendered 'completely frozen' and 'completely dead.' They are under attack from what seem to be extremely fast-growing freezing crystal structures. Shouting and screaming and noisy tape recorders seem to be the only means they have of defending themselves. Zoe is captured by doughlike creatures with rudimentary features and Jamie bravely rescues her.

Dr. Who realises that the clever crystals are after the minerals in the very bodies of the travellers themselves and Jamie sets to work smashing the beasts up with a handy spanner.

THE MYSTERY OF THE MARIE CELESTE

The legendary *Marie Celeste* is discovered on the surface of a world made of metal. Unseen aliens discuss the procuring of specimens from various points in Earth history, much to everyone's chagrin. The Doctor and his friends meet the crew of the *Marie Celeste*, and they manage to slip out of the grip of the methane-breathing Arcturans. But in the confusion Dr. Who has lost his Tardis key! Can he find it again and rescue everyone before the attacking Kraken devours the lot of them?

THE VAMPIRE PLANTS (Picture Strip)

Dr Vane's experimental botanical gardens on Venus are the next destination the Doctor has in mind. They are here to investigate the 'rude shock' that Dr Vane received a few days ago, when he found that his Galea Tentipocus had been scrobbled from its palatial greenhouse. Vane's assistant Regan is attacked by a suckered beast that appears to be the precious plant grown to a monstrous size.

The Doctor and Jamie find a breath-taking forestful of Tentipocus fronds. The Doctor is preternaturally calm: 'Yes. I must think of some way of stopping it before it's too late.' In fact, it's 'incredible' that the solution – i.e., burning the plant down – is so simple. Dr Vane's response to the Doctor's brainwave goes unrecorded. We might note that the Second Doctor has already fought a race of ambulatory vampire plants with fire in an Annual picture story.

GRIP OF ICE

Escaping from the 'ravaging robots of Korad' has caused damage to the Tardis. While the Doctor sets about some repairs, Jamie and Zoe explore the icy planet they've landed on. The suggestion is of a quick walk to the glacier and back for a hot drink. However, a storm with 'evil' intent engulfs them and the Doctor has to set off in a futuristic outfit to rescue his friends. He finds the City of Glace, which contains the Thought Cubes which are all that remain of its original inhabitants.

The Doctor has to face a three-armed being called Cosmos – with his enlarged brain pod and ray gun – and dissuade him from turning Jamie and Zoe into thought cubes like he did to everyone else. The Doctor offers his own brain power in lieu of theirs. Cosmos accedes to this idea, and the Doctor manages to defeat him with the sheer power of his mind.

MAN FRIDAY

Planet Delffo in Galaxy G is a tropical paradise. Dr. Who once promised Toofo of the Creels he would return here one day: to the planet where he learned that beauty is only skin deep. There is a spat on the Island of Devils and Jamie goes stropping off to sun-bathe. It's not long before the Doctor and Zoe meet Goruf, one of the amphibious Creels, who tells them that Jamie has been taken prisoner by a one-legged Blikk. The Doctor and Zoe set off unarmed to investigate, passing through a field of sleep-inducing poppies, and are gathered up by the flying, one-legged giant robot, who takes them down a tunnel to the Hall of Shadows. Here they are reunited with Jamie and learn that the feared Lava People don't really mean any harm.

ROBOT KING (Picture Strip)

Five thousand years in the future mankind is extinct, and the Doctor and his friends are exploring the empty wasteland of a city that was once called Hope. All three encounter a self-proclaimed Robot King, who has somehow survived alone here. He attacks, believing (not unreasonably) that humankind are too dangerous to leave running around. 'Er, no violence please,' frowns the Doctor as they go hand to hand. Luckily, the wily space-time scientist finds the mechanical guardian's off-switch.

SLAVE OF SHRAN

The Garvanes landed their damaged ship on an 'accursed' planet and were 'forced' to invade and enslave its populace. Dr. Who has been captured and brain-wiped and is acting as a servant, repairing their ship. Now they're ready to set off an atomic bomb as soon as they leave this world, rather churlishly destroying all the indigenous cockroach-like creatures in their wake. They are the Shelgars and the 'eldritch glow' from one of their ray guns is all it takes to bring the Doctor back to his senses. When Ekk the Shelgar explains everything our hero quickly rewires the atom bomb so that it will destroy those who attempt to use it for evil purposes.

Ekk's quite keen on freeing all his people from 'the hypnotic power of the computer god,' as well he might be, and the Doctor wants to find Jamie and Zoe. They flee in a hot air balloon and are pursued by giant devil birds – the Dentarops – which they fight with bows and arrows. There are a few very dangerous moments to survive before the Doctor can clasp Ekk's feeler in a gesture of fond farewell.

RUN THE GAUNTLET

It's a jungle out there, and everyone is surprised to see a blue chimpanzee armed with an old-fashioned blunderbuss. Out come the contra-gravity suits (not the contra-grav belts as used earlier, nor the Doctor's much-trumpeted (but soon forgotten) Floater.) When they catch up with the chimp they find he's quite aggressive. He's called Valgar and is quite keen to dissect them. He zooms them to city of Menrox aboard a flying machine shaped like a spoon. The ape men are convinced that the Doctor and Zoe are robots. A spot of recorder music scares their enemies away, long enough for Jamie to arrive. He has rather improbably piloted the Tardis to Menrox. Suddenly the air is swarming with chimps in giant spoons firing blunderbuss ray weapons at them.

A THOUSAND & ONE DOORS

'Of Space there is no boundary,' opines Dr. Who, 'of Time there is no end.' In his very last story the Second Doctor seems determined to expand his young friends' horizons. Infinite universes overlap, he tells them, and there are unlimited dimensions. 'Whisht,' says Jamie, getting a headache.

They soon find themselves in a weird place where they float like butterflies and become caught in a giant and 'enigmatic' net. The Doctor is aware of being discussed by creatures intent on dissecting him. Another lot who want to see what makes him tick! They refer to the Doctor as 'it' and believe that he and his friends hail from somewhere they call 'the Five Hundred and Third Universe.' They are dimension-explorers from the Eight Thousand and Ninety First Universe, apparently. They admonish the Doctor and handle him roughly.

The dimension explorers let something slip about breathing methane and ammonia, which rather points to them being Arcturans with fancy ideas about themselves, but this line is never followed up on. Instead there is wild and fanciful talk of the doorways between dimensions, and the globe-headed creatures continue to be very menacing indeed. When the Doctor rips one of their helmets off he is sick to the stomach. They are utterly alien: with faces like writhing vortices made out of something sticky. The creature dies when it's exposed to our atmosphere and the Doctor and his friends flee. Perhaps the Doctor is less intent on visiting other dimensions now, since the inhabitants are just so horrible to look at.

Other Content

WILL THE CYBERNETIC ANTHROPOMORPHOUS MACHINES TAKE OVER?

It's the best title of any Dr Who thing ever, but sadly Cybernetic Anthropomorphous Machines – or Walking Trucks as they were otherwise known – never really amounted to much, despite once being described as 'real life Imperial Walkers'!

- ARE WE ALONE?
- A MATTER OF GRAVITY
- UNCONQUERABLE SPACE
- STAR FACTS
- PROPHETS OF THE SPACE AGE
- POWER FROM SPACE
- THE SAILOR'S GUIDE
- THE UNKNOWN UNIVERSE
- SPACE QUIZ

Doctor Who Himself

'I was wrong to say I was wrong.' The Doctor makes unequivocal statements rather rashly sometimes, in his haste to tell his two companions what is going on. He has a habit of 'sounding off' 'oracularly'. In their first story of 1970 he declares that they have arrived in the time of the dinosaurs – no, they haven't – and yes they have. This Doctor can be cross, patronising and wry, all at once, but there's little of Troughton's kindliness in the character.

'How you must despise me,' he frowns, when he loses his Tardis key during the affair of the *Marie Celeste*. Again he propounds his belief that Fate guides his every move, and that there is a reason they should be stranded here. He is brave, though. He will always face the unknown unarmed, aware that the presence of things such as ray guns might complicate matters and cause misunderstandings.

The Doctor would 'dearly love' to be 'thrown out of' his native 'Continuum' into a completely foreign dimension. His thirst for new places knows no bounds until he confronts the truly alien beings from the Eight Thousand and Ninety First Universe. They are so nasty-looking that the Doctor is keen to return to more familiar haunts.

Pretty soon he's going to be more circumscribed in his travels than ever before, when the Seventies begin in earnest and he finds himself exiled to planet Earth. It's as if Dr. Who of the 1960s has travelled as far afield as he can manage, at last touching the very limits of his native dimension, and knocking on the doors into the next... and then, having got that far in his first two incarnations, he must turn back, and turn into someone new...

Monsters and Villains

The singing crystal 'people' want to absorb all the delicious minerals contained in the bodies of the Tardis team. The Arcturans are intent on collecting up specimens of the most intelligent life forms from various planets, and come a cropper when they pick on Dr. Who and friends.

The amphibious Creels speak in 'high, thin' voices: 'Is it really Doctor Who?' They live in fear of the dark and shapeless Lava Men who live underground. The Jaibohs are terribly aggressive chimpanzees who want to dissect the Doctor and Zoe. The dimension travellers in the very last story of the 1970 Annual come from a place so far away that even Dr. Who knows nothing about it, and their sheer strangeness seems to disturb him profoundly.

Curious Companions?

Jamie is rather more quick-thinking than he tends to be on TV, noting that, for example, the crystalline structures trapping them appear to have agency of some sort. The Doctor appears to be less fond and forgiving of his young companion – snapping at him and patronizing him rather a lot. In 'Man Friday' the Doctor even tells Jamie that sometimes he wonders why he ever bothered asking him to be a companion on his journeys. This year Jamie has taken to the catchphrase, 'Sizzling satellites!'

Zoe takes a little while to show any kind of personality, but by three stories in she's bragging that spaceships are quite commonplace where she comes from. She finds the idea of visiting botanical gardens on Venus 'jolly interesting,' even as Jamie yawns. In a later story she chides, 'Oh, you make me tired!' when she finds her companions too timid to arm themselves against dangers.

Fiendish Wheezes

The Arcturans are building a zoo containing examples of other intelligent species. The greenish villain Cosmos is turning people into Thought Cubes in order to fuel his own flight into space, away from the doomed planet where he lives.

Anticipating the Future

Prehistoric apemen with weapons and technology who will sleep under the Earth and be missing from the historical record after the Ice Age. There are hints in 'The Dragons of Kekokro' of Malcolm Hulke's later saga of the Silurians.

The mystery of the *Marie Celeste*'s disappearance was solved by the TV show in 1965's 'The Chase', but the Doctor is prone to forgetting that, often invoking

66

the case as a real puzzler. Metal doors open and the Doctor and friends are pushed aboard a sailing vessel by unseen hands. Voices comment on the collecting of human specimens from Earth history. 'Ma certie' (as Jamie would say) this is a future-echo of 'Carnival of Monsters.'

The specimen-gatherers are revealed as the ammonia-and-methane-breathing Arcturans, and so it's tempting to draw a line of connection between them and the Arcturan ambassador of TV's 'Curse of Peladon' some years later.

Egregious errors

The Doctor keeps a 500-year diary, rather than a micro-film library of past adventures. Also, he never calls his recorder a 'music-stick.' And a 'vast knowledge of Galactic tongues' simply isn't necessary for him due to the Tardis' telepathic circuits.

Classic moments

The Doctor being rather nonplussed when the Kraken wakes.

His blinding realization that the rare plants of Venus can be defeated by setting fire to them. No sooner has the Doctor recovered from brain-washing, rewired an atom bomb, and had an idea to bring the cockroach people out of their collective trance, than suddenly he's airborne in a balloon, firing arrows at giant devil birds.
Another classic moment has Dr. Who and Zoe flying through a jungle in contra-gravity suits, chasing a blue chimp armed with a weapon out of Cromwell's time.

Dr. Who's enthusiasm for what in the Seventies Annuals he will call The Omniverse is very endearing. He gets a fright when he encounters the Vortex-faced creatures from another Dimension, though. At the end of the Sixties he realises just how alien and different other dimensions can be. He will spend the Seventies moving from exile in a fixed point in time and space into the most far-flung voyages he will ever make.

What I learned from the Doctor Who Annual 1970

It's just unnatural for plants, crystals and weather to have intelligence and volition. The amphibious Creels measure time in 'ripples.' Dr. Who in the Annuals is often much less patient with his companions than he is on TV. Is it because he thinks fewer people will notice? He keeps micro-film records of the planets and times he has visited. A good way of referring to him is as a 'space-time scientist.' It's easy to rewire an atomic bomb so that it can go off in the faces of those who want to blow up the world.

Space inhabitants are mostly not music lovers, and so it's easy to scare them off with a spot of discordant recorder playing.

There are no limits to the Omniverse. And it's a very scary place.

Illustrations

The same artist as the other Troughton Annuals, it seems, but his likenesses for the Doctor are definitely improved by 1970.

The 1971 Annual

It's an Annual that begins and ends with tales of men bearing the very ordinary name of Fred. But everything between is pretty outlandish.

It's all changed again. In explosive shades of pink the 1971 Annual arrives, heralding a multi-coloured era in which the Doctor has a bright yellow car and a very eventful life on Earth. His new companion – the capable Liz – is promoted to cover star alongside our new craggy, dapper Doctor himself. On TV this changeover made for a new tone of seriousness and a glossy feel to everything. It meant action and grit and stories that took on some of the boldest themes of Wellsian scientific romance and updated them for the nineteen-seventies. I'm guessing that in the world of the Annual, this was also the case..? The end papers promise us soldiers, demons, saucers, reptile men and flailing many-limbed monstrosities, so that's promising.

The Stories

THE MIND EXTRACTORS

We are in England. Bus drivers called Fred mull over passengers' probable destinations and policemen nip through allotments that stand near mental hospitals, finding dead foxes and phoning in reports from Police Boxes that are actually Police Boxes and remain motionless beside bingo halls.

All at once we are in a richer, more vividly realised world than almost any visited by the Doctor Who Annuals of the 1960s. 1971 seems to plunge us into the misty, chilly brew of social realism.

Lumpen faced human dolls blow cigarette smoke into the faces of bus drivers, policemen and Liz Shaw herself – robbing them of their memories. The Brigadier makes his first appearance, visiting poor Liz in the mental hospital. She has experienced giddiness but no brain damage. Lethbridge-Stewart is cross that the Doctor has vanished. He's even posted men to keep an eye on him. Dr. Who's experience with everything odd would be invaluable today.

Dr. Who in his third incarnation makes his first appearance looking rather dishevelled in the allotments, crunching on raw turnip. He's been busy: full of stories about eavesdropping on Russian cosmonauts and his attempts to 'repel a pseudoman.' He and the Brigadier are very concerned about these 'cigarette-smoking pseudos' haunting the place. He picks up the still-bewildered Liz from the mental hospital and finds a shrivelled pseudo lying about outside.

Back at the lab, however, the hideous thing comes back to life… They are the Extractors – and his mind will be the jewel in their extensive collection!

SOLDIERS FROM ZOLTA

An Earth mission to Mars has discovered the presence of Zoltans. They are an alien race that many Earthlings are keen to meet. They even have demonstrations to protest against the various world governments' cautiousness. Meanwhile, wherever the returned astronaut Fairley and his fellows go – on their round of state visits – those expressing anti-Zoltan sentiments are found dead. Fairley himself is killed accidentally –by one of the tiny creatures he has brought back from Mars. The Doctor investigates his bungalow and very nearly falls foul of the miniscule elephant-like insect himself.

THE GHOULS OF GRESTONSPEY

The Doctor's been sucked up in a cloud of smoke by a 'celestial vacuum cleaner!' At least, according to the Brigadier, who seems oddly sanguine about weird events on a Scottish moor not too far from a nuclear power plant. Liz watched in terror as the Doctor vanished, but the Brigadier is confident that his new scientific advisor will be able to sort everything out. Liz knows that there is something underground that is drawing energy from the nuclear station and has Dr. Who 'in its clutches'!

Prisoner of a rather rude member of the Zeld race, the Doctor quickly finds himself losing his temper at these 'ghouls from the stars' and so he starts a punch-up. He manages to somehow rise up through the granite in a queer flying saucer, giving the Brig and Liz quite a surprise. (One of the UNIT troopers' reactions to first sighting a genuine UFO is to fire bullets wildly at it.)

CAUGHT IN THE WEB

The space scientist Rossi is most put out when, upon observing the remarkable properties of some alien dust, the Brigadier insists that Dr. Who is called to his special laboratory in a remote place called Black Peak. Studying the dust back at UNIT HQ with his much-vaunted vibro-bank, the Doctor confirms that it is native to a world called Sequiz and that it's very dangerous.

The Doctor and Brigadier travel to the far north (the Brig in furry parka and huge mittens) and they soon discover the kidnapped Rossi continuing with his ill-advised experiments. He isn't best pleased to see them: 'You can go away and take your Doctor Who with you!' The dust noisily transforms into a hideous Shape from Sequiz, which attacks everyone, until the Doctor saves the day by getting violent with his trusty cane.

INVADERS INVISIBLE

The Brigadier's cross when the Doctor drags everyone out after he sees another of his annoying 'mirages.' It was an ink blot some six feet wide, according to Dr. Who. When they return to UNIT HQ they find that Liz's eyes have gone blank and hard and she's wielding a gun. The Brig thinks it's a mutiny, but the Doctor knows it's an alien invasion. 'The lanky form' of Dr. Who becomes the psychic battleground for dominance over the Earth by an alien aggressor. The Doctor wins and all the slime on his flesh moves sluggishly, apparently to his bottom, in the form of a 'blob of goo.' He puts the whole nasty episode down to aliens invading in the form of mind-altering viruses, which he can combat using X-rays.

THE DARK PLANET

Feeling in the pockets of a young man who has crashed his car on a lonely road, Dr. Who discovers a revolting hair-covered mollusc that is clearly of alien origin. Nearby there's a biologist called Professor Meetchley, whom Liz knows from Cambridge: she believes he might be of help. But when he sets about bandaging the Doctor's injured hand, the Doctor slips unconscious beneath the dissecting table, and Meetchley absconds with the strange specimen.

Dr. Who smuggles himself into Sayles Cottage and finds a man with one arm and suede shoes, who paints landscapes of another world. Now he has precipitated himself in here, it's plain that the Doctor simply has to become 'one of us.' However the molluscs can't communicate with him, and so he will have to be destroyed. For an 'awful moment' the Doctor thinks he's going 'out of his mind.'

Fire engulfs the place, so that there's no record of the strange artwork or samples from the alien planet. Dr. Who thinks the enigmatic molluscs might try to infiltrate Earth once more.

All of the alien menaces in the 1971 Annual are persistent, mysterious and somehow nebulous. They operate from the sidelines and come in the form of insects, viruses, or seafood. And all the while, more overt alien intelligences are still making comebacks even after Dr. Who has defeated them: UNIT are continually holding meetings in order to monitor the doings of the Yeti and the Autons…

CAVERNS OF HORROR

In a moment of fancifulness Dr. Who describes the crystalline caves he and Liz are exploring as 'fairyland.' Liz is grabbed by something with tentacles and faceted black eyes. The Doctor imagines an army of ten-feet tall locusts, stripping the world of all its green plant life. He believes they have mutated in the radioactive labyrinth of this underground world and could wipe out all life on Earth…

He fires his laser gun at them and he gets into a right old tizz. When he sees the Brigadier again, he falls sobbing into his arms. He tells him: 'Pump that hole as full of cyanide as you can.' Here we encounter, for the first time, the Third Doctor's impulse to destroy most alien life forms he encounters. 'Every last one of those foul things must be destroyed.' It's a theme that runs throughout the life of this incarnation of the Annual Doctor. Having previously thought of all life as sacred, he's now changed his mind. 'This time I've got to admit how welcome it is to have a few professional killers around,' is the jaunty line this story finishes on.

A UNIVERSE CALLED FRED

Dr. Who can sense that someone or something is trying to communicate with him, and so he creates a kind of radio for receiving messages from the subatomic level of inner-space. (He had two adventures like this in 1969 and they didn't end at all well. He brushes this thought aside.) The Doctor's gazing at a globe containing a whole, hypothetical universe, just as an orderly called Fred carries in a tray of tea things.

Dr. Who taunts Liz with mind-boggling stuff to do with infinity, wondering what's inside the universe he's named Fred in honour of the man who brought the tea, and what lies outside their own universe. (Again though, if he thinks on: his previous incarnation was rather disturbed to get a glimpse of such things in the dimensions beyond.)

Dr. Who announces that he is proposing to shrink even smaller than Alice ever did, and explore a sub-atomic Wonderland.

It's a wonderful answer to the quandary that the restless Doctor faces as an exile on planet Earth. Where can he explore when he's stuck on one little world? Inner-space beckons him, and in this story – right at the end of 1971 – he seems more excited and engaged than he has in all the preceding adventures.

He tells Liz that if he doesn't return she can have Bessie to look after. She's suddenly thinking melodramatically about life without this man, whose mind can leap 'chasms of creation.' She won't be left out on this occasion, and so they both buckle up in the special belts the Doctor has invented.

He feels a 'terrible squeezing sensation in every atom,' and we assume that Liz Shaw must feel the same as they get hugely reduced in a matter of mere seconds. Down they go into the 'abyss of the sub-atomic cosmos.' (It might be my imagination but the writer or writers involved in the Annual of 1971 might be enjoying mucking about with the language as much as the illustrators are relishing slapping about all the extravagant poster paint colours.)

They find themselves in a world menaced by a blue dwarf star and are met by giant bats with bright pink wings. The Doctor seems positively gleeful to be in such a strange, otherworldly environment for the first time since the Sixties ended. He addresses the belligerent bat-creatures – the Valerons – with 'magnificent dignity.' It is to no avail, however, and they are flown off to the city and shoved in a cell. Liz's scientific curiosity fails her not for the first time in 1971: 'Just get us back to Earth, Doctor. I've had enough.'

They meet Dynil who, as an Antar, has been badly treated by the Valerons and who believes in science rather than sorcery. He hopes the Doctor will help his people and the Doctor agrees, only if Dynil will fly him and Liz to the mountain top where they first arrived.

It's a little surprising then to the reader to hear that the Doctor is appraising his ally – he's elderly and short and clearly no danger – before giving him a sound walloping. Luckily, before that can happen both Liz and the Doctor are whizzed back to UNIT HQ and the ruins of the Doctor's workbench. Thank goodness the Brigadier came in and switched off the Doctor's wretched machine. Presumably the Brig is on an energy-saving mission and as a result has saved the lives of his two most important operatives.

Other Content

- DID YOU KNOW?
- THE PLANET PEOPLE
- THE SUIT OF THE FUTURE
- TWO MOONSTRUCK MEN
- THE LUNAR EXCURSION MODULE
- LIGHTHOUSE IN THE SKY
- THE ROSE RED CITY OF PETRA
- ANIMAL ASTRONAUTS
- TRENDS IN SPACE SUITS
- STAR FACTS
- STRANGE BUT TRUE
- MORE STAR FACTS
- THE WHIRLING WIZARD
- SPACE DICTIONARY
- LAUNCH DAY – CAPE KENNEDY
- ROCKET RANGE
- GUESS WHO
- KALEIDOSCOPE
- THE SPACE CHASE

Doctor Who Himself

Never before has he been so much in danger of 'penetration by a malignant force' when he finds himself involved in the affair of the cigarette-smoking pseudos. He's involved in a terrifying adventure but still feels the 'old excitement' when faced with something outlandish and weird. I get the feeling that quite some time has elapsed since we last saw him in the Annuals timeline, in his adventure of the 'Thousand and One Doors'. This is a Dr. Who hungering once more for the unknown.

After a day of adventures his elastic-sided boots start to pinch. His retorts to the Brigadier are often acidulous. Catching sight of his reflection in a mirror in a dead astronaut's bungalow, Dr. Who finds his new features 'pleasingly novel.' For the first time in the Annuals he is admitting to not being human. His blood and heart aren't human, he tells Liz and the Brigadier in 'Soldiers from Zolta.' He has apparently told the Brig that he is the 'most transcendent scientific genius of all time,' which makes me picture him blowing his own trumpet rather brashly at his UNIT job interview.

When Liz is possessed by an alien force that turns her brusque and nasty, Dr. Who finds it in himself to knock her out with a chop to the neck. This is the first instance of the Third Doctor's habitual slapping or hitting his female companions.

Another of his habits is always to carry a little piece of wire in his pocket.
It's altogether – and quite endearingly – typical of the Doctor that, while he's excited about getting himself and Liz shrunk down into the Universe called Fred, he has a nagging feeling at the back of his mind that returning them to UNIT HQ isn't exactly going to be a doddle. But he keeps quiet about that for now, as they deal with a deadly expanding star and some cross men with pink wings.

Monsters and Villains

The Extractors are hideous beings, extruding long thin pipes from their mouths and cornering human beings one at a time in order to steal their minds. The Zoltans are intent on colonizing Mars and invading Earth by currying favour with credulous locals and stinging dissenters to death with

74

tiny, poisonous elephants. The boastful, arrogant, humanoid Zeld are collecting human beings deep underground in Scotland and leaching away their psychic energy.

The Sequiz dust when experimented on by Dr Rossi starts to transform into a hideous Shape that scares even Dr. Who. His reaction is such that it leads me to wonder if he's seen another of the vortex-faced dimension-travellers from the end of the 1970 Annual, to which he also had an aversion.

Hideous, hairy molluscs on a completely dark alien world come to Earth in order to delegate their cosmic responsibilities and to commission some rather dingy paintings. In the tiny bottled universe called Fred, the men with pink wings mostly think the Doctor is a magician and he is making a blue star come down to destroy them all.

Curious Companions?

Liz Shaw is clever and wonderfully spirited, railing at the Doctor and Brigadier's assumption that, wherever there is life, there must also be killing and war. She's a 1970's dolly bird with pacifist leanings and a PhD. As advanced as her qualifications are, she is still 'awed' by the Doctor's scientific knowhow and his equipment, which includes the fascinating 'vibro bank,' which he produces with a flourish of his silk-lined opera cape.

She sees him as half towering scientific genius, half elf. By the end of her year with Dr. Who it's obvious that she has had enough. Their sojourn in the universe known as Fred does her head in. Upon returning to UNIT HQ she wants to deny it all and feels quite tired and overwhelmed by recent goings on. She allows the Doctor to drive her home in Bessie and it's easy to believe that she just never goes back.

Brigadier Lethbridge-Stewart appears for the first time as head of UNIT and Dr. Who's boss. Already, in the very first story of 1971, he is chasing the Doctor and demanding to know what he's up to. When the Doctor asserts that aliens are behind the current situation, the Brigadier is grudgingly accepting. 'We realise now that Earth has probably always been under surveillance.' We become aware that these are very early days for UNIT. Lethbridge-Stewart still seems a little sceptical about the kinds of things the Doctor takes for granted. According to him, Dr. Who's job is to 'ferret out' all kinds of strange happenings. They are manageable and can be dealt with, these happenings, because they are in Great Britain, and not on some outlandish planet of the type Dr. Who 'prates about.'

The Brig's question about what the occupants of a Number 59 bus and Russian cosmonauts can have in common gets to the very heart of the UNIT stories in any medium. Everyday places are right on the front line when it comes to the alien incursions of the nineteen seventies: the more banal the better.

The Brigadier's concern when he thinks the Doctor has fallen foul of the Extractors is very touching. He offers the best help that Earth can provide. A nurse scoffs at the way he phrases this, but the Brigadier knows exactly what he's saying. He's got a Duty of Care to his strange, extra-terrestrial friend.

'Pooh!' the Doctor dismisses the Brigadier's prosaic, earthbound attitude. However, as he confides in Liz, he believes he may be improving Lethbridge-Stewart. He may make a scientist of him yet.

For all his apparent cynicism and sarcasm, the Brig is developing a fondness for both Dr. Who and Liz: 'The odd pair he was saddled with were at it again,' he groans, when he hears them going on during the adventure of 'The Universe Called Fred.'

Fiendish Wheezes

The Mind Extractors loiter about in raincoats smoking what appear to be cigarettes that exude a mist that robs human beings of all their marbles. Miniscule stinging insects from Mars are just the thing for bringing down oppositional voices at buffets and official receptions all around the world. The molluscs from the Dark World just want someone to look after their planet for them once they have slithered off this mortal coil, but they seem to have a very odd way of going about it.

TV Feedback

A UNIT captain has a surprising flashback to the moment that Dr. Who was found babbling outside his Police Box. He was talking all about having a new face and coming from space. Completely batty, of course.

These early stories for the Third Doctor appear to be happening against a backdrop of renewed bids for global domination by the Nestene Intelligence. While the Doctor hops over to Italy, Liz is still at UNIT HQ, looking for clues for how to defeat the Autons once and for all. Later, the Brigadier seems preoccupied by what appears to be a 're-emergence' of the Yeti…

'The Mind Extractors' features Auton-like monsters who manage to be even more disturbing than TV's famous waxwork dummies. These creatures look almost as if they've had bad plastic surgery, and they produce endless, engulfing smoke from their cigarettes.

Humans returning from missions to Mars slightly tampered-with and causing trouble puts us in mind of 'The Ambassadors of Death.' Similarly, 'Doctor Who and the Silurians' is evoked in 'The Ghouls of Grestonspey' with its subterranean creatures leaching power from a nuclear plant.

Anticipating the Future

Venturing into caverns to meet giant insects with chitinous skin is something the Third Doctor will be called upon to do in later TV adventures.

Classic moments

The Doctor stares in horror at the face of the Extractor in his lab as the thin white tube emerges from its mouth, growing longer than a cigarette, then longer than a spaghetti strand... oozing smoke and inching towards him.

The Doctor glimpsing his new face in a mirror and being pleased with what he sees – even in the midst of an adventure – is a rather nice moment (later echoed in TV's 'Rose.')

The Brigadier in Arctic gear and furry mittens, freezing next to Dr. Who in his opera cape, as they investigate in frigid temperatures.

The Doctor's gleefulness at opening up the world of the sub-atomic particle and discovering the universe of Fred is a delightful moment.

What I learned from the Doctor Who Annual 1971

Don't hang around near allotments. Any strange light in the sky is almost guaranteed to be a flying saucer in 1971, probably belonging to an alien species intent on invading.

It's very easy to siphon off energy from a nuclear power plant, for whatever nefarious purposes you fancy.

Any Earth probe sent into space is going to come a cropper, and your astronauts are going to come back doo-lally and / or possessed.

There are infinite worlds, much smaller than this one and one of them is called Fred, after the man who brings in the tea.

Illustrations

The Annuals for the Pertwee years – 1971 to 1975 inclusive (there was no Annual in 1972) – were illustrated by Steve Livesey and Edgar Hodges.

The pictures are multi-coloured. There is a hint of photo-realism coming in, as well as psychedelia. As TV *Doctor Who* moved from black and white to colour broadcast, an extra dimension of sophistication takes over in the Annuals. The drawings are less slapdash and naïve. The pages actually feel stylish and thoughtfully designed. The colours throughout the book are beautiful.

NB. Due to disappointing sales, there was no Doctor Who Annual for 1972 (but see Appendix 1).

The 1973 Annual

Barry Letts' glorious novelisation of 'The Daemons' begins with the absurdly upbeat sentence: 'Doctor Who was a happy man.' He's doing up his antique roadster, Bessie. There's that tang of oil in the air as he works in the UNIT garages. The whiff of spring, perhaps. And Bessie herself is daffodil yellow. Doctor Who is with his good friends Jo Grant and Mike Yates and the two of them are burbling like dafties about black magic and the Age of Aquarius. They're at the start of a terrifically exciting adventure that will combine sci-fi and Gothic horror. What's to be unhappy about?

I think of all *Doctor Who* during this Glam Rock epoch in that tinselly, golden light. The UNIT chums were having a terrific time defending the Earth against alien incursions. And they were very successful at it, too. They battled forces from outer space and the Earth's inner crust. Week after week they'd knock these terrors back with ingenuity and bravery and good-humoured fun. The era has a kind of tremendous glow suffusing it.

The 1973 Doctor Who Annual? Not so much. I don't think the UNIT family are having quite as much fun as all that. Though there's nothing madly wrong about the continuity details in these stories, there is something completely off-kilter about the whole thing. It's in the attitudes of some of the characters – principally the Doctor.

I'll try to explain.

The Stories

DARK INTRUDERS

Dr. Who, Jo Grant and the Brigadier are aboard an aircraft carrier in the Pacific, watching a manned space capsule splash down in the water. Astronauts Curley and Dermann have returned from Mars rather stiff and zombie-like. Soon guards and biologists are being found unconscious around the place. Examining the capsule the Doctor finds alien dust particles, which he pops into an envelope to examine at his leisure in his cabin with his 'vibro bank.' Then he finds that a shadowy figure has tried to make off with that very same device.

The planetary dust makes a mosquito-like hum and the Doctor is amazingly quick to identify it as belonging to Minos. He surmises that a scoutship from Minos was hiding on Mars and waiting to pick up Earthmen. Minoans are calculating, ruthless and old enemies of Dr. Who. What is more they are somehow *inside* the Earthmen. They are after the brains of scientists. "The Minoans are great brain stealers!' declared Doctor Who.'

The Doctor swaps cabins and puts himself next in line to have his brain plundered. The Minoans have a go, but he resists their mesmeric techniques. Ghastly mental wrangles ensue. With his vastly powerful mind Dr. Who is able to force his enemies to retreat and the astronauts plus all the scientists are saved.

WAR IN THE ABYSS

Jo and the Doctor travel to Antarctica, where her Uncle Grant (Grant Grant?) has gone missing. He's the manager of an oil rig. The Doctor is concerned with various aspects of climate change, and strongly suspects that the Earth is being moved closer to the sun. This idea is met with scepticism by Major General Carter.

The Doctor and Jo steal a Snow-cat and nip off, both wearing rather fetching furry parkas and boots. They find pipelines with no oil flowing, and an awful crevasse, which their purloined craft topples into. At the bottom they find Uncle Grant and his oil rig crew locked inside a metal room.

Things locked them up. Machine-like beings called the Klatris. The Doctor decides that they must be a robotic civilisation who live inside the Earth. He rashly reaches the conclusion that these subterraneans are intending to emerge and invade the world above.

As it turns out, the Klatris don't give a hoot about the world's surface heating up as they nudge it closer to the sun. The Doctor is apparently right to be cynical about them because they reckon on wiping out humanity.

Delightedly, the Doctor discovers that the oil rig is built upon a dormant volcano. He plans to reactivate it sharpish, using dynamite. Even without having met the Klatris, he is keen to set off the explosion that will seal their fate. Boulders of ice and pink lava rain down as the volcano brings about awful destruction. Jo laughs and joshes with her Uncle.

Our UNIT friends seem like horrible, thoughtless people. Worse than that, genocidal maniacs. What's more, none of them have done a stroke to prevent the Earth's perilous drift towards the sun.

HUNT TO THE DEATH

Witnessed only by sheep, a terrible metallic thing materialises on a Yorkshire moor. The Kelad looks very much like a steel praying mantis. Four aliens with ray guns – Fhibo and his pals – are hunting the creature.

Jo and the Doctor are driving in Bessie to an experimental radar station when they come across a distressed Mancunian potholer, Harkin, in the road. His friend is stuck down Tumbling Pot with a broken leg, and the Doctor is keen to go down to rescue him, even though he 'isn't exactly dressed for it.' When they find the heavily-armed Fhibo the Doctor recognises and calls him by name. Naturally, the Doctor has visited Planet Llios, where he fought 'spindly monsters' with 'warped robot minds'. But now he learns that, after he left, the monsters came back! (This seems to be another occasion in an Annual story when the Doctor left a job half-done. This is becoming a theme over the years. Does he ever actually defeat anyone? Does he ever see things through? And is this why he has recently taken to blowing things up? Is he perhaps looking for more of a sense of closure?)

In that previous adventure the Doctor helped them to build a Time Transporter, but it seems that the Kelad has used it in order to transport itself to Yorkshire in order to stir up bother. Down in the cathedral-like caves they discover the Kelad in all its terrifying glory, and the Doctor gets them to whistle and thus scramble its radar. Fhibo and his comrades gang up and shoot the robot in the head until it blows up. Then they take the bits back to Llios.

DOORWAY INTO NOWHERE

Dr. Who and Jo are travelling in Bessie, map-reading and getting a bit lost. The big question is whether the Master has kidnapped Dr. Who's friend Giles Winston, a great physicist. Jo grumbles a bit when they get to a disused factory. The barbed wire isn't doing her 'blouse and slacks' any good at all.

Suddenly our heroes are clambering about in the catwalks and steel girders and ladders that summon up the very feel of early Seventies *Doctor Who*. British industry in the real world might have been in turmoil during that period, but in the world of Dr. Who, those factory complexes were kept quite busy with the manufacture of devil dolls, evil slime and green werewolves.

The reader could just about cheer when the Doctor declares: 'I am convinced the evil hand of the Master is in this!' We can't wait to see what his current 'nefarious undertaking' will consist of. 'Silky and suave', he jumps out and greets them almost at once, gloating that they have fallen into his trap.

There's a surprise twist, though. He lays down his 'glittering weapon' and proposes an alliance with Dr. Who. How does joint domination of the solar system sound? He lets them into his secrets. He has found a Gateway into another dimension that even the Time Lords don't know about. Cue lots of snarling and sneering between the Doctor and the Master – as good and tense as anything on TV. There is a lot at stake here, we realise. Feelings run high. The Master taunts him about the loss of his Tardis.

The Master intends, of course, to conquer the new dimension that lies behind that steel door. He opens it to reveal a paradise world in daylight. It has two suns and flying dragons. The Master's scheme involves leading the monsters through the Gateway and into England. He wants to conquer Earth, as well as the world through the door.

Jo kicks the Master violently, and he accidentally shoots his (violet) ray gun at his own control panel. The Gateway vanishes, foiling the Master's plan and leaving him stuck in the world of flying dragons.

THE CLAW

Mike Yates is accompanying Jo and the Doctor to Scotland in a UNIT staff car. Sea mist comes down and they are brutally attacked by the claw of a gigantic lobster. Evasive manoeuvring from Tibbins the driver saves their lives, and rudely awakens Dr. Who.

The Brigadier is in charge of an investigation on a remote island where weapons are being tested, and where men are going missing. The Doctor and friends meet an eccentric native – a fisherman called Macfee – who apparently has lobster pots on the island of Inishgrian. Mike's cross because that's a restricted area. Macfee has been fishing for lobsters all his life, and won't be put off by armed guards.

Reunited with the Brigadier, the Doctor sets to wondering: 'Was it really sea-mist, or some sort of emanation?'

Watching Macfee pulling up his lobster pots, they see him messing with crystals. These contain power drained from the atomic base. Challenged by the Doctor, Macfee transforms into sea mist, and then into that giant claw. Dr. Who grapples gamely with this, but next thing, he's inside a space ship. A lobster addresses him by name.

The Doctor is intrigued to find that this space ship is actually the lobster pot itself, and the lobster is after some advice from him. Macfee was forced to flee his own world, and came here after locating the nuclear power source on this Scottish island. He disguised himself as a comedy Scotsman and his ship as a lobster pot. He liquidated several men. Also, he knows Dr. Who because he is legendary among time travellers (the Doctor preens somewhat at this) and Macfee got the idea for disguising his spacecraft from the Tardis. Now he's offering the Doctor the chance to come with him into space.

The Doctor explodes into action. He often leaves these moments quite late in Annual stories, with the result that his solutions to quandaries tend to be rather violent. He sabotages the spaceship with a piece of bent wire from his pocket. Everything blows up and Jo finds him, shortly afterwards, face down on the beach. The alien lobster pot is in scattered, smouldering pieces.

SAUCER OF FATE

Somewhere in the Cotswolds a farmer watches a flying saucer land on Druid's Table. It's a very small one, so he takes it home and puts it on the kitchen table. His nephew Ernest is a reporter, who brings it to UNIT HQ, but unfortunately he vanishes in the car park. The Brig takes hold of the saucer and he vanishes as well. But he's left a crude doodle behind.

It seems that anyone who touches the saucer gets whisked away into captivity. Dr. Who isn't entirely sure, but it could be the Triolites from Ur behind it all.

(A brief aside. Writing this bit, I'm sitting in Nexus Café in the Northern Quarter in Manchester just before Christmas 2013. Everything is retro-style and Mott the Hoople's 'All the Young Dudes' is playing out of the speakers. Has there ever been a better conjunction of reading matter and musical accompaniment?)

The Doctor gets dissolved and zapped onto a spaceship, but he has brought a device with him in preparation. It turns out that the Triolites are 'shapeless grey masses' and they're very impressed by people who dress as impressively as the Doctor does. In their control room they've got three men strapped to couches. The Doctor lets himself be taken captive and placed with the farmer, the reporter and the Brigadier. Once he's in position, he reaches under his cape and switches on the device he's brought. It zaps them all back home to Earth.

THE PHASER ALIENS

Dr. Who is in a helicopter in Australia, trying to show Professor Hart invisible aliens through the bizarre spectacles he has invented. Australia has its own version of UNIT – the ICA (Institute Contra Aliens) – and the Doctor has his own lab here, too. There are aliens with a base in the desert, but they haven't done much beside produce a few funny flashes.

Dr. Who is a bit grumpy in this story, since no one in Australia seems to fully trust his word. His 'fancies' are being 'indulged.' He christens the creatures in the desert 'the Phaser Aliens'. He puts Jo in charge of manufacturing the special spectacles, and he goes out with a pilot to observe the alien ship. The photos he takes makes the truth plain. Jo has a look and sees vague, smoky shapes. They look to her like poached eggs. The Doctor is disturbed by the thought of invisible, intangible egg monsters zooming about over Australia. He gets back to work on inventing his Phaser gun.

Dr. Who has become intent on destroying 'these… these… things.' He's become less tolerant and more bloodthirsty as this Annual has gone on. Is it just a manifestation of his fury at still being exiled to Earth? He's intent on blowing up and shooting every alien that comes near. He seems to feel that they're deliberately flaunting their prowess with inter-dimensional gateways, time travel, transmat, and invisibility almost as a way of mocking him.

The Doctor admits that these Phaser Aliens haven't harmed anyone and they appear to be unarmed. But he must defend his adopted planet against potential menaces, and he's piqued that these creatures have stolen every single diamond in the world. So he has his Phaser gun mounted upon a helicopter, sets it off, sparks are shooting out everywhere and all the aliens are killed. Weird, leathery creatures lie about dissipating on the desert sands.

And that's another curious ending for one of the Doctor's adventures in 1973. He kills them and plans on stealing the diamonds back. All the way through this Annual Doctor Who and his friends have meted out rough justice to a bunch of extra-terrestrials who have only wanted to address global warming, take him on a trip, steal jewels and pick up men.

The Doctor dreams of returning to the stars, but by the end of 1973's adventures I'm wondering whether the cosmos will be ready for him when he gets free to wander once more.

What on Earth has become of Dr. Who?

Other Content

A PEEP INTO THE FUTURE

Another attempt by the writers of the Annuals to predict future technology, including colonies inside asteroids and the food of tomorrow (very like the food of today, apparently – porridge, vegetable soup and buttered peas!).

Most excitingly though, is the suggestion that one day, in the not too distant future, 'an American businessman is going to be able to write to an associate in Europe and get an answer the same day'! Sadly, the writer believes this will be due to mail being delivered by rocket ship and has not dreamed up the concept of email decades early!

- STAR STUDDED FLAGS – Flags with stars on them.
- ESCAPE TO FREEDOM – Famous escapes from history.
- THE WAY TO AN ASTRONAUT'S HEART – Food in space.
- UP IN SPACE – Space based quiz.
- MYTHICAL MONSTERS – Lavishly illustrated article on Greek and Roman myths.
- MONSTERS THAT REALLY LIVED – A selection of dinosaurs.
- THE SUN, THE MOON, THE STARS – Quiz.
- STAR GAZING – How to star gaze guide.
- A JINGLE OF JOES – A quiz based on the name Jo.
- WORDS WITH DR. WHO – Crossword.
- THE MONSTER GAME- A board game in which Dr Who and the Brigadier search for Jo Grant.
- THE SEVEN WONDERS OF THE WORLD

Doctor Who Himself

He's very snappish when there are other scientific experts on hand. He likes to be the centre of attention, which is why he wears an opera cloak and a frilly shirt all the time. He's terribly impatient and full of urgency. His demands 'brook no delay.'

Other scientists have heard of Dr. Who. They watch him curiously, half-amused by his manner. He is conspicuous on Earth, in a way that the TV show doesn't always stress. He's always saying weird things. In 'Dark Intruders' we get a flashback to how the Third Doctor first arrived on Earth, lying on the floor beside a Police Box and babbling about wearing a new face. It's clear that the scientists around him think him bananas, but they also know that he's extremely important. In the text he is referred to many times as 'the scientist', and we are reminded that this is a Dr. Who with an Earth-bound job.

The Doctor knows everything about every alien race and has met each of them. Those he doesn't already know he will make massive assumptions about, usually that they intend to invade the Earth and do great harm to humanity.

He is unequivocally on the side of humanity against foes such as the Klatris. The situation is quite different to 'Doctor Who and the Silurians' when, upon encountering a forgotten, underground species native to Earth, he was intent upon doing the best thing for everyone and brokering a peaceful solution. That's not how he is here. What has happened to him?

Now, as readers of the 1973 Annual we might just put this down to careless writing. The Doctor is badly characterised here, and these stories don't have the intriguing shades of grey / green of a Malcolm Hulke TV script. But if we take it at face value, then we get a Doctor who wasn't prejudiced against a race of intelligent lizards, but is extremely prejudiced against metallic beings and artificial life.

It leads me to wonder whether his (admittedly unusually intense) past experiences with varieties of cybernetic life and wayward super-computers have led to this attitude of his. In 'War in the Abyss' he is quite gung-ho in his determination to set the volcano off. Does he see the metal creatures as not actually being alive? But even so, surely the Doctor we know would be terribly keen to make a study of them?

His rashness and bloodthirstiness are worse by far than anything he ever accused Lethbridge-Stewart of. Even though he hasn't yet clapped eyes on the demon-like metal men from under the ground, he still wants to destroy them out of hand with an almost neurotic zeal. He makes sure that he is the one to push the plunger for the dynamite. This is extraordinary behaviour for the

Doctor who felt so betrayed by the Brigadier's actions on Wenley Moor, surely?

But this is action hero Dr. Who. He is gruff. The text even refers to him, butchly, by his ostensible surname when 'Who' points gloatingly at the destruction he is wreaking.

Received wisdom is that the Third Doctor on TV is a paternalistic, patronizing fop. But he almost seems liberal compared with the version from the Annuals. (It's interesting, perhaps, to think of the Annuals as producing exaggerated, distorted, Hall-of-Mirrors versions of the characters we know and love.)

Is the Dr. Who of the Annuals an unthinking bully? What will redeem the kind of behaviour we see here in 1973?

There is a touch of pathos in the way he tells his old friend Fhibo in 'Hunt to the Death' that, after he leaves a planet behind and time passes, he expects to fade into a fairy story in that world's memory.

This Doctor always seems to know exactly which set of alien menaces he is facing, given even the tiniest of clues. He's very keen to trumpet his intergalactic knowledge. It strikes me that this might be an act of over-compensation on his part, and a reaction to his current Earth-bound life? Either way, his certainty is amazing. (We must watch what happens to this unswerving faith in his own knowledge as the Seventies continue. Will self-doubt creep in, I wonder?)

In 'Saucer of Fate' he twirls a cane and his handkerchiefs are frilled with lace. This Doctor is becoming more foppish with each adventure.

He claims that long life teaches you that no theory is ever too outlandish.

Monsters and Villains

The Minoans are famous for stealing the minds of brilliant scientists. They are adept at infiltrating the bodies of their victims. The Klatris are metallic demons who live deep under the Earth and who drink crude oil. The Kelads are giant anagrammatic robotic praying mantises who the Doctor once defeated on the planet Llios. Now one has come to Yorkshire, possibly to find Dr. Who. But before anything significant can happen, it gets blown up. The Master has discovered a Gateway into other dimensions and is so excited by the possibilities he wants Dr. Who to share his good fortune. The Triolites send miniature saucers to Earth which invite you to touch them, and when you do, they zap you aboard their spaceship. The Phaser Aliens hide in the desert with stolen jewels and twinkle occasionally but, mostly, cannot be seen.

Curious Companions?

Jo Grant is happy to be on a ship that's Hawaii-bound. She basks in tropical sunlight wearing groovy sunglasses. While the Brigadier and Dr. Who 'prowl restlessly' up and down the deck she knows how to enjoy herself. She doesn't care much about signs of global warming, such as rising tides and the swelling of the sun. She's more concerned that her Uncle is stuck on the oil rig he manages in the Antarctic.

She's still getting used to the Doctor and finds him bossy and childlike. By the end of the 1973 Annual she knows him well enough to know that he'll never explain things immediately, and that he's liable to lapse into 'great, deep thoughts about the universe and space and time and dimensions and all sorts of things that most people hardly know exist.' Interestingly, she even thinks of him as 'satanical' when his cloak flares about him as they rescue a potholer in Yorkshire. On that occasion Jo is firm about wanting to go down Tumbling Pot with the others. She will not be left out of adventures.

She comes across as a bit thick in 'The Claw', asking whether anyone thinks the mysterious disappearances on the island have anything to do with the giant lobster that attacked the Doctor's party as soon as they arrived? Perhaps she's not thick so much as a bit dozy. In 'Saucer of Fate' we catch her staring dully out of the windows of UNIT HQ and, just when something mysterious is about to happen, she is distracted by a passing heron, of all things.

Brigadier Lethbridge-Stewart's speech is quite archaic – especially when he describes situations as 'dashed odd'. Watching the Mars space capsule land in the Pacific Ocean he enthuses over a 'perfect splash down.' He's used to being commanded by the Doctor, who makes 'curt requests' when he's on one of his searches for truth.

The Brigadier is constantly suspecting 'enemy agents' at work. He has a good dose of Cold War paranoia about him. He is always wanting the space-age Doctor to get back down to 'brass tacks.'

In 'Saucer of Fate' we glimpse a UNIT HQ that isn't a Victorian mansion. It looks instead like any nineteen seventies municipal building. It looks like the school I attended, Woodham Comprehensive school, or any other late Twentieth Century Comp, with its utilitarian design and wide windows.

Mike Yates makes a rare but welcome appearance in 'The Claw', when he is entrusted with getting Dr. Who and Jo to a remote corner of Scotland. As usual, Mike tries his best to be helpful, but he puts his foot in it – as when he keeps mentioning Jo's car sickness. Endearingly, Mike continually tries to impress the Doctor – with things like the tightness of his security. But the Doctor is always nonplussed by the things Mike says. Mike, in his turn, finds the Doctor whimsical – wondering why, for example, in all the drama, the Doctor's going for a stroll along the shore?

Fiendish Wheezes

Alien beings are very intent on getting hold of super-advanced human scientists all the way through this Annual. We meet a parade of Professors who have become embroiled in extra-terrestrial doings. The Minoans are keen to steal the minds of scientists. The Klatris want to take the Earth closer to the sun and warm everything up so they can live on the surface. In 'Hunt to the Death' we are left wondering what it is that the Kelad actually wants. It used the Doctor's Time Transporter to come to Earth in 1973, so we wonder whether he was seeking the Time Lord for some reason? This seems intriguing, but the story itself is short-circuited by both bloodlust and page-count.

The Master discovers multiple dimensions beyond this one. Does 'Doorway Into Nowhere' pave the way for a future, more complicated Whoniverse? The Neuronic Zone of 1976 and E-Space in 1981 are both pocket universes that the Doctor slips into. Here in 1973 the Master is crowing about finding a doorway into a wider, madder, more multifarious 'omniverse' (the term gets used in the 1975 Annual) than we've ever had before. The Doctor seems to know more about the 'multi-dimensional character of the cosmos' than even the Time Lords. He has already been caught up in such spaces during his previous travels. In a sense, this current wheeze of the Master's is nothing new to him.

Another offer of free travel off-Earth comes the Doctor's way in 'The Claw', when comedy Scotsman / alien lobster Macfee goes to some trouble to get the Doctor inside his lobster pot / spaceship. These baddies seem to go to quite a lot of effort just in order to hang out with Dr. Who.

What exactly *is* the Triolites' scheme in 'Saucer of Fate'? Have they simply developed an elaborate method of picking up men?

Dr. Who seems to find it easy to tackle the plans of the aliens in this Annual. Anything they have devised is easy to reverse. His enemies all seem a bit stupid and, whatever they manage to do, he finds it easy to undo. In a sense, these are the fairly untroubled adventures of Dr. Who and his friends. Whether the monsters are from space or inside the Earth it's quite easy to blow them up. However, even if they're blown up, they'll come back eventually anyway.

TV Feedback

Here we are the very heart of the cosy UNIT years. We're watching them tackling alien invasions, surreptitious incursions, monsters from the deep and, of course, the fiendish Master. All the ingredients for somewhat slightly familiar fun, fun, fun.

The Mars Capsule occupants returning to Earth with something wrong with them echoes 'Ambassadors of Death.' Jo Grant's Uncles in high places are something we've already heard about in 'Terror of the Autons.' The metallic Klatris inhabit the world underneath the ground, just like the Silurians. Volcanoes going off and our UNIT chums being a bit nasty reminds us of 'Inferno.'

The Master's scheme in 'Doorway Into Nowhere' is a cracking one. It's like he's nabbed an inter-dimensional version of the Time Scoop from 'Invasion of the Dinosaurs'. His plan is to harness all the monsters and plot points from every Malcolm Hulke story and unleash them on Earth in 1973..!

'The Claw' and those nasty pincers unavoidably remind us of 'The Macra Terror'. The disappearances in 'Saucer of Fate' come about in a similar way to those in 'The Three Doctors.'

Anticipating the Future

There are lovely forward-echoes in 'The Claw': from the missing persons and deadly Scottish sea mist of 'Terror of the Zygons' to the astonishingly aggressive alien seafood of 'The Invisible Enemy.'

I wonder if the Doctor's strangely brutal and genocidal impulses glimpsed in 1973 presage the bizarre behaviour we get from him later on. The shenanigans of the 'Dark Doctor' in the Virgin novels between 1991 and 1997, for example. Or the Tenth Doctor when he goes disastrously off the rails and loses his moral compass in the 'Gap Year' specials of 2009. The Doctor has been a bastard before and after 1973, it's just gobsmacking to see the UNIT years turn sour like this.

Egregious errors

The UNIT years turning sour like this. The Doctor deliberately blowing things up.

In 'Doorway Into Nowhere' the Master claims that he too has been cruelly exiled to Earth by the Time Lords. From the TV we gained the impression that he had *chosen* to slum it down here, taunting the Doctor with his various schemes and intergalactic lifestyle.

Classic moments

The arrival of the robotic Kelad on the Yorkshire Moors. It's an opening scene worthy of the TV show at the time. The Master getting terribly excited about his Gateway to another dimension.

What I learned from the Doctor Who Annual 1973

Space travel is injurious to human health. Astronauts always come back with something nasty wrong with them.

When bad stuff is happening always look around for the most dandified scientist. He might look bonkers but he's the only one who actually knows something.
Never get into a battle of wills or a duel of mental powers with Dr. Who. Don't let him jump to rash conclusions about his enemies. Most often he's right, but what about the times he's wrong?

Don't live deep under the ground and emerge expecting a warm welcome.

A bent piece of wire kept in the pocket of your velvet smoking jacket will always come in handy. Perhaps for jabbing into the control panel of an alien spacecraft and causing it to explode. You can always ask a female assistant for a loan of a hairpin. (Though, really, given the bouffant Dr. Who's sporting these days, he's more likely to have a supply of his own than she is.)

Illustrations

The art is mostly wonderfully graphic and colourful, as befitting the vibrant look of the show in 1973. Some of the stories ('War in the Abyss' and 'The Claw') have a rather more muted, conservative look and stand out as rather dull, compared to the swirling acrylic splashiness going on elsewhere.

The 1974 Annual

'A weird eldritch glow suffused the pods…'

We're getting the juicy stuff in this Annual. Pods and seeds and mysterious spaceships crash-land or surface or inveigle their way into Earth's defences. Aliens make contact via secret communications devices or they declare themselves openly and land in London parks so that everyone can see them. Advanced beings from the future come to warn us, invade us, or to change our future or their pasts. Everything is radiating or vibrating or quivering with weird intimations of extra-terrestrial life.

We are in the very heart of Dr. Who's UNIT years. And the Doctor is excited by all of this stuff going on around him. In other recent years he's been grumpy and intent on blowing everyone up, but the Doctor in 1974 is excited by the prospect of new life forms and finding out about things he doesn't know. He is excited about discovering dimensions that lie beyond this one, and positively refreshed by a curious side-trip he makes into a timeless realm beyond anything he has ever experienced. In 1974 he is patient with Jo and never slaps her once. He depends upon her good sense. Even the Master doesn't seem to rile him as much as usual. The lurid colours of this Annual are basked in a genial glow. Tyrants are only gangsters, he tells us, at the very end of the book. We can defeat them easily with our intelligence or – failing that – a good sock on the jaw.

The Stories

LISTEN – THE STARS

Mrs Prentice – the heavyset UNIT cleaner – arrives to dust round Professor Veitch's 'little sanctum'. She trips over her own shoelaces and accidentally activates the Professor's 'ionic vibrator', with which he hopes to 'reach beyond this galaxy.' Unseen, the Master is spying on all of these events, quite dispassionately, through the scanner in his Tardis. He is astonished when Mrs Prentice seems to make contact with a being called Zex in the System of gger. The wily Master wastes no time in taking over the cleaner's mind and offering her body to the alien, if only he'll help with the Master's ongoing efforts to conquer the Earth.

Soon Jo and the Brigadier witness Mrs Prentice and her sonic mop attacking UNIT HQ – accompanied by the Master. Dr. Who is soon located and brought up to date with an audio recording of everything that's happened in the story so far. He makes one of his amazing scientific lash-ups from random objects, including a fork as a 'vibro-flange.' It's a handy 'astro modulator', which proves efficacious in sending Zex back where he came from.

OUT OF THE GREEN MIST

After a day out 'in town' Jo returns to UNIT HQ at midnight to find all the men asleep on the job. Only Dr. Who is awake, in his laboratory, which is filled with an eerie green glow. Jo is astonished to hear him arguing with a strange intelligence, and she interrupts by shouting. Apparently the green entity was about to show the Doctor some of the 'wonders of existence' and at first he seems miffed that she has spoilt everything.

Suddenly they are interrupted by the Master – disguised as the Brigadier! Not only isn't he embroiled in skulduggery on Pluto, he's back here at UNIT HQ and excited by the Doctor's new device which can contact many different dimensions. The 'writhing green mist' starts coming out with all kinds of semi-religious, quasi-scientific guff about the world Beyond that has everyone most intrigued. Jo is guided to operate the weird machinery by the power of the Doctor's thought, and there is a loud and mysterious 'TWANG!'

The Doctor vanishes but is back before his coffee is cold. He has been somewhere for an unknown span of time and he has seen fantastic things, but they are fading from his memory already...

THE TIME THIEF (Picture Strip)

Anachronistic planes and ships are attacking and looting vessels stocked with the latest scientific equipment. The Brigadier dispatches Dr. Who and Jo to look into it. On the way, our heroes discuss how phenomena such as UFOs, monsters, etc are often just fleeting projections from life in other dimensions. Rather excitingly, the Doctor and Jo scuba-dive to examine a recently-wrecked ship but are attacked by a savage Ekayprian sea beast. Luckily, Mike Yates discharges a beam of ultrasonic waves in the nick of time.

Nevertheless, Jo and the Doctor are transported to the wildly alien world of Ekaypia, where, in a gloomy fortress, they are unsurprised to find the Master in charge of everything. He has constructed a giant time machine that will transport alien hordes to Earth all at once, thus beginning his 'era of conquest and glory.' Luckily the Doctor gets a chance to tinker with his circuitry...

THE FATHOM TRAP

En route to a conference at UNIT HQ General Byland has vanished under the sea! Our heroes are aboard a tiny submersible looking for plane wreckage and – far beneath the surface – the Doctor jumps up and thinks he's sighted something under the 'globiginera ooze.' Their young pilot Burton engages in

93

technical discussion about mud-pumping while the Brigadier grows exasperated. But underneath the mud is a hatchway which opens to reveal a mysterious shaft and into it the submersible *Pisces* is ineluctably drawn...

The humans awake muzzily in a metallic pentagonal chamber and learn that the Doctor has already met their captors, the Kluss, who are ululating serpentoids with moustaches. The Doctor knows them of old and doesn't think they killed the General, or intend to torture everyone, despite the fact they're brandishing ray guns about. Dr. Who communicates with the Kluss via a sucker clamped to his head and learns that they crash-landed here, and having found bodies in the wreckage have delayed tending to their injuries until another human 'model' could be found. The Brigadier gallantly volunteers to help, while the Doctor finds a way to fix their engines and send them on their way.

MENACE OF THE MOLAGS *(Picture Strip.)*

Every city on Earth is visited by strange, low-flying rockets and the Doctor and Jo are keen to go and meet the aliens. For once the visiting extra-terrestrials aren't being terribly secretive, and they broadcast their demands over loudspeakers. When the Doctor and Jo take a helicopter up to meet them they find that the aliens resemble the devil as depicted in the myths of many cultures. This, as they themselves recognise, disadvantages them slightly in discussing matters in a level-headed manner with mankind.

They are here to help. A shower of dreadful space seeds have arrived on Earth – and from them grow the Molags: hideous prehistoric creatures who turn everything they touch to ashes. They attack London at the very same moment that the devil-like aliens choose to present themselves to the world's leaders in a London park. As everyone flees, not unnaturally suspecting the doings of Beelzebub, the Doctor has calmly assembled the equipment needed to rid the Earth of the Molags, courtesy of instructions from what must surely be the Daemons.

TALONS OF TERROR

On the Yorkshire Moors a bloated creature a single eye and a talon is attacking poor old Bessie from behind! Luckily Dr. Who can 'conjure' great speed from under his car's 'prim-looking bonnet'. They are rescued by men who emerge from a futuristic saucer, shoot the creature with strange weapons and address the Doctor as 'Premier Lutz.' The men are Kreffs from the future, come back to save the world from the Perigons. Now that she thinks about it, Jo admits that Dr. Who does look a bit like Premier Lutz, who is going to be at the Crag Hall peace meeting. They can't convince the Kreffs that they have made a mistake.

Aboard their ship the Kreffs describe how important Lutz's contribution is to creating peace and prosperity on their future Earth. They are grateful to him for bringing the Galaxy Peace Force to Earth in order to defeat the Perigons. The Doctor and Jo and the others are almost killed in another attack by the bloated beasts quite close to the conference venue. The Doctor and his doppelganger – the genuine Premier Lutz – face one of the nightmarish Perigons up on the moors with only a silk-lined cape to save them… and to prevent the fiendish creatures from changing Earth's future history.

OLD FATHER SATURN

In the mid-Atlantic the Doctor and his friends witness the sudden emergence from the depths of a Kraken-type creature. The whole thing goes off with the most enormous bang. The Doctor observes that the giant shrimp appeared to be holding a craft of some kind, dredged up from the Atlantic ocean, containing living beings. He's rather excited – wondering aloud whether it may have come from outer space or maybe Atlantis. Barely able to contain himself, he jumps overboard and swims up to take a look through a port-hole. He spies a man inside, wearing a hot pink space suit.

It's a tragic story, for these men have come from one of the moons of Saturn and have lain at the bottom of the sea for millions of years. They are waking up to find that their world was lost many aeons ago, becoming part of Saturn's famous rings. Also, Earth air is incredibly poisonous to them.

GALACTIC GANGSTER

The Brigadier is cross because the Doctor has dragged him and his men out to an abandoned airfield, where some kind of encounter is due to take place. Jo Grant has vanished and the Doctor is faced by a queer kind of vacuum. Suddenly there is a multi-coloured vision before his eyes: a mirage of some vast space war.

All at once a nine-foot tall alien creature appears, holding Jo aloft and shouting about enslaving all mankind to make him Lord of the Galaxy. The Doctor determines to sort out this 'insane scoundrel' and to free his assistant in the process. The Brigadier seems to be in thrall to the creature: 'This is fantastically impossible!' cries the man not given to excitement. Meanwhile the Doctor punches the alien creature on the chin, frees Jo and wins plaudits from a second, newly-arrived alien, who is impressed by the simple straightforwardness and skill at fisticuffs as displayed by Dr. Who.

Other Content

A SPACE AGE CHRISTMAS

Just what about Christmas will have changed by the year 2003, asks one Annual writer? Dinner will be cooked by computer, but Christmas trees will

95

be made of plastic as 'there will probably be very few trees left in the world', Christmas cards will be a thing of the past (replaced by videophone messages) and gifts will mainly be handmade, due to the 'sheer unattractiveness of many mass-produced goods'.

- IN OTHER WORDS – Space related definitions (plus 'Sloshing')
- SIGNS IN THE SKY – Fairly random sky related facts.
- EURKEA! – The lives of great scientists.
- TWO MILES UP – An article considering the problems inherent in two kilometre high skyscrapers.
- TOMORROW'S HISTORY – The time capsule buried as part of the New York World's Fair in 1964.
- ESCAPE TO MARS – One day the Earth will be too hot to live on (though that won't happen for 4-5 aeons, thankfully) and we'll all have to move to Mars.
- PIONEERS OF SPACE – Biographies of three lesser known space pioneers.
- MOON ROCKET MEMO – The Apollo/Saturn rockets.
- A COLLECTION OF CITIES – City based quiz.
- MALEVOLENT MONSTERS – Mythical beasts like the werewolf who, allegedly, 'terrorised hundreds of people until they were finally conquered'.
- MARATHONS IN SPACE – How to deal with boredom on long space journeys.
- DR WHO'S FACTS AND FANCIES – Famous tales Dr Who tells to entertain Jo.

Doctor Who Himself

According to Jo Grant he's 'half towering scientific genius' and 'half pixie.' He's protective of his young companion: 'She is young and innocent and she stays that way!' he rails at an unknown, glowing green menace. The Doctor discloses that he is 'potentially immortal'. He is still concerned with the existence of infinite universes and dimensions (as glimpsed in the final adventure of his previous incarnation.) Discoveries Dr. Who has made about the Omniverse make the Master positively 'drool.' It's a 'multi-dimensional super-universe which is the Whole of Being', apparently – and this has the Doctor just as much agog as it has his wicked counterpart.

He slips into a dimension beyond everything, outside of time and space, and is back before his coffee can cool, but he is reassured and exhilarated by the wonders he experiences in that realm. This is a much more cosmic – even spiritual – Doctor than we knew on TV at the time. While that one raged against his confinement to Earth, this one finds contentment in the idea of infinite dimensions and possibilities beyond the common rut.

He gets cross when he thinks the Brig and his cronies automatically equate anything strange with war and weaponry and fighting.

Monsters and Villains

The Master has a mind that drools with anticipation at the thought of mucking about in other dimensions and dominating alien worlds. He hangs around UNIT HQ on the off-chance of getting Dr. Who to help him.

Zex from the System ggr seems momentarily intrigued by the Master's scheme to take over the Earth, but is soon put off. Other creatures – such as the Daemons and the Kluss – though frightening to look at – turn out to be peaceful and helpful. Some aliens – such as the travellers from Saturn's long-lost moon, or the Master's servants the Ekayprians, are quite hapless. The Perigons are as wily as they are nasty-looking, however – determining to travel back in time to change history and prevent their own defeat in taking over the world.

Curious Companions?

Jo Grant seems a bit more autonomous. She's helping out Professor Veitch (another scientific advisor to UNIT?) with his experiments and she's having days out 'in town.' She is a bona fide genius, according to the Doctor, because she always comes up with the common-sense idea that has eluded him – in 'The Time Thief', for example, she points out that surely he can hypnotise the Ekayprians if the Master can.

Brigadier Lethbridge-Stewart seems to be under a lot of pressure from Whitehall. VIPs are constantly going missing in mysterious circumstances, the Master is determined to take over the world, and the Doctor is continually attempting to contact other dimensions.

I'm intrigued by the UNIT sergeant who is apparently known to all as 'Sparky.'

Fiendish Wheezes

The Master's doing his best in 1974. He can spy on the Doctor's UNIT laboratory via his own Tardis scanner screen. In order to gain an advantage over his hated foe, he'll even tap into the mind of cleaning ladies, as easily as he will alien intelligences. Later, on the planet Ekaypia, he creates a giant time transporter to bring armies of aliens to conquer the Earth. His schemes grow more grandiose, but no more subtle.

TV Feedback

The sheer dogged persistence of the Master and his schemes for taking over the world is very in tune with the TV show in about 1972. The benign though quite satanic-looking aliens in the picture strip, 'Menace of the Molags' are quite clearly drawn literally from the Daemons in the eponymous TV adventure. No credit is given to the show's writer, but it's an interesting development of the idea, and another aspect to the species that is shown here.

Time travellers from a future Earth coming back to the present day to interrupt a conference and kidnap a particular VIP is clearly an echo from the fairly-recent 'Day of the Daleks.' This time the travellers want to ensure that the politician's plans actually work out as he intends.

Egregious errors

'The Fathom Trap' has the Doctor reveal that his memory has been wiped not only of the necessary equations and knowhow that would allow him to pilot the Tardis out of this time zone and world, but also of details of his travels. Only now are his memories of those amazing journeys starting to return. This is at variance with established TV lore.

Classic moments

Mrs Prentice the cleaner and her lethal mop, marauding through the corridors of UNIT HQ is a wonderful moment. Also fabulous is the Doctor and Jo being drawn into an underwater cave and transported to the very alien surface of the planet Ekaypia. They strip off their wetsuits and the Doctor casually reveals that he's still wearing his perfectly tidy velvet jacket and frilly shirt. Why did this never happen on TV?

The Brigadier, Jo and the Doctor waking up in the undersea base of the serpent-like Kluss and mistaking them at first for deadly enemies is a perfect *Doctor Who*-ish moment. Only the Doctor realises that these hideous, undulating, ululating beings are actually benign.

What I learned from the Doctor Who Annual 1974

The Master can see all. But he can't communicate with as many dimensions beyond all time and space as Dr. Who can. There is a timeless realm beyond the galaxy that the Doctor visits for an unspecified amount of time, which he says is rather pleasant. The Kluss – though hideous – are very thoughtful serpentine aliens. Most baddies are just gangsters and bullies.

Illustrations

The artwork seems to be the product of several different hands in 1974. 'The Time Thief' strip in particular is an accomplished piece of work – reminiscent of Frank Bellamy's *Doctor Who* illustrations for the Radio Times. Very dynamic, very colourful: this is one of the most visually appealing of all the Annuals.

The 1975 Annual

In many ways this was always my favourite of the Doctor Who Annuals. I was too young to have received it on publication. It was immediate pre-history for me, coming from the time of the Third Doctor, whose velvety presence I only vaguely remembered gracing our colour TV. The 1975 Annual gave a glimpse of this raffish Doctor's past and I bought it some time near the end of the Seventies at one of the very first jumble sales I (who was to become a lifelong rummager and hoarder) ever went to. This was the first Annual I bought for myself as an act of Collector-ish passion, rather than one I simply received on Christmas morning as a present. Buying it was the decisive act of a fan and a committed reader of untelevised *Doctor Who* adventures and, really, a kind of turning point for me. I was deliberately taking a step into a world of *Doctor Who* stories that were off the beaten track.

A shadow world of tiny print and sheer oddity.

The Stories

THE HOUSE THAT JACK BUILT

The Doctor and Jo are kidnapped and transported to a deadly dimension where they are forced to undergo various tests of endurance involving spinning, hypnotic mirrorballs, carousel horses, deadly chess pieces, a fake Tardis and an infinity of mirrors. The wily old Doctor discovers that a wicked computer – possessed of a sense of humour – is behind the whole scheme, kidnapping folk from all over time and space in order to 'test' them. Having done so, it drains their brains of useful content and then disposes of their witless forms.

'Jack' has bitten off more than he can chew in choosing Dr. Who for his subject. The Doctor manages to drive the computer crazy with a seemingly impossible chess problem, and makes his escape along with Jo down a celestial corridor generated by opposing mirrors.

The Doctor and Jo make their way through their nightmarish and surreal puzzles that can't help but remind us of the classic *Avengers* episode of the same name. In that case, a computer capable of independent and nasty thought was behind the plan, too. The Doctor being trapped inside a mad world of gigantic puzzles and surreal situations reminds the TV viewer of 'The Celestial Toymaker', 'The Mind Robber', 'Carnival of Monsters' and 'Death to the Daleks', all of which would have aired by the time of this story's publication. Still to come on TV, however, 'Pyramids of Mars' would echo the madman's labyrinth of logic games which the Doctor and friend must traverse and 'The Five Doctors' would reprise the notion of the deadly chessboard.

There's a particular charm to this tale, however, and I've always attributed it to the fact that it was written by sixteen-year-old fan Keith Miller, who had been running the world's first *Doctor Who* fan club since January 1972. This is clearly the work of a committed, knowledgeable enthusiast. He captures Jo's slight dappiness along with her loyalty, in the way she gallantly claims responsibility for causing their predicament. He even has the Doctor rubbing the back of his neck thoughtfully as he considers how to win the day. This is closely-observed Dr. Who and a surreal side-step adventure during a humdrum day at UNIT HQ.

It also conjures a lovely picture of Dr. Who's omniverse as a place in which alien nasties – computers, goblins, mad demi-gods and aliens – are forever waiting in the wings, intent on abducting the Doctor and his friends from their everyday lives and doing unspeakably awful things to them.

REVENGE OF THE PHANTOMS

Drawn by signals for help, the Doctor and Jo arrive in a hideous, clammy wasteland, where Jo finds herself beset by the shrieking cries of phantoms. Inside a rather nasty building they are confronted by paintings, statues and tapestries that show alien beings with lunatic, demonic eyes. In a circular room at the top of the tower they meet a shrivelled creature on his last legs, who tricks the Doctor and expresses his determination to possess the Time Lord's body. The gallery downstairs is a kind of exhibition of all the other purloined forms the wicked creature has ever had and their spirits are the wailing phantoms outside. The ranting alien is quick to deliver all of this backstory, and then goads Jo into doing his will – giving the suddenly 'empty-minded' girl a carving knife with which to do the Doctor in. A tussle of wills ensues in which Jo, of course, refuses to kill the Doctor and the evil homunculus soon croaks himself 'wildly' into death.

THE TIME THIEF

Afternoon tea aboard the Tardis is interrupted by a call from Karr, a Time Lord friend, who asks the Doctor to deal with renegade Time Lord, Madrigor (whose name is suggestive of the unholy product of a mating between the Master and the Royal Beast of Peladon, Aggedor.) The planet Lunargov III is revealed as the villain's mobile home, complete with plastic flowers. Madrigor seems very charming – almost like a more successful and better-adjusted version of the Master, perhaps – but he soon gives away the fact that he wants to take over Gallifrey. The Doctor manages to deactivate his deadly Terrestoids temporarily and, following an undignified tussle, there's a chase back to the Tardis.

101

DEAD ON ARRIVAL (Picture Strip)

The planet Mezlob has a gravity some twenty seven times more powerful than that of the Earth. Returning home, the Doctor is encouraging Jo to enter a 'molecular adjuster' machine that will recalibrate her weight. She's wearing a very fetching pink trouser suit but comes a cropper as the Tardis sweeps through a cosmic dust cloud. Jo finds herself on Earth, but she glows and hovers around and passes through walls like a ghost. She witnesses – with a shock – the Doctor laying flowers before her own open casket. But only she can see the almost parodically-stereotypical green invading aliens – the Breelians – who are trying to rip a hole in time and space in order to invade the Earth.

The Doctor winds up communicating telepathically with the Breelians and comes over very queer at UNIT HQ, much to the Brig's consternation. And ghostly Jo is delighted to find that she's been joined in limbo by her best friend. He whisks her back aboard the Tardis and, though it's not explained how, once within they become corporeal once more. Perhaps they use the newly-introduced molecular adjuster? In which case it's more than proved its usefulness within the space of three pages. But these are mere quibbles beside the fact that the Doctor manages to rig up a force field to prevent the Breelian ship hurtling out of their dimension into our own and ensures that the fiends are blown to smithereens. The noise of Breelians exploding in the vortex is: THAKKABOOM.

The Doctor explains to Jo that the molecular adjuster went wonky at the start of the story and shot her into an alternate dimension. Cue lots of dense speech bubbles of technobabble from the Doctor about mirror universes that I, frankly, would have skipped had I been Jo. At the end her cosmic counterpart on Earth 2 is being lectured at, as well. The Brigadier's rubbing his chin like a well-meaning buffoon and Jo elects to make them all a nice cup of tea.

FUGITIVES FROM CHANCE

One of the Annuals' most fantastic tales, as the Doctor visits a world in which various maritime battles from Earth's history are re-enacted by sailors whose very flesh has been transformed to living glass, jade or metal. Befriending John Mander – a pirate made all of gold – the Doctor is taken to the city of the bird people, high above the clouds. There, the quite snappish and stork-like Melovians announce their discovery that mankind is actually quite awful, and they intend to blow up the Earth in order to do the universe a favour. This makes the Doctor furious, and he wants to wring the necks of these 'overgrown budgerigars.' He does the next best thing and outwits them, fairly easily.

AFTER THE REVOLUTION (Picture Strip)

Welcomed to Freedonia – site of an earlier adventure during which the Doctor helped legendary Kamoa with his revolution – the Doctor finds himself suspicious. He soon discovers that everyone has been replaced by cyborgs and all the real Freedonian populace are either living in the hills or being sacrificed to a giant robotic lizard. At the heart of the fake paradise Kamoa's still-living brain is in complete control of his world and it turns out he's got a piece of his own mind inside every one of his subjects. Jo does the talking and convinces Bolgar the misguided to do the right thing and unplug the living brain's life support mechanism. The Doctor – clearly miffed that Jo has provoked a better revolution that the disastrous one he helped with – ends the adventure hurriedly and quotes Hamlet at her for no apparent reason.

THE BATTLE WITHIN

The Doctor slips into a coma and finds himself in the 'evil swamp' and rocky inclines of his own subconscious. Here he meets a cloaked and shrouded figure who claims to be his own alter ego – a malign incarnation of his own drive towards death and self-destruction. At the head of a horde of hideous beasts – gargoyles and demons and giant parrots – this implacable enemy makes it clear that, while the Doctor has travelled everywhere in 'the omniverse', it was only in order to escape his own inner demons. And now at last they've caught up with him.

Meanwhile, aboard the Tardis, Jo Grant watches over the Doctor's lifeless body and prays for his soul. Her love and faith are what return him to the 'real' world, and ultimately defeat the nasties that his waking mind usually manages to keep at bay.

On TV the Third Doctor faces malign mythological creatures as he pays his visit to Metebelis Three in 'The Green Death.' There he steals the famous blue crystal – having climbed a mountain and beaten off beasties – and later he presents it to Jo Grant as a wedding gift. This proves his undoing, of course, as the crystal later goes bonkers and facilitates the summoning to Earth of the giant Metebelis spiders, which is bad news for everyone. His quest on Metebelis is a hubristic one and, in 'The Battle Within', the taunts of his alter ego seem to make it clear that his attempts to ignore his psychological demons are hubristic, too. There's no getting away from them for the rather-too-sure-of-himself Third Doctor.

In the years to come the Doctor would be shown having similar internalised battles. Later in Seventies TV *Doctor Who* we'd learn about the Matrix – the organic super-computer containing the minds and souls of all the Time Lords gone before. When the more self-questioning and philosophical Fourth Doctor eventually visits his home world in 'The Deadly Assassin' he enters the super-computer itself – and faces another anonymous enemy in a fantasy world of terrifying situations, imminent death and disaster. 'The Face

103

of Evil' will present us, in the very next TV adventure, with some of the most frightening imagery concerning the Doctor's facing his own darkest tendencies. The next year when he enters his own inner spaces, in 'The Invisible Enemy' he finds that his mind has been invaded by an evil space prawn. Other tales take up the theme, but stress the psychological dimension – 'The Ultimate Foe' on TV and Paul Cornell's first Virgin novel, 'Timewyrm: Revelation'. In each of these stories it is revealed that the scariest place in the *Doctor Who* universe is inside the Doctor's own mind, and there is some pretty ghastly stuff that he's repressing.

'The Battle Within' from the 1975 Doctor Who Annual seems to presage all of this.

Also, by having Jo Grant hovering over his lifeless form and begging him to come back to her, we have the idea of the Doctor's companions being the ones whose faith keeps him going, and can literally give him the strength to face his foes and carry on. Jo did similar – if more prosaic – nursing of her beloved Doctor on TV in 'The Daemons' and 'Planet of the Daleks', both of which would have aired by the time of this Annual's publication. In this story it's more complex. She is lending spiritual, psychic help to draw him away from his internalised foes.

Later on TV, Sarah Jane Smith would find herself crouching next to the Fourth Doctor's lifeless form on a pretty regular basis. Almost every story would see her willing him to live again. ('I thought you were dead!' she accuses him in 'The Brain of Morbius'. 'You're always doing that!' he says, jumping up jauntily, just as the next danger presents itself.) Much later, the Fourth Doctor is leant support in his final moments before regeneration by memories of his dearest friends. And, a little later still, the Fifth Doctor is guided towards his even bumpier transformation by what appears to be spiritual and telepathic succour from his own friends and companions.

Two important things are made evident by this five page Annual story. The Doctor has terrible demons that he spends his life running away from. And he is dependent upon the travelling companions with whom he surrounds himself for spiritual and psychic strength.

In defeating his self-destructive enemy the Doctor asserts his own will as embodying 'life itself. The wish to grow and love.' Here's a hint of the Doctor's own awareness of himself as folk hero; as a fragment of myth at large in the universe. But he contains darkness and monsters – and it's amazing to find that the infernal landscape of his subconscious looks just like a rocky gravel pit. Almost as if all those hostile alien terrains he visits on TV are just physical manifestations of his own darkest places…

This strange Annual story gives us our first glimmerings of the Doctor as a much more complicated person than we knew about at this point, and is pointing towards his own developing understanding of his place in 'the omniverse': one that will tend towards the megalomaniacal and messianic impulses experienced by, at one time or another, both the Seventh and the Tenth Doctors.

The Doctor of the Annuals is, perhaps, more mythic in his conception than his 1975 TV persona.

BEFORE THE LEGEND

The Doctor and Sarah visit England during its primitive past and find that the local populace are being ruled over by aliens known as Lantan, who have pointed heads and plastic uniforms. They live in a 'huge metal complex' and see no reason why they shouldn't go on dominating all life on Earth well into the future. The Doctor is quick to disabuse them of this notion, pointing out that no Earth records ever really mention the Lantan invasion. As if to underline the seriousness of his future-knowledge, the rumbling of earthquakes and approaching tidal waves trouble the would-be invaders. Several days in prison ensue for the Doctor and Sarah before they can make good their escape, secure in the knowledge that the Lantans are mostly wiped out.

SCORCHED EARTH

In one of the least spectacular stories in *Doctor Who*'s history, Sarah Smith accompanies Dr. Who to an earth-like world where they hope they can have a little break. They find a civilization something like Britain's own agrarian past, and a small population ruled over by a Marshal Zona. Some kind of plague or virus is destroying the soil and ruining the crops. Somehow it is being brought by streaks of fire from the sky. The Doctor is charged with coming up with a scientific solution or being put to death. Sarah accidentally provides the solution when she voices her desire for fish and chips – with lots of salt and vinegar. The Doctor has a brainwave – yes! Salt will cure the agricultural woes of his desperate foes. And so, bargaining for his life, he teaches them how to irrigate their fields with seawater. Plus, he also teaches them that fish – which they have up till now been quite afraid of – are, in fact, edible.

These helpful suggestions made, Dr. Who seems quite keen to whisk Sarah back into the Tardis to try another world. It's as if he himself realises that this hasn't been the most impressive of adventures for his new, novelty-seeking companion.

It's almost a bum-note that the 1975 Annual ends on, but fortunately 'The Secret Steps' on the end-papers proves more thrilling. It's a board game for two players involving the barbarous Aktexians, human sacrifices atop the Ixis monument and a sacred diamond, all proving far more exciting and evocative than that drab story about soil.

105

Other Content

- OUR SPECTACULAR SUN – Earth's sun.
- UP IN SPACE – Another space based quiz.
- NOT JUST AN EMPTY SPACE – For the second year in a row, a depressing article on the fact that Man will need to leave the Earth eventually.
- EARTH OF THE FUTURE – A partial reworking of last year's TWO MILES UP, predicting the world of the 21st century.
- IN THE FUTURE – Inventions designed to thwart criminals or help humanity.
- DR WHO'S SPACEAGE CROSSWORD – Crossword.
- SECRETS OF THE MOON ROCKS – Article on the rocks brought back from the Apollo missions.
- DECISIONS, DECISIONS – Brain teasers.
- ESSENTIAL LIFE SUPPORT SYSTEMS – The environment inside a spaceship.
- FUTURESCOPE – More useful inventions.
- TORO THE TINY MOONLET – A now out-dated article on the near Earth asteroid 1685 Toro.
- TEST YOUR KNOWLEDGE – Quiz.
- THE SECRET STEPS – An overly complicated board game

Doctor Who Himself

He is a Time Lord with a sense of urgency, forever keen to get on with things. 'We've done enough yapping. Now let's find out what's happening.' He can be quite curt with Jo, but is devastated when he thinks he's killed her stone dead in his molecular adjuster machine. Still and all, she is given to hysteria and, in two stories at least, the Doctor fails to resist the urge to slap her face until she calms down.

He has afternoon tea and scones aboard the Tardis while the auto-pilot does all the work, and he treats travel to other times and places quite casually. A visit to the paradise where the villain Madrigor lives is a pleasant opportunity to avoid all the rain they've been having recently in England. Even with his galactic liberty only recently regained, this Doctor is quite breezily at home in the wider universe.

He can be quite irritable when confronted by bad behaviour in alien races. When the Melovians threaten him thus, 'Take care, fancy one!' he is quite livid and expresses his desire to wring their necks.

Monsters and Villains

The alien computer 'Jack', which kidnaps creatures from other worlds and makes them submit to tests of intelligence and endurance; the deadly chess-pieces inside the House that Jack Built; the shrivelled baby-sized alien who tries to purloin the Doctor's body as he has so many others in the past; renegade Time Lord Madrigor, who uses his scientific knowledge to nick stuff throughout time and space; the lizard-like Breelians who hide behind bushes in public parks and who have a spaceship that goes THAKKABOOOM when the Doctor blows it up; the snitty and superior birdmen known as the Melovians who kidnap sailors from all eras of Earth's past; the cyborg inhabitants of Freedonia who refer to the Doctor as 'the white thing' and try to feed him to their giant lizard; the still-living brain of Kamoa of Freedonia; the hideous mythological beings within the Doctor's own soul – gargoyles, demons, a giant parrot; the Doctor's own Death-Wish, manifest as an evil counterpart who wears Jon Pertwee's face and opera cloak and hangs around in the cloying mist of his subconscious; the Lantans – high-foreheaded and plastic-uniformed – who claim to have invaded Earth during the dark ages. (Unfortunately, so obscure is the era they've colonised that no one will ever remember either it or them.)

Curious Companions

Loyal Jo – a bit more elfin-faced and wimpy than her TV self, though she does have the wherewithal to draw the Doctor back from the brink of mental breakdown. She is absolutely unbeatable: 'Even if I am just a ghost,' she says to herself, glowing in a darkened chapel beside her own coffin, 'I must find a way of warning the Doctor (about the hideous green, scaly aliens intent on invading Earth that only I can see)!' In her sensitivity to new environments and the plights of others, Jo often feels as if she's 'trying to wake up from some stifling anxiety dream.' Jo's humanity and compassion frequently save the day, and the Doctor's neck – never quite gaining her the gratitude that it ought to.

Sarah Jane (while looking a lot like Jo Grant in the illustrations) is quite evidently the newish girl when she's introduced in 'The Time Thief.' More forthright (and feminist?) than Jo, she makes the Doctor sit down and explain his full back story, involving the Time Lords, Gallifrey, his exile and all his previous adventures before she'll stir her stumps and help in his quest to put a stop to arch-villain Madrigor's schemes. She talks him into letting her come along on dangerous assignments. She won't be left somewhere safe or fobbed off by the paternalistic fop. She is, however, always amazed by his ability to pull off the impossible stuff. Her visit to Madrigor's mobile homeworld is clearly her very first trip to an alien planet, given how much amazement and wonderment she experiences in the course of 'The Time Thief.' Later, visiting another – though admittedly mundane – alien world, she'll bemoan the fact she can't get fish and chips in outer space.

Fiendish Wheezes

An alien computer with an evil sense of humour kidnaps the Doctor and Jo in order to test their intelligence and drain their brains; an alien body-hopper lures the Doctor to his ghastly world in order to steal his form; Madrigor and his robot Terrestoids want to take over Gallifrey and facilitate their ruling of the galaxy with the Time Lords' recently-invented Time Ioniser; the Breelians want to punch a hole through the fabric of space and time in order to steal the Earth from the 'soft and flabby' human beings; the Doctor's own inner demons want to hold him hostage and then return him to the everyday universe as a thoroughly unpleasant person; bird people kidnap sailors in order to learn about the human race and learn enough to want to commit genocide; a disembodied brain wants to create a race in his own image; on an alien world, the human inhabitants are quite cross about agricultural matters.

TV Feedback

The Annual begins with the Doctor still trying to fix the Tardis and the control console standing in his UNIT laboratory; our heroes are dragged into an alien dimension where they must face various tests, some of them surreal in nature; the Doctor and Sarah have convivial drinks with the villainous Time Lord Madrigor, just as the Doctor and Jo once paid a similar visit to the Master in 'The Sea Devils' on TV; the Brigadier looks somewhat piqued by the endless flashing and bleeping of lights of the Doctor's laboratory equipment while its owner is out gallivanting; the Time Lords live on a planet known as Gallifrey which fact had recently been established in the TV story, 'The Time Warrior' (and also in the comic strip from TV Action issue 126 in July 1973); the companion begs the near-dead Doctor to return to life; the time-space vortex in which both the Tardis and the Breelian ship travel appears to be the *Doctor Who* TV title sequence circa 1974 – popularly known to fans as 'The Time Tunnel'; 'The War Games" influence is clearly felt in 'Fugitives from Chance', but this time all of the combatants are involved in games of a nautical nature. In the face-splittingly dull 'Scorched Earth' Sarah Smith yatters on about wanting fish and chips with lots of salt and vinegar, unwittingly providing Dr. Who with the answer he needs. It's an echo of Jo's clumsiness with the mushrooms in 'The Green Death.'

Anticipating the future

The Doctor enters a surreal dimension and finds it inhabited by something very nasty; the Doctor falls for a plot to steal his body and have his mind replaced by something very nasty; arrival on a seemingly pleasant world is spoiled by discovery that the flowers and plants are plastic, betraying the hidden presence of something very nasty; the Doctor having to tell his companion that he'll 'explain later' because first he must do something about a menace that intends to do something very nasty; a brilliant leader's brain survives his body's death and sets about making plans that are very nasty, plus creating cyborgs in his own image who are also very nasty; a revolution helped along by the Doctor only succeeds in creating a future civilization he is sad to discover has turned very nasty; the Doctor enters his own mind and finds it inhabited by something very nasty.

Egregious errors

The idea that the Tardis travels through space like a rocket does, encountering cosmic dust clouds and troubling its occupants with the very notion of boring things like unfamiliar atmospheres and gravities. Sarah (Jane) Smith is introduced as Jo's replacement, even though Jo isn't written out, and Sarah Jane appears to look, dress, behave and sound exactly like her predecessor. I can only imagine that the name was changed late in the day, giving credence to the ridiculous idea that the girl companion characters are somehow interchangeable. What this means is that the stories are presented out of order. The book begins with the Doctor still trying to repair the Tardis, and later on he is travelling freely in time and space. He enjoys adventures with Jo and Sarah Jane completely out of order. Perhaps the events of 'The Battle Within' do something to scramble his perceptions.

The Time Lords seem very polite, almost loathe to ask the Doctor to go on a mission for them. Neither the TV audience nor the Doctor himself are used to such kid gloves from his mysterious superiors. This leads me to suspect unseen Time Lord-ish developments happening in the background of this Annual, the events of which seemingly take place between 'The Three Doctors' (at the end of which his exile is lifted) and some time after 'The Time

Warrior'. Are the Time Lords feeling particularly contrite towards him during this period? And I wonder if we'll ever find out why..?

What I Learned from the Doctor Who Annual 1975

Tricking the evil computer by being both more clever and more tricky; alternate dimensions are not necessarily places where good and evil are radically reversed and everyone wears eyepatches. Sometimes the differences between quantum universes are subtle and quite hard to pick up on; evil alien intelligences possessing the minds of others will always give themselves away because their eyes look nasty; if in the process of tangling with a super villain do find your way straight to their control room and muck everything up for them – computers, consoles, etc – before they can find and capture you again; alien villains are often verbose. Use the time they spend waffling on by thinking up your plan to defeat them. You can rile them quite easily by tossing a few witty insults their way. Always try to make friends with one of the baddies because one day your intrinsic humanity might convince him to turn against his crazy master and thus save the day while at the same time sacrificing himself, ensuring that you don't have to. Love and loyalty always overcome the baddies, even when you are your own worst enemy. You can easily defeat alien invaders in history by threatening them that you'll take them forward to 1975, where they will be ridiculed and locked in a sanatorium for the clinically insane. Whenever you arrive anywhere in time and space you will soon be embroiled in some kind of hand-to-hand fighting, which will end with you being taken captive and brought before the brutal ruler of this place. There will be some kind of scientific quandary that only the Doctor can solve and he will be taken to a laboratory to sort it all out, while you watch on admiringly.

Classic moment

The Doctor drags the unconscious Jo across a giant checkerboard towards a fake Tardis while gigantic chess pieces attempt to kill them; on a wild and wuthering moor Jo is beset by phantoms and becomes hysterical and only a slap from the Doctor can free her mind; Jo follows the Doctor into a village church, only to find that he is laying flowers in front of an open coffin casket that contains... her corporeal body! The Doctor climbs a mountain to escape a horde of hideous monsters representing his own most horrible thoughts; the

Doctor and Jo confront wicked birdmen in a cloud city, while in the company of pirates made out of gold and other precious metals.

Illustrations

Wonderfully sketchy, vibrant pen and ink. The Doctor has, at times, a look of John Le Mesurier. There's a lovely fluidity to the drawings, though, which seems to stem from the fact that Edgar Hodges took his own 'telesnaps' to base his likenesses on. The illustrations don't seem as rigid and awkward as in other Annuals, which seem at once too tied to photo reference *and* too remote.

It's the wonderful colourfulness of the drawings in this year's Annual that stands out. The Liquorice Allsort pink of Jo's trouser suit and the glowing gold of the transformed Pirate Captain, and all that greenish fog and pulsating purple and blue of the Time-Space continuum. For me, growing up, *Doctor Who* was always the most vibrantly-hued of TV shows and this particular Annual captures that very nicely.

On at least four occasions that same publicity photograph of Jon Pertwee and Katy Manning is used as reference for the artwork. The one where he's working on his dematerialisation circuit while she looks on admiringly. It comes in very useful for those moments when the Doctor is called upon to do something fiddly and scientific and Jo – or Sarah – stands by and watches with great interest.

111

The 1976 Annual

The Fourth Doctor arrives and what changes?

1975 was very true to the Third Doctor's personality as seen on TV – brilliant, paternalistic, boastful, easily piqued and keen to impress his travelling companions. Determined to police the universe and punish wrong-doers. The Fourth Doctor of the Annuals is, perhaps, something of a slacker in comparison. A dilettante. A roving intellectual… Does he have a mission? A sense of purpose? The final story of this book has him saying, right at the end: 'We have all the time in the universe.' And what he wants to do with that time is study. He wants to investigate new cosmic power sources and to stare at the feet of giant robots and ponder imponderables.

The Fourth Doctor's life in the Annuals is the longest, just as it was on TV. And it's stranger. Right from the first, from 'A New Life' in the 1976 book, the ground is shifting. He rockets off from Earth and UNIT HQ with Sarah, hoping for a holiday among extra-terrestrial chums – leaving the miffed Brig and clueless Harry behind in his wake. Following his unseen regeneration he wants to get into the universe again – and be at large in this grand, glorious place where his last incarnation felt so at home. But… he at once finds a paradise world denuded of friends and familiar faces. Straight away he is alienated from his cosy cosmos. Behind his back, everything has changed – and we, the readers of the 1976 Annual knew this before Dr. Who did. We had already checked out the strange pictures before diving into the text. The world of the Annual felt so different. Dingier and more lurid. A thousand times more frightening and unsettling…

It's also about really alien places. In 1976 we travel to properly exotic and bizarre worlds. On TV we always had a lot of metal corridors, spaceship interiors, cave walls and gantries. In the Annuals there is no limit to the landscapes we can inhabit. There is no stock scenery. Anything is possible. In 'The Sinister Sponge' we get to see eight feet high mushrooms and huge red flowers with tentacles and grabby mouths. (Though, to be fair, 'Meglos' on TV had a brave stab at presenting similarly menacing flora.)

These radically alien planets can be rather bleak. War on the world of Bremton a hundred million years ago reduced its inhabitants not to dust, but to 'mindless parodies of the creatures they had once been.'

Everyone gets their minds messed about with in the 1976 Annual. Some of that mind-boggling is perhaps down to scale. The scale of things has changed.

Aliens can be more than 85 feet tall, the Tardis can be the size of a fruit pip. Time itself becomes elastic – as indeed it should in stories about the Tardis, and millions of years can pass in the reduced space of a five page short story.

The Stories

A NEW LIFE

The Doctor takes Sarah off for a holiday to the idyllic world of the Lexopterans, where he hopes to introduce her to his old friend, Miranon. The Doctor hasn't been here for 102 years though and is surprised to see things have changed. Sarah is disappointed to be shown a seemingly deserted – though tidy – alien world. Behind a hidden panel they find Miranon's dead body. It is Sarah who picks up the clue that allows the Doctor to work out the mystery. The Lexopterans used a scientific formula to avoid conflict with an alien race by transforming themselves into vegetation. Miranon was the last man standing, but was killed before he could turn everyone back into their rightful selves. Lucky for the Lexopterans that Dr. Who happened by!

THE HOSPITALITY ON HANKUS

The Tardis deposits our three travellers in a very unstable alien environment, where the sky is dark red and the land is a green mish-mash. All is upheaval and flux and the Tardis experiences violence like we've never seen before. The three travellers are rattled around and we witness Harry swinging Sarah by her ankles, Sarah jack-knifing through the air, and the Doctor sitting on the ceiling, watching their antics. The Tardis is being flung about, we are told, like 'a cork in a washing machine', which is an image that stayed with me for years after I first read this book as a kid. It spoke volumes about the violence of time travel, and the fragility of the travellers inside their apparently indestructible craft, and also the insignificance of them against the hugeness of the cosmos.

We are on the planet Hankus in the Maston Galaxy, and the people are reptiles with antennae. Jen-Ka and his family are awaiting the arrival of the Doctor and his friends. Jen-Ka pops out to catch some 'spads' in a pond nearby, in order to impress Dr. Who.

The Doctor, meanwhile, menaced by a gigantic four-headed lobster, realises his mistake. He has materialised the Tardis at the wrong scale. They have arrived in a miniaturised state on a fruit, almost been eaten by Jenn-Ka and have been spat out into a pond. It's all soon remedied and they return to normal size and everyone has a good laugh about it over dinner.

THE PSYCHIC JUNGLE *(Picture Strip)*

Sarah says the jungle on the world they're visiting is horrible. She's talking mainly about the snakes and the horned demons creeping about everywhere. Is she imagining them? But all three can see the hideous giant spiders who, in their turn, believe themselves to be on a desert world and menaced by the Ventros, who are giant birds. The Doctor invites them into the Tardis to escape the hallucinogenic effects of the planet, which is alive and psychic and sensitive to the primal fears of visitors. Dr. Who cleverly saves the day with a 'biotronic neural attachment' to remove the spiders' fears temporarily so that they can fix their ship and escape. We are left wondering, were the giant spiders actually giant bunnies? The story ends with Sarah asking the Doctor what horrible things he saw in the Psychic Jungle, and he's very evasive.

The disturbing nature of this picture strip makes feature articles such as 'A Short History of the Pressurised Spacesuit' seem even more banal and irrelevant. These stories are revealing a different kind of *Doctor Who* – more about psychology than astrology. We're becoming more interested in inner space than outer.

THE SINISTER SPONGE

Here's one of the show-stoppers of the Annuals. Bear with me on this one.

Visiting the planet Inscruta, Dr. Who once again hopes to meet an old friend – this time, the leader of the Inscrutes, Elkalor. Almost as soon as they arrive on this colourful world our friends are alert to a greenish-yellow cloud heading towards them. 'That's no cloud!' 'It's more like a… a sponge!'

Narrowly escaping being absorbed by the sponge (which has a look of the sponge people of Femizor, six billion light years away) our friends are trapped inside a red-petalled plant which tries to dissolve them with acid. The Doctor facilitates an escape by singing 'Land of Hope and Glory' very loudly.

Soon the Doctor's old friend Elkalor is found hiding inside a giant cabbage. He looks awful, with his feathers dropping out and his flesh turned transparent. When Dr. Who and Harry join him in the interior of the cabbage, the once proud leader describes a noisy feminist uprising. The women were found to be harbouring a sentient sponge in the Council Hall and 'consorting' with it. They soon evicted all the men, and banished them to the cabbage patch.

Elkalor will not accept Dr. Who's offer to help: 'Though our very bones are turning to jelly, I cannot entertain your kind offer.'

But by now Harry is turning see-through, too. Our heroes are involved whether Elkalor wants them or not. Clever Harry fashions ear-muffs out of tough cabbage leaves to protect him from the hullaballoo of the women. Pretty soon, though – the women are right there, banging pots and pans and Sarah is amongst them, hypnotised and vengeful for all the wrongs done to her gender.

114

The Doctor intervenes by communicating directly with the Sinister Sponge, utilizing Femizonian Aurapathy to discover that the sponge wants to return to its distant home of Femizor by creating a 'transformer.' The sponge has caused friction between the Inscrute sexes as a result of absorbing Oriolic dust beams en route to this world. These beams have had a deleterious on his male hormones, and also those of the local Inscrutes. (Dr. Who asks: 'Have your own hormones been affected?' and the Sinister Sponge is furious at being quizzed about such things.)

The Doctor's solution is to produce from his pocket a Rhao, or space mouse. They are the sworn nemeses of Sinister Sponges the galaxy over. The Doctor is keen to point out that the sponge isn't evil. He's young and amoral and oversensitive. He has accidentally shot himself across the galaxy and caused this mess. In the face of the Time Lord's implacable good sense the Sponge becomes apologetic. The Doctor reasons that cabbage juice is just the thing to cure the disintegration caused by Oriolic dust.

The liberated ladies of Inscrute make cabbage tea in order to end the war between the sexes, and the war within the very fibres of the Sinister Sponge. Dr. Who sends him home with a Molecular Speed-beam aimed directly at his home world of Alpha-Mardis 2.

With all this done and dusted, Dr. Who decides to go fishing. He displays a breezy lack of panic and concern. He doesn't sermonise or bask in the glory like the Third Doctor might. He just goes off to enjoy himself elsewhere.

NEURONIC NIGHTMARE (Picture strip)

Perhaps the strangest of all the Doctor Who Annual stories. The Tardis is in a very odd region of space indeed when our friends are brought to visit Skizos – a flame-headed skeleton in sepulchral robes. He explains that his world is divided into two and this is Skarol and the other bit is Lektra, and there they cultivate humanoids in farms. Apparently the point is that Skizos and his people generate excess energy in their very persons and they like to siphon it off onto the human beings, who then die.

Harry seems to save the day, but he turns out to be a Neuroid in disguise, who explains that, actually, the siphoned energy gets dispersed into the neuronic biosphere, harming no one. So that's okay then.

The real Harry has been spending time on the farm, reappearing in a very natty blue and black striped blazer. Neuronic space seems to be a very queer place to be, and the strip ends disquietingly with the Doctor concerned about being able to navigate the Tardis safely out of it.

It almost seems to this reader that Neuronic space is where all these 1976 stories are taking place. It's a place where humanoids suffer terrible things, and have alien psychic energies pumped into them whenever they least expect it. They can't even trust their own eyes. It makes me wonder whether Dr. Who ever actually manages to get the three of them away from that noxious zone.

'Neuronic Nightmare' raises the tantalizing possibility that the Doctor and his friends are stuck forever in this psychedelic zone.

AVAST THERE!

Another tale in which Sarah and Harry are perfectly well characterised. They slip out of the Tardis in order to warn the Doctor of the danger he faces. The Tardis has materialised aboard a pirate galleon floating through space and he has the wicked captain on his trail. Sarah and Harry are the ones forced to walk the space-plank however. Luckily the Doctor carefully manoeuvres the Tardis into just the right position to save them.

THE MISSION

These stories are following the TV show's lead and determinedly leaving Earth's orbit. They are even more intergalactic than Tom Baker's early years on TV, though, taking us to wildly improbable worlds and adventures that are set over vast time periods. This story begins with a prelude in the pre-history of the planet Tyrano, showing us how Tamrike the Bremtonian died as he attempted to claim the world for his people, and how he didn't quite manage to activate his Giant Robot to do the work it was built to do.

Then, about a thousand million years later, we catch up with the Doctor, Sarah and Harry having a bop in what appears to be a Tyrano Night Club. Sarah is boogying with two men with fins and the Doctor and Harry are both dancing with the same girl.

A random set of electronic signals reactivates the Giant Robot, which has sunk deep into the soggy earth. The robot wakes and starts to attack – and even Rama beams and sonic lances are no good. The Doctor and friends investigate and he soon discovers that the robot is trying to carry out its age-old mission – way too late. His instruction was to take control and pilot this whole world to a cooler region in space so that the Bremtonians could comfortably invade. Some buttons are quickly pressed and the Giant Robot is easily switched off.

Other Content

- PECULIAR KILLER PLANTS – Specifically, the Venus Fly Trap.
- FIT TO BE AN ASTRONAUT – The requirements to become an astronaut.
- GREAT JUMPING JUPITER – History of the Pioneer 10 spacecraft.
- PUZZLING PLANETS – Planet based quiz.
- SPACE TALK – Fairly random space related information.

- DRESSED FOR THE JOB – A short history of the pressurised spacesuit.
- STORIES IN THE STARS – Another piece on the signs of the zodiac, which Annual writers seem to think counts as science.
- IT'S A FACT – Further random facts.
- MAZE OF MADNESS – A board game, featuring a foam rubber avalanche.
- MOON STRUCK – Quiz.
- A GALAXY OF STARS – Quiz.
- THANKS TO SPACE RESEARCH – Everyday items we owe to space research.
- SPACEWORD – Crossword.
- ABC OF SPACE – An ABC of Space.

Doctor Who Himself

This Doctor – just like Tom Baker on TV – wants to get away from Earth, UNIT HQ and the Brigadier's apron strings. He dashes off to another planet with Sarah to visit old friends. He wants to visit Miranon on his peaceful world after a gap of 102 years. Perhaps he wants to surprise him with his new face: 'I've changed again! What do you think of this one? Look – some scarf, eh?' Other stories remind us that the Doctor has friends on other planets who we haven't met yet, such as Jen-Ka and his family in 'Hospitality on Hankus'. I love the idea of Dr. Who's endless friends in outer space, whom he periodically revisits. I like the way Jen-Ka's mother fusses about readying the spare rooms and how she calls them 'dwelling units'. I get a particular frisson of readerly pleasure from that combination of the space age and the domestic.

Later, in 'The Sinister Sponge', Dr. Who is at home on an alien world once more. On the planet Inscruta he already knows Elkalor the Inscrute leader, and is amazed at finding him reduced to living inside a giant cabbage.

This Fourth Doctor truly is one who 'walks in Eternity', just as the Fourth Doctor on TV was about to tell us, sometime around 1976. He casually namedrops amazing-sounding aliens and worlds and the reader longs to see and hear more of them. Our minds are boggled by mentions of the Cloud Men of Multar, the wondrous Diamond Highway of Zimmar, the colourful Widge Men of Neuronis and the Imago Cascade of Ferras.

The Doctor is very evasive on the subject of his primal fears. He won't tell Sarah what he sees in the Psychic Jungle. Years before mention of the Fendahl, or the Dark Times on Gallifrey, or the Other or the Pythia,

Lungbarrow or the Time War, the readers of the 1976 Doctor Who Annual are being introduced to a Doctor with a subconscious and a personal and ancestral history that he doesn't like to talk about. This picks up on 'The Battle Within' from the previous year's Annual, and fills in more of the picture of a Doctor who's more complex and troubled than the one we saw on Seventies TV. Doctor Who is a haunted man. He has friends all over time and space, but he also has stuff inside that he's trying to run away from.

He's keen on going, 'Aaaah,' in that mock-pompous fashion, just like Tom Baker, and he's very fond of gizmos called things like 'Oscillating Reverberator Units.'

Monsters and Villains

We seem shorter on villains, all of a sudden. Faceless marauding hordes, blundering four-headed lobsters, sentient sponges who are prey to their hormones… all of these things are just creatures doing what creatures do, and their victims are those who happen to be around at the time. We have less of the bwa-ha-ha super-villain in the mode of the Master or Madrigor this time around. The closest, perhaps, is Skizos, at the heart of the Neuronic Nightmare, with his skull-like face in flames. He's pretty terrifying, and he's doing pretty awful stuff. Perhaps he's all the baddie one Annual needs?

Curious Companions

Sarah and Harry are very true to themselves in this. This isn't what people usually say about the Annuals – especially the late seventies ones – but I find them consistent with their TV selves, and at times even more interesting. Sarah is the Fourth Doctor's first choice for a companion, and Harry is added into the mix later on. There is none of that sense from TV that Harry Sullivan is any kind of encumbrance, however. He takes an active role in these adventures. In a story like 'The Mission' he is even helpful – when the Doctor asks him to bring in his Naval knowhow for the cracking of codes. I like this version of Harry because he is interested in other worlds and peoples. He tries out Virtual Reality gear and learns about the history of Tyranian civilization. His TV incarnation's adventures were played out at breakneck speed, with no gaps between. He barely got time to change his blazer. Then suddenly, he was gone from the show. The 1976 Annual presents a Dr. Who, Sarah and Harry team that gets to stay together a bit longer in order to explore a psychedelic and perplexing universe. They even get to go to a dance.

Sarah, meanwhile, is quite a calm and domesticated person. She'll still stand up for herself and argue and get scared, but she seems a mature, well-seasoned time-and-space traveller by now. At one point in 'A New Life' she suggests they return to the Tardis so that she can make something to eat, and they can figure out their mystery calmly. The avowedly feminist companion takes on an almost wifely role to the Doctor here. However, she has other facets in this book, too – joining the hormone-crazy ranks of noisy, brainwashed women in 'The Sinister Sponge' and disco-dancing in a threeway with two of the flippered men of Tyrano. Her relationship with Harry seems consonant with the irked fondness that we get on TV. When he tries to protect her from danger he gets lambasted for treating her like 'a piece of quaint mindless pottery.'

Even so, these are terrifying and violent adventures that Sarah and Harry are being involved in, through their connection with this rather blithe and casual Doctor. In one particularly hectic moment Sarah feels like 'a blind woman on a plane that is fast running out of fuel and must find somewhere to land.' The hideous things they undergo in both the Psychic Jungle and inside the Neuronic Nightmare would give any prospective Tardis team-member pause for thought. The worlds of the 1976 Doctor Who Annual seem particularly frightening to me, for some reason. I think, perhaps, because as a child I pored over the strange illustrations for many hours, trying to figure out what on Earth was going on in them.

Fiendish Wheezes

The Lexopterans turn themselves into flowers in order to escape rapacious invaders. The Sinister Sponge messes about with gender dynamics on the Planet Inscruta, hoping to build a 'transformer' to take him back to his home world. Skizos and his people breed human cattle into whom they siphon off their excess, deadly psychic energy. The Bremtonians send an eighty-five foot tall robot to the planet Tyrano, so he can pilot it to a cooler spot, and they can invade. In 1976 we are a bit short on fiendish wheezes – though the ones we do have are pretty wild. Most of the things that happen do so not because of a Machiavellian genius at work, but because of random mischance. The TARDIS turns up and it's the wrong size, or the planet makes visitors' unconscious fears apparent, or living sponges soak up the wrong sort of cosmic dust. In the second half of the Seventies this is a scary, amoral, disorganised universe.

TV Feedback

The Doctor and his friends turned up in a miniaturised state back in the Sixties in 'Planet of Giants'. The tiny Tardis springing up to its rightful size in an instant is very like that moment in 'Carnival of Monsters' when its sudden appearance surprises everyone.

The Doctor and Harry being almost eaten by plant life in 'The Sinister Sponge' has echoes of their tussles with Mutants and giant clams in 'Genesis of the Daleks.'

The Giant Robot on Tyrano in 'The Mission' is a clear echo of the robot K-1 in Tom Baker's debut *Who* TV story. The illustrations show that photographs of the TV version were clearly consulted. This Bremtonian titan bears the same baleful metal face and the same boxlike feet. It's tempting to link them in your mind: these devoted, loyal, unthinking creations trying to get on with their work.

Anticipating the Future

'A New Life' is the Fourth Doctor and Sarah's first space trip alone together! Well before 'Planet of Evil' on TV. It's not **quite** as exciting…

'Hospitality on Hankus' weirdly anticipates TV's 'The Invisible Enemy' with its rare and curious combination of bodily miniaturization and deadly seafood.

In the years between this Annual's publication and 2005 the concept of chairs with safety belts in the Tardis console room would have counted as an egregious error. However, once New *Who* started – there they were! Like the battered seats out of a trashed Ford Cortina, welded to the rails around the console. These seats seem to be the product of a writer or designer thinking – what if this was all real? What would these travellers actually need aboard a machine like this?

The 'Neuronic Zone' is a region of time and space where everything is a bit messed up. It's somewhere the Doctor isn't sure he can navigate the Tardis away from. The question of whether they will ever return to their native universe anticipates the E-Space story arc of Season 18 on TV, a few years later.

Any mention of a Pirate Captain can't help but put us in mind of the marvellous specimen from 'The Pirate Planet', still a couple of years away. Also, antique galleons floating through deep space is an image later used to great effect in TV's 'Enlightenment' in 1983 and Michael Moorcock's 2010 novel, 'The Coming of the Terraphiles.' In each case the aliens are dressing up like this out of affectation.

The Giant Robot on Tyrano – waiting patiently to come back to life in order to fulfil his mission – is a reverse echo of the Melkur from 'The Keeper of Traken', who also found himself spearheading a very gradual invasion, slowly growing mossy and defunct.

Egregious errors

Was there ever a gap between TV stories of this era for these tales to fall into? The Doctor, Sarah and Harry tumble pretty swiftly between Nerva Beacon, Earth, Skaro, Voga and Loch Ness, but I don't care. This is a lovely, more leisurely version of their time together.

The Tardis travels through the 'transdimensional flux', which is a grey nothingness. This is the most terrifying version yet of what Terrance Dicks often calls 'that mysterious region where time and space are one.'

In 'The Psychic Jungle', and most stories here, Sarah and Harry really don't look like themselves. Harry has a touch of Oliver Reed or Ernest Hemingway about him at times, and he is often seen sporting a Seventies porn star moustache. Both companions have the bland good looks of shop dummies or catalogue models. Harry appears to be dressed as the Milk Tray man and I wonder if, in the Psychic Jungle, their altered appearances are down to the weird telepathic stuff going on. Am I reading too much into it..? Maybe the artist is just using stock images that don't even come from *Doctor Who*? Or maybe he's getting his friends to pose. 'Stand over there and try to look as if you're being harassed by a Sinister Sponge.'

What I learned from the Doctor Who Annual 1976

When he tells you he's taking you to a beautiful world inhabited by friendly pacifists: watch out. Even the most innocuous worlds can be terrifying, especially if you materialise on the wrong scale and fall into a pond. Also, it isn't just the monsters and stuff marauding about that can do you harm. Some planets are alive and telepathic and can bring your worst fears to life before you. Sponges can be sentient but not necessarily evil. Watch out for noisy feminists. Cabbage tea can do wonders for hormonal imbalances. The Neuronic Zone is a very strange and scary place. Watch out for being zapped into a human farm and receiving the excess psychic energy of flame-headed skeleton people.

There's an intellectual cynicism at work in these stories. The Bremtonian Giant Robot wakes up to fulfil its mission millions of years late, and only because of random mischance. The 1976 Annual as a whole seems to tell us that yes, there are monsters and villains – but there are huge, complex forces at play in the universe and we puny humanoids will never fathom them out. Dr. Who might understand some of what's going on, but he'll never explain fully. All you can do is decode the scrambled messages left in the lurid mess of the galaxy, and hope to survive. It's nice to have friends to go and visit.

Classic moments

Confronting the giant hairy spiders in the Psychic Jungle and realizing that they aren't in fact illusions is a moment that stayed alive in my imagination for a long time. Sitting inside a makeshift house in the heart of a giant cabbage, hearing how the battle of the sexes is going on the Planet Inscruta. And hearing that it's all down to a giant and Sinister Sponge who's consorting with all the women. The Doctor's lack of fear when confronted by the frankly terrifying Skizos: 'Ah! So you have decided to come out?' 'Why not? I'm Doctor Who!'

Illustrations

The artist for 1976 and for much of the rest of the Seventies was Paul Crompton. Paul Green also contributed some work to the 1976 book.

The illustrations make Dr. Who's world look as if it is molten. No less colourful than in previous years – but darker. Obscure. Harder to make the details out. A much less certain universe. We seem to be getting a bit of multi-media and collage, too. This is Doctor Who Annual as Fine Art.

There is a curious blend of photo realism and a more expressionist psychological realism, which results in something very unique – especially in what is essentially a book for children. We have less clear cut illustrations, a less cartoony and comic-strippy universe. The accent is no longer on literal representations of what is happening in the stories, but rather on ambiguity, murkiness, hesitation, equivocation, indeterminacy and a deliberate blurring of detail. There is a feeling that you're not quite sure what you're reading... the rules have changed. This is postmodern realism in the world of *Doctor Who*.

The obscure and mostly-dark pictures often show hands and floating heads. Faces are seen in rictuses, screaming and suffering. And when we see the Doctor's face it's not like his previously avuncular, reassuring presence – it's just a baleful boggle-eyed stare, propped up on loops of woollen scarf. Just watching out of the darkness in quite an unnerving fashion.

In 'Neuronic Nightmare' – perhaps the most extreme in terms of narrative and artwork – characters look like zombies, like flayed, bloody bodies, and are cast in luridly coloured light. They phase in and out of existence and never seem wholly present or substantial. This gives the story a thrilling, dreamlike quality, entirely fitting for the curious year of 1976.

The Amazing World of
Doctor Who

I sometimes feel that the years of my childhood were about seven times as long as years nowadays. And as if in support of that idea, here we find a year with two Annuals: a year hidden inside a year. 'The Amazing World' was an extra book, initially produced as part of a promotion for Typhoo tea, along with a set of collectible cards and a wall chart. How wonderfully appropriate it seems for *Doctor Who* to be involved in promoting tea. I wish there was product placement in each of the stories, with Sarah pausing to fill a flask or the Doctor calling a halt to proceedings while everyone has a cuppa.

In those days collecting picture cards given away with packets of tea was quite a big deal. I remember having cards to do with World Wildlife, Space Travel and Mythical Creatures. You'd have to send off a postal order for the book to paste them into, and the whole thing would smell wonderfully of tea leaves. I wasn't aware of this *Doctor Who* promotion at the time, during the long, hot year of 1976, but if I had, I would have thought of it as the most exciting tea-related special promotion ever.

The book has a number of factual articles and this time they're even about *Doctor Who..*! They discuss various enemies and adventures from the show's past, which must have been exhilarating for young fans in those days before *Doctor Who Weekly* and its ilk made discussion of past adventures commonplace. There are reprises for two of the most memorable recent prose stories ('The Sinister Sponge' and 'The Mission') and two of the best – and strangest – picture strips ('The Psychic Jungle' and 'The Neuronic Nightmare.') All of these stories come from the previous year's Annual, which reminds us that, in those days, the Annuals were seen as ephemeral. They were in bookshops and newsagents during the run-up to Christmas and then gone again. The stories took place in the blink of an eye. Just in the way that the TV show was shown once and – apart from perhaps two stories getting a repeat in the summer – the episodes were gone (supposedly) forevermore after that. Back then, the whole of *Doctor Who*'s history didn't exist as one continuous, ever-present, simultaneous narrative for the delectation of fans, and it wasn't being pieced together lovingly by learned experts like the partly-ruined scrolls of some ancient cycle of myths. That's not how this cultural phenomenon was experienced then. Everything was a lot more throwaway in the nineteen seventies.

Among the repeats in the 'Amazing World' of 1976 there were two new stories.

The Stories

THE VAMPIRES OF CRELLIUM.

Visiting the world of the snailmen of Yula, the Doctor and Sarah find that the famously harmonic group-mind has been disturbed by psychic power emanating from the planet Crellium. Sarah is apprehensive as they pay a visit to this lifeless, greasy, fetid world with its stunted vegetation. They hear a distant sob and Sarah is reminded of the Sirens from Earth mythology. What they find is a faceless woman lolling in a tended garden of flowers, beside the lifeless body of an old man.

The woman is Marsalla, who has been a servant to the man called Krem-ling – ever since she was a child and he brought her from the planet Juksta. In his life he has taken many forms – Heemies, Worgs, Benlithulans, Suasian Norbs and, most recently, a bearded human male. 'Next he will adopt the snail flesh of the Yulians.'

The Doctor becomes terribly angry about all of this feeding on innocent alien victims. He describes Krem-ling as a psychic vampire, and recognises him as one of the emissaries of Drakka, who don't have their own forms and must devour spirits and adopt bodies to stay alive. If Krem-ling is allowed to invade the Yulian Common Will with his Drakkan brethren, he will be able to suck the essence of a whole world at once! The Doctor realises that the other Drakkans are disguised as flowers in the small garden here. He urges Sarah to rip them all out by their roots but before she can, the flowerbeds convulse and the soil gives up the forms of 'slimy, squat automatons.'

The Doctor works on getting Marsalla to help defeat the vampire Drakkans, even if it means her own death. He persuades her with a speech that seems to me worth quoting in full:

'Is this your life, this black abyss? Is this your future? A desolate, never-ending trail of violations? Do you not remember Juksta? Was your childhood so empty? Do you not remember playing in the sunlight? Do you not remember your mother, your father, your family? That is your life, Marsalla, not this evil.'

The Doctor's saying this to the faceless companion of an eternal monster, goading her into action against the homunculi that threaten a whole world. It can be read as the Doctor's entire lives' mission in a nutshell. This short speech is what he is continually saying, in all of the stories he is involved in. It's a rallying cry and a prompt to action and bravery. It's life affirming and nostalgic and all about taking responsibility. It's what lies at the heart of any *Doctor Who* story worth its salt.

And what a funny place to find it. Way off the beaten track. In an extra story in a book that isn't even a proper Doctor Who Annual. Just a book produced to advertise a brand of tea. There's something very fittingly eccentric and even perverse about that.

And I'm quoting it in full and dispensing with my usual silly categories to do with 'fiendish wheezes' and 'what we learned' etc, because when it comes to 'The Amazing World of Doctor Who' from 1976, my usual way of appraising these books seems rather facile, all of a sudden. All I want to do is draw your attention to what the Doctor says to Marsalla. All you need to know about *Doctor Who* on the TV or in books is there, I think, and you don't need me being clever and ironic and silly about it.

1976 and the couple of years that follow it seem to have been a time for bold, sometimes earnest statements, and about people in *Doctor Who*'s Amazing World really thinking hard about the way they want to live their lives.

In the story itself, the speech does its work. Marsalla does what she knows she must, and physically enters Krem-ling's body in order to stop his plan for psychic domination of the world of the snailmen. The emissaries of Drakka are lumbering towards the Doctor still, with their arms outstretched... and he runs after Sarah, to escape into the Tardis. At just that point Marsalla produces a device that blows the whole lot – vampire homunculi and herself and enchanted flowerbeds and stunted trees – sky high.

Back on Yula, the group-mind of the snailmen is changing in response to this adventure. Perhaps it has grown too complacent in its peacefulness? The Doctor detects a new influence at work on the Communal Will, and thinks it might well belong to the spirit of Marsalla.

ON THE SLIPPERY TRAIL

A much less cosmic and spiritual tale in which Sarah and Doctor land on a new planet, slide about on what seems to be a giant snail trail, and then get attacked by a huge slug-thing. Sarah almost gets sucked up along with all the vegetation, and the Doctor drags her into a cave. There he sets to crumbling up soft grey rock, shinning up a chimneylike hole, and sprinkling the crystals out of his hat onto the slug monster below. Of course, it's salt, and the two friends watch the monster thrashing about oozily and turning into a dead, withered balloon.

The locals – the Anthrons – dash out to thank Dr. Who and his friend. They've been plagued by this slug thing for many a moon.

Strange, to have slugs and snails as the focus of the two extra stories in this bonus Annual. In one the creatures are transcendent beings, living in spiritual, communal harmony, eliciting admiration from Dr. Who and noble sacrifice from secondary characters. In the other they are garden pests, essentially, and the Doctor has to sprinkle them with salt.

It's the sublime and the ridiculous; the cosmic meets the banal.

126

The 1977 Annual

I feel like we're travelling deeper now, and into some of the odder corners of the omniverse. Even here the Doctor is known. He's revered in some quarters, and hated in others. Each story is lobbed out like a stone being skimmed across a placid lake. Each brief contact creates ripples that roll outwards. Each story is illogical but weirdly suggestive, too. I feel as if we're only getting part of the story each time. There's a whole lot of murky stuff underneath.

Of course it's the Fourth Doctor who takes us into these stranger recesses of time and space. He's nonchalant and not easily impressed. He's often bored and forever striding onwards, keen to see what's next.

In 1977 it really feels as if he's letting us come along on the trips he dreamed about when he was exiled to Earth in the Glam Rock years. These are the journeys he thought about when he was chafing against the Brigadier's rules and regulations. These curious planets are Dr. Who's natural environment. In this era of disco and punk, at times it's like we're getting to walk in eternity alongside him.

The Stories

WAR ON AQUATICA

The Doctor, Sarah and their friend – scientist and amateur space traveller Professor Vittorio Levi – are being held captive in the kingdom of Medusia on the planet of Aquatica. The serpent-haired Medusians are quite keen to crack the secrets of the Tardis. Our heroes escape through ornamental gardens to sleep on the beach, where they are woken by Phyllos, god-like Master of the Phyllosians, with his silver hair and shining sapphire eyes.

He takes them home to meet his wife, Dyonne, and while she cooks breakfast, they learn about the sources of tension between the peoples of Aquatica. The Medusians are stealing glyt from the glyt-mines by mesmerising the Mattermonks of Matterdom and, what's more, they're spiriting the Lumidolphs of the Phyllosians away from the Lumid sea.

I can just hear Tom Baker's explosive retort: 'WHAAAAT?!'

Next we learn that the Medusians are training the space-dolphins to carry explosive warheads. Outside again, the Doctor and friends witness a tank of Lumidolphs being hoisted onto the backs of ships ready to sail.

Dr. Who and the others take a motorboat to see King Chympanzo – a blue, Simian monarch – and they observe the tragic sight of dolphins being projected at great speed at the Medusians' enemies. Phyllos tries to persuade

127

the apelike king to set his pets – the Mongs – onto the Medusians. They descend by dissolving parachutes and attack. Defeated, the Medusians suggest Phyllos, his wife Dyonne and Dr. Who should negotiate peace on Aquatica. So, then everything is sorted. The Doctor, Sarah and Vittorio decide they quite like it here – on this odd, E R Burroughsian world – after all. But it's really time to return to Earth in 1977.

CYCLONE TERROR

Dr. Who wants a holiday, but he and Sarah have wound up on Zoto in the galaxy of Zaurus in the year 4000 and it's all very bleak. A cyclone arrives and blows them five miles away. When they find their way back to the Tardis it is surrounded by admiring Zotons, who recognise the Doctor and know of his exploits.

The Doctor offers to get to the bottom of the cyclone mystery which is forcing the Zotons to hide away down pits. He doesn't take very long to discover reptilian creatures called Zanons (who he also recognises) operating a powerful wind machine from behind some trees. The machine is set to produce perfectly regular and deadly cyclones.

The Zanons – who are famously scared of weapons – are defeated by the Doctor whittling a piece of wood into the shape of a ray gun. And also, by Sarah jumping onto one of their backs. They are soon chased off by their own wind generator. But will they ever come back?

THE TIME SNATCH

A saucer lands in the middle of the dustbowl, startling gold prospector Ben Hunter. He is subsumed by a hideous red blob creature. Nearby at UNIT USA on Last Hope Ridge, Gustav Bhoul is examining Crystal Z, which has come back aboard an unmanned space probe.

The Doctor and Sarah are here and, finding that the precious crystal reminds him of something, the Doctor slips it into his pocket. Just then a dusty, shambling figure emerges from the desert and walks straight through both the electrified fence and the laboratory wall. He demands the crystal: 'We have come to take it back.' He isn't the first zombified human to burst into a UNIT HQ, and it's not till he paralyses them all with a jab of his finger that anyone takes him seriously. The shambling brute leaves behind him a small transparent cube, 'to hurl you into the Time Zone – and the crystal with you.'

At this surprising turn of events, Dr. Who, Dr Bhoul and Sarah are sucked into the vortex. It is a 'mind-searing journey'. The Doctor kicks over something that tinkles and amazingly – it's the Time Cube! Which he describes as a miniature Tardis. Suddenly, out jumps a caveman, which is scary for a few moments until a mammoth jumps out. This almost tramples the Doctor and Sarah, plus the rather unwary Dr Bhoul.

The Doctor activates the Time Cube and they are whizzed back to the present and the dust bowl, where they find Ben Hunter unconscious. And the crystal is okay.

We are left thinking: what is the point? Why do they even care about this crystal? Mightn't the aliens need it? And don't they have a right to it? And, actually, where have those red blobby aliens gone at the end of the story? Have they just given up? And what was the whole thing with sending people back into the past? And what has happened – unseen – between the Doctor and Sarah? I feel that their relationship has changed somehow.

THE BODY SNATCHER (Picture story)

On the way to Mitra B, Dr. Who gets waylaid (apparently he's going there to discuss their 'moral progress.' I've no idea what this means. Perhaps it's another onerous mission he's been sent on by the Time Lords. This time they are acting less like cosmic policemen than galactic vicars and the Doctor is their chosen expert on morality. It's all most curious. I can't imagine the Fourth Doctor being exactly cock-a-hoop with such a mission. The most laissez-faire and liberal Doctor of them all would inevitably cause an unwelcome rumpus at such a sombre-sounding event.)

He winds up on Axa, which is a moon belonging to the planet Torm. Sarah and Harry (Harry's back!) are vanished away and the Doctor is taken deep underground, where he meets a huge foe with a skull-like face, sitting on a throne. This is Rascla, who has interrupted Dr. Who's travels simply in order to kill him. Actually, it's worse than that, because first he is going to take over the Doctor's body and pilot it into the midst of the sanctimonious inhabitants of Mitra B and destroy the lot of them. Rascla knows that without Mitra B the whole of this galaxy will become chaotic and his Tormian toad-men will be able to exploit that to their benefit.

While his two companions are hypnotised, the Doctor's body is taken over. There is a surreal montage brilliantly depicting the Doctor being evicted from his own mind. The comic strip is disrupting straightforward narrative flow in favour of juxtaposed imagery, nightmarishly poetic interiorised dialogue, and mixed media collage.

The toadmen wish their leader luck, but he won't need it. He will release awful germs as soon as he arrives, making all the Mitrans indulge in 'a self-destructive frenzy of murderous hate.' Rascla sets off, regretting having to take two human companions with him. He gets the Tardis zooming towards the 'Mitra B Committee for moral welfare', which has to be one of the dullest destinations the poor Tardis has ever been sent to.

When the disguised Rascla is poised with his vial of deadly poison he suddenly freezes. The Doctor speaks to him inside his head. It seems that he has managed to slip himself safely into Sarah Jane's sleeping psyche in an act of self-preservation. And so a mind duel breaks out, with Rascla insisting he is the heir to the universe, and the Doctor telling him that his spirit is puny. And he's no match for Dr. Who in a battle of wills.

Rascla is driven off into a 'shadowy world of phantoms' and, before the committee's astonished eyes, the Doctor regains control of himself. And the poor two-headed Mitrans – so keen for moral guidance from the famous Dr. Who – seem only too familiar with his habit of never explaining everything at once: 'Perhaps you will explain it to us later.' A more cynical man than Dr. Who might suspect them of satire.

The final frame of this psychedelic and rather frightening adventure is a coda aboard the Tardis. The Doctor apologises to Sarah for hitching a lift in her head. She wants consulting next time, she tells him. She says this as she tends to Harry – who has been oddly reticent during this escapade – and who seems to be vomiting into a bin.

THE EYE SPIDERS OF PERGROSS

The Tardis is dragged off course and with a 'terrifying twang' it lands upon a world inhabited by spiders. On closer examination it seems that the spiders' bodies are enormous eyes. They are the Shioheng.

Our friends leave the Tardis by swinging on cobwebs through lilies and orchids, and they are drawn by colourful rays emanating from one of the eyes. They enter the dilated pupil of one of the eye spiders themselves, floating down a breezy tunnel and 'along a psychedelic corkscrew' and eventually winding up in the creature's green-veined brain chamber. The Doctor declares the being 'very evolved indeed', which is high praise coming from him.

Sarah finds a large TV and the Doctor hopes to see brain clips of past experiences of the eye spider. To his excitement that is exactly what happens. He even recognises pictures of his Greek friend Xerxes Periopolos, who invented the Astralfutoro-rocket back on Earth. They watch Xerxes visiting alien planets – dancing the Glubja-roo with the Lucilians and playing a rugby-like game with luminous octopi. Then they see him coming to this spidery world, where the Doctor's old friend and all his crew were transformed into eye spiders.

It's Sarah's idea to go back in time to prevent this from happening. The Doctor agrees and the screen flashes up 'THANK YOU.' They quickly exit the brain, the 'breezy corkscrew' and the eye itself and head back to the Tardis. They hurtle back through time to the year 3000 and greet Xerxes and prevent him turning into a giant eye with spidery legs. Now he can be sent home to his lovely wife Maria and his children – and the Tardis *waltzes* back to 1977.

DETOUR TO DIAMEDES

The Tardis is sent off course again, this time to a steaming swamp world. They are grabbed by massive copper-green furry creatures who throw them over their shoulders and tramp through the horrible-smelling swamp. 'Don't worry,' the Doctor tells his chums. He doesn't think they mean any harm. Giving it some thought, the Doctor decides that this must be the planet Diamedes, and the creatures carrying them are the nice-but-slow Slodes. They must beware the 'nasty grey lumps' in the swamp below. They are the Carks, and best avoided.

Everyone gets a fright when Harry and his Slode are almost pitched into the marsh. Luckily, Sarah's screams distract the Carks and the Doctor manages to pull Harry to safety. Their journey continues to the Slodes' dwellings and there they meet an elderly human male, grey and on the point of death. Incredibly, the Doctor recognises him as Zyphos, his old friend and the finest captain of the Tandian fleet. He was marooned here years ago and his crewmembers were gobbled up by the Carks. He's been happy here among the Slodes but now wants to go home to die amongst his own kind. Dr. Who asks Sarah and Harry if they'd mind making another detour?

MENACE ON METALUPITER *(Picture Strip)*

The Tardis crew are visiting Metalupiter, where the inhabitants are by all accounts attractive and charming, even if they're robots. Dr. Who, it seems, has overcome his aversion to mechanical life, which was at its most pronounced in 1975.

On arrival in this strange world of classical ruins and futuristic townscapes, Harry is attacked by one of the leopard-like natives. The Doctor builds a device to immobilise all Metalupitrons in their vicinity, and this allows Harry to drag one into the Tardis. The Doctor examines the cat-faced android and finds that its brain is made out of rubber.

He gets the memory and the voice box of the robot working and Puskeet introduces himself, telling the tale of how his people were interfered with when an alien craft entered the orbit of their world, stole their memories and replaced them with rubber, and turned everyone into slaves. They forced the Metalupitrons to build nuclear reactors which, when detonated by their ships' weaponry, will create a chain reaction, fusing the entire planet into a gigantic crystal, which the aliens will then turn into an indestructible space craft.

Everyone takes a moment to absorb this and the Puskeet the robot leopard announces that this plan reaches its fulfilment on this very day..! The Doctor and his friends need to get to the Centre, avoiding on the way all leopard-faced robots, who have been programmed to kill intruders. Puskeet leads the way, advancing bravely and withstanding the firepower of the four-armed invading aliens. He fights back and meanwhile, clever Dr. Who shuts down all the reactors just in time. And then he restores the Metalupitrons' memory banks and the robots turn out to be charming after all.

131

DOUBLE TROUBLE

As the Tardis arrives back at UNIT HQ on a pleasant summer's day after a trip to the planet Dumok Sarah is looking very pale. The Doctor goes off to see Lethbridge-Stewart and Sarah is told by Harry that all her cosmic 'gallivanting' seems to be taking its toll on her. She flares up at him in the UNIT canteen. She also appears to be staring fiercely at a random soldier, and there's a funny light in her eyes.

The Doctor comments that women are all moody, and Sarah Jane is no exception. His attitude makes me think that there is definitely something up between the two of them lately. I think it might have to do with short-lived travelling companion Vittorio Levi. The way he appeared and then was suddenly gone is highly suspicious. I think there was a dalliance of some kind that no one is talking about...

Harry spies on Sarah, seeing that she's walking jerkily and acting distracted. She's also sending surreptitious messages into space. When he tries to stop her it's like he's been electrocuted. The Doctor soon finds the unconscious Harry, just as the Brigadier runs in, claiming that Sarah is beating up one of his men.

Two shadowy, bluish figures emerge from the bodies of Sarah and the soldier she is tussling with. These are two aliens from Dumok: one of them a murderer who stole aboard the Tardis. The other is Theon of the 'disciplinary council', who followed and took over Sarah's body and thus came to Earth.

A cigar-shaped craft from Dumok lands on the grass outside UNIT HQ. Blue creatures dash out to take away the limp homicidal alien. Sarah wakes up cross.

SECRET OF THE BALD PLANET

The Tardis crew arrive on a world smooth and featureless as a white billiard ball, where footsteps sound like slamming doors in a long corridor. When they fall down an unexpected shaft they find giant, multi-coloured earwig creatures staring at them. They are taken to a spherical room and meet the Parads of Paras and their purple-shelled leader, Gresk.

Second in command Ramstra shows them his laboratory, which is filled with delicate devices. Eschewing the usual telepathy, Ramstra urgently communicates using actual words that come out of his 'small, hairy mouth.' He needs their help and doesn't want Gresk to hear. He explains that, when they reach the age of sixteen seasons, all Parads are sent into the Rectulator machines, the function of which is lost in history. All Parads but Gresk have undergone this mysterious process and disappeared. Legend has it that they get whizzed to the twin planet of Bossgar. When it came to his turn, Gresk rebelled, killed the elders and took over. Now he's turned purple, his body's grown feeble, but his mental powers have become formidable and dangerous.

Dr. Who isn't sure who to trust on this bald planet of earwigs. For once he seems reluctant to take sides. Could this be an after-effect of how violated he felt when Gresk communicated with him telepathically? The Doctor comes across as oddly vulnerable in this story. Has he, in Gresk, discovered an enemy with a mind that he feels he couldn't defeat in mental combat..?

He takes a look at the Rectulators, which are transparent capsules, big enough to hold a giant earwig. He translates a tablet engraved with their history (it's in Xylian, a language the Doctor can read but the Parads can't.) He learns that after sixteen seasons Parads tend to go a bit loopy and it's a part of their natural spiritual development that their psyches get sent to the twin moon of Bossgar. Only that way, by leaving their shrivelled bodies behind, can they hope to evolve towards perfection. By resisting this, Gresk is perverting the course of his own and everyone else's development. The Doctor fiddles with the Rectulator capsule and Gresk vanishes – off to Bossgar – in a yellow ray.

With everything sorted out on the bald planet of the earwigs, the Doctor reveals to his companions that he believes he has got them lost again in time and space…

Other Content

- MAZE OF MYSTERY – A map-based maze.
- REACH FOR THE SKY – Man's attempts to reach space.
- TWINLE, TWINKLE LITTLE SATELLITE – A history of satellites.
- THE AIRSHIP RISES TO FAME – A history of hot air balloons and airships.
- SPACE HAS A WORD FOR IT – Space acronym based quiz.
- MORE TO IT THAN MEETS THE EYE – Visual puzzles.
- SPACE SCRAPBOOK – Some space related facts.
- ASTRONAUTS SPELL SPACE – Five facts spelling S.P.A.C.E.
- SPACE FACTS AND FANCIES – Random vaguely space related facts.
- A SPACE RIDDLE-ME-REE – Riddle.
- PICK THE PLANET PEOPLE – Space quiz.
- SKYLARK SOARING HIGH – The Skylark rocket.
- THE TERROR TRAIL – A board game, featuring giant insects.
- PROBLEM OF THE PAINTED PLANET – Drawing puzzle.
- DR WHO'S CROSSWORD – Crossword.
- SPACE TALK – Space facts.
- OUT OF THIS WORLD! – Cartoons.
- DRUM BEAT IN SPACE – The Pioneer 6 space drum.

- PICK THE PLANETS – Planet based quiz.
- MOONING ABOUT – Moon based quiz.
- THE NAME'S THE SAME – Planets which share their name with mythological creatures.

Doctor Who Himself

Quite at home in matters of intergalactic diplomacy, Dr. Who is often called upon by aliens to negotiate peace between bizarre species. He is forever shoving things into his pockets which, eventually, turn out to be useful.

In 'The Body Snatcher' Dr. Who meets even more good friends he hasn't seen in hundreds of years. I can't help feeling that he's a forgetful and neglectful friend. He only ever returns when there's been a ghastly changeabout. As a friend you only see him again if he's been possessed, or you have. It's as if he's always telling us: nothing can ever be the same. At the same time, however, there's hardly ever a dull reunion in the world of Dr. Who.

He tells Harry and Sarah that one day he will write his own science fiction novel, which presumably will give new meaning to the phrase, 'You couldn't make it up.'

New heights are reached in this Annual in terms of the Doctor knowing people in even the remotest corners of the galaxy. When he and his friends are watching the telly inside the brain of an eye-spider on Pergross, the Doctor recognises the Greek man who appears on the screen. If I were Sarah or Harry I'm not sure I'd always believe him. The Doctor himself is so surprised and excited by what he sees projected upon the eye spider brain screen that he ejaculates, apparently.

Gresk the Parad seems a powerful foe, and the Doctor feels his mental force touching his 'personal emotions.' In a very Fourth Doctor-ish moment he tells everyone to fend off the giant earwig's telepathic feelers by imagining the taste of ice cream and kippers and onions all at the same time. In order to avoid combat with Gresk's mutated mind the Doctor's moves like crazy: like a high-speed film of the London to Brighton car race…!

Monsters and Villains

Aquatica teems with creatures at odds with one another: blue apes, exploding dolphins and snake-haired Medusians. The Zanons are reptile men who don't

134

go anywhere without their havoc-causing wind machine. Skeleton-faced giant Rascla of Torm is an impressive baddie, achieving that acme of villainous schemes – the body-swap. His toadmen lackies aren't very scary, however. These lissom youths slouch about in bathing trunks, casually leaning on walls while their crazed madman of a leader goes off to do the dirty work. The eye-spiders are frightening but not villainous. They just want to drag you into their brains and make you watch their endless home movies. The earwigs of the bald planet are extraordinary creatures, transporting themselves into the unknown when they reach the age of sixteen seasons. They are looking, it turns out, for spiritual perfection.

Curious Companions?

Sarah has to admit that wherever the Tardis takes them, it's always more exciting than a day at the seaside. She proves herself quite game, yet again. She jumps onto the back of one of the reptilian Zanons, and holds on, even though she almost faints at the nasty feel of it. In 'The Time Snatch' she stares at the blue sky of the desert and finds herself longing for the cool grey of Britain. And again, she's keen to join in physical fights. She picks up a stone in order to brain a caveman. At times she's even snarky with the Doctor himself, commenting tartly on his inability to pilot the Tardis home.

Sometimes in 1977 the Doctor and Sarah are weirdly formal with each other. 'Don't you exert yourself, my dear,' he says, sounding more like himself as he was when they first met. She comments – stiltedly – 'Goodness knows what period of Time we've been hurled into.' Putting aside the fair supposition that these stories have been written by someone out of touch with these characters, what can we as readers make of these odd exchanges? Has something perhaps happened between the two of them, to make them talk this way to each other? Maybe they have retreated from each other, after growing too close, and are taking refuge in the old formalities. Perhaps they are parodying themselves, in some kind of Doctor / assistant kinky role-play?

The Doctor finds Sarah quite moody throughout much of 1977. Her body is possessed by disembodied intelligences twice in these stories, and this might have something to do with it.

Giggling polymath Professor Vittorio Levi pops up out of nowhere for 'War on Aquatica.' Who the devil is he, this unnecessary replacement for Harry Sullivan? He's one of the many Earth scientists that the Doctor seems to enjoy knocking about with. There are dozens of them in the Annual stories, all indistinguishable. Levi stands out a little because we are told he is an amateur space traveller, and this boggles the mind slightly. I see him as a Latin version of Zaroff from 'Flash Gordon', building his own spaceship in his garage. I derive a certain amount of pleasure from imagining the circumstances in which Dr. Who became aware of Levi's experiments and offered him a trip or two aboard the Tardis. It's not everyone he allows aboard. There must have been a reason for it.

Though, there is something devil-may-care and – dare I repeat the cliché? – Bohemian about the Fourth Doctor. Professor Vittorio Levi is perhaps the space-scientist equivalent of a mate the Doctor's dragged home from the pub with him. 'Just wait till you see *my* spaceship!' I can just picture Sarah's face when she wakes up and hears them clattering about in the console room.

It's so lovely to have Harry Sullivan back for several stories in this Annual. He reads Asimov aboard the Tardis, which seems such a Harry-like thing to do – it's as if he's conscientiously mugging up on outer space. He comes out with things like, 'Blimey, Doctor! … It's A.D 3872!' Faced with enemies like gigantic earwigs Harry clenches his fists and grimly prepares to punch their lights out. He is endlessly brave and gallant.

When they are trying to block their minds to mental attack from Gresk the giant earwig, Sarah and Harry think pleasant thoughts. She imagines Harry in the bath, and he imagines himself the hero of the last spy-thriller he read. This moment is one of the clearest insights into both characters and where they're at in 1977.

Fiendish Wheezes

Shooting explosive dolphins at your enemies is very fiendish indeed. Blowing your enemies about with a wind machine seems less fiendish, but the Zotons' lives are made a misery by the Cyclone Terror. As fiendish wheezes go, Rascla of Torm's mind-swap idea is a good one. He plans to exploit the faith that the people of Mitra B have in Dr. Who. The best villainous schemes tune into the Doctor's strengths and turn them into a weakness. No one is expecting him to turn up and be a bastard.

The four-armed aliens who enslave the leopard-like Metalupitrons have devised an outrageous plan to turn the whole of the planet into a giant crystal that they can pilot about the universe.

TV Feedback

On the whole the 1977 stories are nothing like anything on TV. Though we *have* had crystals in UNIT laboratories brought back from outer space and causing chaos before. Also, Davros and his hypothetical vial of poison is evoked in 'The Body Snatcher' – a tale in which Rascla has exactly what Davros imagined in his nasty little mitt. The moody and violent Sarah Jane double wandering about at UNIT HQ is a reminder of the recent 'The Android Invasion' on TV.

Anticipating the Future

UNIT has a base in the US. In 1977 it is on Last Hope Ridge. The Fourth Doctor turns 'bad' in 'The Body Snatcher' when his form is taken over by Rascla. On TV we will glimpse the same Doctor acting very badly in stories such as 'The Deadly Assassin', 'The Face of Evil', 'The Invasion of Time', 'The Armageddon Factor' and 'Meglos.' As Terrance Dicks once said, of all the Doctors, the Fourth is the one you imagine somehow turning most frighteningly and convincingly evil.

Egregious errors

Does the inclusion of Vittorio Levi count as an error? I think we're getting a glimpse of other friends and companions in this alternate, fragmented timeline for the Fourth Dr. Who. I imagine Professor Levi fetching up at Nest Cottage, say, for a Christmas glass of sherry with Mrs Wibbsey, the Brigadier, Mike Yates, Romana, K9, Amelia Rumford, Beep the Meep and Sharon from the *Doctor Who Weekly* strip. I've come to think that there are no such things as continuity errors. Just branching lines of all kinds of apocrypha and opportunities for further stories.

The earth scientist Xerxes Periopolos gets preferential treatment. Is it because he's an old friend of the Doctor's that the Time Lord changes history so that the Greek scientist doesn't, actually, get transformed into an eye-spider? Why would the Doctor do this for him and no one else? Again, is it just an error on the writer's part, or does it point to something else? Is there some cosmic reason that Professor Periopolos should have a second chance?

Classic moments

Phyllos explaining the crazy politics of Aquatica over breakfast and then everyone jumping aboard a motorboat to watch exploding dolphins is somehow the epitome of the very phrase, 'World Distributors Doctor Who Annual story'. Another good example is the mental war between the Doctor and Rascla in 'The Body Snatcher', where the surrealism and experimentalism reaches new heights. Only to be topped, pages later, by the Tardis team's descent into the pupil of an eye spider and their discovery of the memory cinema in its brain.

What I learned from the Doctor Who Annual 1977

The deeper you get into outer space, the stranger the alien species become, and still Dr. Who is pretty blasé about everything he sees.

What's more dangerous than evil space lizards who hate you? Evil space lizards with a wind machine who hate you.

Beware of return visits from your old friend Dr. Who. He doesn't ever have quiet weekends away. If he turns up on your doorstep again, something hideous is about to happen.

It really isn't worth getting into a battle of mind-power with Dr. Who. He will most definitely kick your mental arse.

Illustrations

The vividly smeared impasto acrylics and splattered muddy then brilliant water colours all through this Annual are great fun. They're the perfect accompaniment to the wonderfully silly, silky and crunchy wordplay in evidence in stories such as 'War on Aquatica.' I can't help wishing that the pictures related a little more closely to some of the images conjured up by the text, however.

The 1978 Annual

One of the more fraught years for Dr. Who, this.

His adventures are all in outer space, and he keeps arriving on worlds that are rather grim and ghoulish. There are often skeletons strewn about the place and civilization lies in tatters. If he was expecting to bump into an old friend he most often finds them changed, embittered, dead or worse – they've forgotten him. His friendship with Sarah is a little strained throughout these six adventures in space. She's weary of his sense of humour and his endless dashing across these bleak landscapes.

Dr. Who begins this Annual by reflecting happily on days of yore, when his adventures were relatively carefree, and he ends the book essentially wondering whether he has actually gone insane.

It's not the most festive of Annuals.

The Stories

THE SLEEPING BEAST

In his second incarnation Dr. Who met Swee the Guerner – a turtle-like creature with a very long nose – on the planet Rimba and they got along famously. They met when Swee and his people were preparing to move to a new planet, having eaten everything on their current one. They are creatures of prodigious appetites and are known for gobbling up worlds and moving on.

Skip to the present and the Doctor and Sarah come face to face with Swee, who is quite unfriendly, claiming not to remember the Doctor at all. In fact, all the Guernerans are agitated and heavily armed. The Doctor is quickly accused of being the mastermind behind the gigantic stone robot known as the Sto-Cat which has been attacking the Guerneran ships. There's a gloating answer phone message left by the giant creature. Communicating with the Sto-Cat, Dr. Who learns that there are a thousand million of the unfriendly things scattered throughout the galaxy, awaiting their orders to awaken. This particular giant robot was brought back to life by the landing of Swee's ship. The Doctor manages to make him see sense and go back to sleep. And there is a big surprise when he turns out to look just like the Sphinx on Earth.

THE SANDS OF TYMUS

The Spartrons are having a tricky old time on the inhospitable planet Tymus, what with its three suns and seas of dust. Many of them have had to start wearing artificial limbs. Their Professor Branxion is busily building them new, solar-powered 'forms' they can wear: whole new bodies that will enable them to get about better on this unfriendly world.

The Doctor and Sarah are captured in the desert by native Toregs and taken to a city carved out of stone. Promax, leader of the Spartrons, seems very pleased to find that one of the prisoners is a lady. She'll come in most useful in Professor Branxion's 'female renewal programme.' Off she goes to the workshop, which is a horrible place littered with spare arms and legs. The Doctor is keen for Sarah not to be stuffed into a tube and forced to undergo whatever mysterious thing Professor Branxion is planning. When she pops whole and alive out of the machine he is pleased to find she's the real thing, and not a duplicate. However, the clever Spartrons intend to make a whole lot of new Sarah Jane Smiths. All the female Spartrons have died and will now be replaced by clones of Ms Smith. The Doctor and Sarah don't seem at all bothered by this, surprisingly.

THE RIVAL ROBOTS (Picture Strip)

On the planet Vona – where Sarah fully expects the inhabitants to be very sensitive – she is grabbed by a giant claw almost the very second she steps out of the Tardis. The Doctor is just about smashed to smithereens by a giant metal bee. He's then quite surprised to bump into his old friend Orlak – a man with a nose like a tusk. Orlak reminds Dr. Who that his people are served by two lots of robots – the Yeng and the Domos. The first lot defend the world and the Domos look after the Vonans at home. It turns out that both grades of robots are at war.

Off they go to the city of Retz to find the kidnapped Sarah. An attack is imminent. The Doctor and Orlak access the city via an air vent – which is ironic, given that ventilation shafts are Sarah's usual preferred route into just about anywhere. Everyone in Retz is pretty much content, unaware of impending attack by giant metal insects. There's an intruder alert sounding and suddenly it's all going on. There is wild talk about each of the robots having a neutron bomb in their brain, since in order to protect the Vonans it might be necessary to blow them all up.

Dr. Who ties the Yengs up in one of his clever logic traps (just as his last incarnation used to love to do) and underlining the fact that the robots are supposed to protect their masters and keep them alive. Eventually he gets them to deactivate themselves, and the relieved Vonans decide in future that they'll have just the one kind of robot to see to all of their needs.

A NEW LIFE

Arriving on a peaceful world, the Doctor and Sarah find that the foliage is twisted and distorted. Then they start discovering ruined buildings and skeletons lolling about the place. They start to think there's been a terrible war. Down they go into the underworld via a crumbling manhole cover. They find darkness and a boat to take them down a rushing river, where they are soon menaced by creatures that are a hideous cross between dogs and fish, snapping and snarling at them.

They are rescued by humanoid creatures who fling spears at the fish-dog monsters, and take Dr. Who and Sarah to their identical-twin leaders, Matalus and Jometh. The leaders are very old and pale after long years hiding underground. They refuse to believe that the newcomers could have come from the surface. Nothing could survive up there after the war. The Doctor is delighted to tell them that things have changed. Life is springing back to the world above. He is rewarded by being chained, along with Sarah, and placed right where the fish-dogs can get at them.

They are rescued by Barda, who heard what they had to say to the elders, and believes them. He goes up to the surface with them and feels the sunlight on his face for the first time ever. The Doctor and Sarah slope off and leave him to it.

THE TRAITOR *(Picture Strip)*

At the edge of the Sigimund Galaxy the Doctor and Sarah have come to witness the Aurora Artialis. The spectacular event is interrupted by the crash landing of a rocket on a nearby world. They follow in the Tardis in order to help any survivors. Once there they are told they must help the survivors quickly before the Lokans arrive and destroy the rocket.

Zemos and his fellows explain that they are marooned scientists who have been prisoners of the Lokans. They want to capture the ship that comes to service the Lokan robots – will Dr. Who help them to take control of it so they can escape this planet?

They nobble the robo-guards in order to bring the Lokan ship. Two days pass and then they can attack the Lokans – rather violently ('Thunk!') When one of the Lokans wakes and the Doctor explains how he's helped Zemos and his pals get away the Lokan explodes: 'You fool! Those men are no scientists! They are liars and psychotic killers!' And what's more: 'They are totally and permanently insane!'

We are told that, on their home planet, their bodies reflect their mental health. And sometimes the Lokans produce hideous people with fangs and bulging, bloodshot eyes: 'evil is apparent in their appearance.' So they are sent off into exile, to this planet, where the three suns apparently nullify their 'disorder'.

141

The Doctor and Sarah have been hoodwinked by a sob story. They're always arriving on planets and helping people out. Now they have fallen foul of trickery. Zemos and his friends will revert to ugliness and evil and cause havoc. The Doctor phones him in space.

We get an image of evil, ugly psychotics aboard their stolen rocket. They have become drooling primates and they make noises like this: 'Kaarrr' and 'Kreeee' in one of this Annual's more disturbing moments.

However, their purloined spacecraft glides too close to the Aurora Artialis at just the right moment and the extra burst of sunlight turns them nice, gentle and handsome again.

The Doctor begs Zemos to return. He lays a trap. He has betrayed them. He says, 'I did as I had to, Zemos.' Zemos remarks bitterly that he and his fellows threw away their freedom to return the Doctor's favour and now they must be prisoners again. The Doctor cannot, will not, help.

As they leave in the Tardis, Sarah is upbeat. But – in an extremely unusual moment at the very end of this most intriguing and morally complex of Annual stories – the Doctor weeps for what he has done.

THE SEA OF FACES

The Doctor and Sarah look at the Tardis scanner and can see nothing but a sea of expressionless faces. Outside they are surrounded by gently breathing, stocky, hairless humanoids with no ears. The Doctor's telepathic gift allows him to tune into the hubbub of dreams in all the dormant minds around him. The children alone seem able to move around. They see one, frightened and hungry. A huge low-flying spaceship passes very slowly overhead, leaking a green gas that seems to induce the population's sleeping sickness. Sarah breathes the gas and the Doctor can see her dreams in which she wears a star-spangled costume and rides a chariot pulled by a flying white horse.

The overhead spaceship is so slow-moving the Doctor can grab hold and haul both himself and Sarah onto its back. The Tardis is soon lost to sight in the mass of humanoids below. The Doctor starts worrying: what if all of this is his own gas-induced dream? What if he's only having delusional fantasies of taking 'heroic action'?

He wakes up inside a mother ship in orbit round the planet. There are many of the slow ships contained here. He finds more skeletons. This is an Annual haunted by skeletons and worlds that are dead before the Doctor even gets there. There is a recording by the last of the 'free-speech Kendorians.' The Doctor learns their history, and how they cured disease and fell victim to an over-populated world. They'd murder each other for the sake of having a tiny bit of privacy. The scientists on the moon invented a gas that would induce a kind of sleep that allowed people to live entirely inside their own dreams.

The Doctor sets to work on coming up with a solution to the Kendorians' ossified plight. He rescues Sarah by hitching a ride on the slow-moving rocket and picking her out of the endless crowd. She comes to her senses once he has administered her with a 'blood-purifying pill.' The Doctor plans to give the Kendorians the choice between carrying on in their dream-state or coming to their senses and building an actual future. He announces that over-crowding will no longer be a problem here, since many of the dreamers have (conveniently) died.

Sarah is glad that he's sorting everything out. She had a wonderful dream of her own (he knows). Just like when she asked him what terrifying things his mind conjured up in the Psychic Jungle of 1976, she asks him now why he wasn't affected by the dream-inducing gas.

His reply freaks her out. 'Maybe it all just went on in my mind. Maybe this is my dream.'

And so ends his final Annual story with Sarah Jane Smith. And this is actually worse than being stuck in that 'Neuronic Nightmare' of two years previously. Here it's possible that Dr. Who is dreaming forever that he has rescued Sarah and saved her life. It's only in his imagination that they're setting off again for endless adventures aboard the Tardis. But it's altogether possible that they are both two more faces in the sea of humanity: slack-jawed, swaying, passive zombies on a dead planet.

It strikes me that the world of the 1978 Annual is a cruel and bleak one. There is nothing reassuring at the end. Sarah doesn't have a chance to undercut his sombre, existential musings with her usual, 'Oh, *you!*' The book ends with him suggesting that they are stuck forever, never knowing what is real and what is dream.

Is this, after all, the 'New Life' that the Fourth Doctor promised Sarah when he took her away in the Tardis in 1976? The same title recurs in this book, too. Sarah's new life is one of indeterminacy, uncertainty, radical confusion. Is she Wonder Woman, is she a zombie, is she merely going home to Croydon? And are they still best of friends?

Other Content

- LOONY LAFFS – Cartoons.
- MYTHICAL MONSTERS! – The usual assemblage of mythical beasts.
- APOLLO MANNED MISSION EMBLEMS – The crews and emblems of the Apollo missions.
- IF – Relative sizes of planets of the solar system.
- A RACE AGAINST TIME – A board game of almost no imagination.
- CELESTIAL SQUARES – A space-based quiz.
- MYSTERY MESSAGE – Decipher the code.
- SPACE NAMES – Name based quiz.

- THE LIFE CRYSTAL – Puzzle.
- MERRY DANCERS OF THE SKIES- The Aurora Borealis.
- SCIENCE LENDS A HAND – Inventions, none of which appear actually to have come to anything.
- DR WHO ALPHABET- An alphabet based on space and mythology and religion and any old gubbins which came to the writer's mind.
- ARITH-MENTAL INTERROGATION – Number puzzle.
- OBSERVING THE STARS – The Siding Spring Telescope.
- PROBLEMS, PROBLEMS! – Brain teasers.
- PEACEFUL SOLUTION – Maths puzzle.
- SPACEWORD! – Crossword.
- TRUE OR FALSE? – Quiz.
- ORBITING TELESCOPE – The possibility of putting a telescope in space.
- IT'S IN THE STARS – Star facts.
- SPOT THE DIFFERENCE – The difference at the bottom of each picture is more interesting than these things usually are.
- ESCAPE FROM THE GREEN VOLCANO- A board game.

Doctor Who Himself

He's keen to journey far afield in the universe. But even out here there are old friends to surprise with a visit. He and Sarah are starting to chafe against each other like an old married couple. He despairs of her lack of manners. In 'The Sands of Tymus' he is laconic and sarcastic with her, but still desperate to save her when she's taken off by the Spartrons. He's quite a taciturn figure, Dr. Who in 1978. It's tempting to wonder if he's feeling tetchy as a result of all the repetition – he keeps finding that Sarah's been captured and has to go looking for her. Some of the story-elements he's encountered in 1978 seem similar to those he found in 1976. Is he becoming jaded?

He is still interested in exploring and studying. In 'The Sea of Faces' he talks about his fascination with people and beings of all kinds: 'The ebb and flow of words and feelings fascinate me.' He also claims never to have been to a party, which we know can't be true.

He hasn't lost his idealism, though. He is easily hoodwinked by Zemos and friends in 'The Traitor.' His sense of injustice is pricked by their apparent plight and they play him like a fool. In the end, though they think him their friend, his sense of moral purpose forces him to betray Zemos et al. The end of that picture strip sees him weep because of what he has done. We hardly ever see Dr. Who weep. 'The Traitor' sees the Doctor's moral compass wobbling. He can't trust his own instinct for making friends any more.

This is a big story in terms of ideas about liberty and the things he really believes in. Setting aside the interesting (and deliberately superficial-seeming?) idea that the Lokans have a changeable physicality that reflects their mental state this is a story about the Doctor's attitudes to personal liberty and punishment. Is he perhaps thinking about his own escape from his stifling home-world, as he helps the lost scientists free themselves? Is he wondering about what constitutes criminality when the Lokans guilt him out about what he has done? Maybe he's reflecting on the onerous exile to Earth in the early Seventies his previous self was forced to undergo as a result of his own supposed criminal activities? Set free, Zemos and his fellows turn into monsters – but isn't that what the Time Lords believe Dr. Who became? And is that enough reason for him to become complicit and condemn the 'criminals' and trap them again? Is he crying for them at the end, or is he crying for himself?

Here's another moment in a seemingly throwaway Annual that feels like a cornerstone in the Doctor's characterization, and a moment missing from the TV series.

'The Sea of Faces' has more of those glorious moments in which the Doctor doubts himself. Presumably he's still rattled from the mistakes he made in 'The Traitor'. He is questioning the assumptions he makes about the universe. But – he reassures himself – at least his dreams and delusions are of being heroic. He doesn't give in to inactivity and passivity. His endless momentum is always Dr. Who's salvation. He always keeps on running and trying.

Monsters and Villains

'Ha! Another one destroyed! Another victory for the mighty Kryptolian race. One more step on our glory trail across the universe!' It's the wearisomely shouty Sto-Cat, of which there are a thousand million, waiting to wake up and start yelling on your answer-phone and destroying things. The Spartrans are ailing on their over-warm adopted world of Tymus. They're going about with artificial limbs and they're desperate for cloned women. They can't quite muster enough energy to be truly bad. The robots of Planet Vona – the Yeng and the Domos – are at war and both are quite frightening, in their deadly literal-mindedness. Zemos and his psychotic mates are very frightening – one moment pretending to be peaceful scientists, the next crazy men with fangs. They even manage to fool Dr. Who.

Curious Companions?

Poor Sarah isn't feeling very curious at all in the 1978 Annual. In these cosmic adventures – perhaps the most cosmic Dr. Who has ever had, with no returns to reassuring old England – Sarah seems to be feeling the strain of several years of interstellar travel. Though at the start of the book she's quite perky, cheeky and impatient – this soon turns to her feeling browned-off. She's approaching the end of her adventures with Dr. Who and she's looking pretty gloomy as she surveys another sandy planet. Quite often she feels herself wishing that they'd 'never left the cool safety of the Tardis.'

Her adventures with Dr. Who are starting to feel a bit arduous. There are miles to be trekked. Days pass between events. Everybody they meet seems to be rather hard work these days. When the Doctor suggests that all the clones of Sarah on Tymus might be as bad-tempered as the original one, she throws a shoe at him. It's 1978 so it's probably a cork-soled platform sandal. 'A New Life' has her bursting out that another hour 'cooped up in the Tardis' with Dr. Who will drive her mad. She is tense and finds him unfunny.

She isn't at all keen on robots. In the tale of 'The Rival Robots' she declares that she'd rather see them all on the junk heap. It's amusing to imagine the Doctor taking careful note of her hostility to our metallic friends. Quite soon she'll be back in Croydon, and he'll be sending her a robot chum of her very own quite shortly after that.

It strikes me that Sarah Jane's endless speeches in 'The Sarah Jane Adventures' on TV about the marvellous and wonderful things she saw during her space adventures must have been about things seen mostly off-camera. Perhaps she is referring to things like the spectacular Aurora Artialis that Dr. Who takes her to see in 'The Traitor.' Certainly, there's more to it than the dullish corridors and ventilation ducts that she mostly saw on the telly. She seems quite enthusiastic about watching stellar events in the 1978 Annual. It's about the only time she isn't completely mardy.

In their final Annual story together Sarah reflects that the Doctor will never understand the average person. But so what? If he was different then he wouldn't be doing what he does, and neither would she. At the very end we learn that Sarah still values this life with him, and this chance to explore.

At the start of Dr. Who and Sarah Jane's final Annual story together, they hug each other before leaving the Tardis and encountering 'The Sea of Faces.' This reminds us that they are, after all, the best of friends.

In her dreams Sarah is Wonder Woman. Embarrassingly, Dr. Who reads her mind and learns this. But perhaps he always knew?

It's a relief to know that, in the world of the Doctor Who Annuals, 1978 isn't the end for Sarah Jane. She returns to us in 1983's 'K9 Annual.' There, she's at home in England and quite real. It's okay. It turns out that there's nothing as safe, prosaic, logical, dependable and everyday as a talking robot dog.

Fiendish Wheezes

Taking over the universe can be easily accomplished by fashioning a thousand million stone lions and hiding them underground and making them go to sleep. In 'The Sands of Tymus' the wheeze is pretty straightforward. Kidnap Sarah. Stick her in the machine. Clone her as many times as you like. Because, actually, she's not particularly bothered. Zemos and his gang tricking the Doctor into helping them escape from their prison world is the best wheeze going on in 1978. They play upon his good nature and his gullibility and his need to do the right thing. Their Lokan overlords are even more slippery, however, in getting the Doctor to do their bidding and trick Zemos into returning willingly to the prison world.

Is your world suffering from chronic over-population? Invent a gas that sends everyone to sleep and lets them dream their lives away.

TV Feedback

The combination of Egyptian artefacts and sci-fi trappings in 'The Sleeping Beast' is familiar to TV viewers from the then-recent 'Pyramids of Mars.' The Doctor and Sarah's laissez-faire attitude to cloning in 'Sands of Tymus' is curious, given that they were livid about the replicants in 'The Android Invasion'. Also, the workshop of spare limbs hanging about can't help but remind us of the Doctor and Sarah's visit to Karn on TV in 'The Brain of Morbius.' The spectacle of dead worlds littered with skeletons is apparent a couple of times in this Annual. 'The Sea of Faces' with its corpses and its recorded message about the history of the world is a reminder of 'The Hand of Fear' on TV.

147

Anticipating the Future

'The Sea of Faces' seems to anticipate a number of elements present in the Steven Moffat TV era. The recorded messages left behind by the last of the Kendorians, for example, as the Doctor stands amongst the skeletons, is very like the numerous examples of supposedly dead things still having a voice in latter-day TV *Doctor Who*. This story is shiveringly close to 'Silence in the Library' at times – not least for its evocation of a hushed world in which all the humanoids are trapped inside their own dreaming universes. Images of life continuing through death and inactivity abound in Moffat's writing, and here in the 1978 Annual. Very often machines keep on working after human life has gone, creating and exacerbating a nightmarish state.

Egregious errors

I'm not sure that anything goes against TV continuity or conventions or characterization of the two central characters. We are in a separate timeline, in which Dr. Who and Sarah Jane Smith travelled together for longer, and into further distant galaxies.

Classic moments

The 1978 Annual begins with a flashback to happy days in 1968 and the colourful adventures of the Second Doctor. He was fighting giant, stinging butterflies and then he met Swee the Guerneran. It was all good fun back then and this Proustian moment for Dr. Who is a delight for his fans.

The moment in 'The Traitor' when the Doctor learns that Zemos has tricked him into doing his will is a classic one. Sarah stands there in her pink mac, completely gobsmacked. 'But they were so gentle and nice!' And we learn how awful these psychotic monsters really are... This story ends with the Doctor weeping about what he has been forced to do. It's a very striking moment for the series and the character, in any medium.

What I learned from the Doctor Who Annual 1978

When you go looking up old friends, prepare to be disappointed. People change. They forget you. They move on. They can go to the bad. When you travel with human beings, they soon get tired of very dusty hot planets with three suns. They quite like going back to Earth every now and then, no matter how much they tease about wanting to be somewhere exotic. Just because someone says they're a peaceful scientist, don't believe everything they say. They might well be psychotic killers, even if they're not ugly on the outside. In fact, don't listen to anyone. Do your own thing. We can't ever be sure whether the world we're in and the further adventures we're heading into are actually real, or whether they're just a heroic dream that Dr. Who is having. Never mind!

Illustrations

There's a lot of dark and smudgy Paul Crompton artwork in this Annual, reflecting its themes of atrophied invaders and chemical warfare and nebulous psychological states. Heavy, dark pencil and black pen and ink are the order of the day. Lots of the images are extreme close-ups, rather like those photographic puzzles in which you have to guess which household object you're looking at. It all feels rather cold and dark. Some of the illustrations are in smudgy, smoky charcoal. The Doctor is seen in quite good likenesses of Tom Baker, but at times he is completely blacked out in ominous silhouette. Sarah never looks anything like Elisabeth Sladen. She is to be found in a pink mac and mini skirt, very bored-looking, as if modelling outdoor wear on alien worlds.

'The Traitor' picture strip contains the most beautiful art in the whole of this Annual. It is lurid and cinematic and rather violent in places. As a child it reminded me of the sophisticated and very adult artwork in the Hamlyn 'Encyclopaedia of Science Fiction' edited by Robert Holdstock, which was published shortly after this Annual.

The tiny text is printed on very dark tinted pages making it all quite uninviting to peruse.

The 1979 Annual

Right at the start we are told that the Tardis has gone awry because the Doctor forgot to fill the Actualising filter with Essence of Vallo. In the old days it was Fluid Links filled with Mercury. It was the Dematerialisation circuit, or it was the Polarity of the Neutron Flow. Is it just me, or do the Tardis and its 'innards' seem a little less scientific in these heady days of the late nineteen seventies? The Essence of Vallo sounds like something from a fantasy saga. It has a touch of alchemy about it.

Plus, the very idea of a filter that *Actualises* things – a device aboard the Tardis that has the critical function of doing stuff to Actuality itself – seems very evocative and suggestive to me. Does it filter the Actual out? Or does it filter it in? Does it draw impossible people and events out of the raw stuff of imagination? Or does it distil fantasy into something more tangible? Even within the first column of text in the 1979 Annual someone is casually messing with our minds.

Perhaps this is a low-tech, magical version of *Doctor Who*? With his space charts and his wooden-walled Tardis interior, he's becoming more of a wizard or a guru than a scientist… he's using trickery and psychology to bring about peace and ending famine; he's working with sentient pansies to get a ruthless killer to quietly leave their world alone.

The 1979 Annual is taking us into murkier waters than ever – sexual jealousy and genetic experimentation, cannibalism, black magic and sacrifice all loom large in the far-distant worlds we are exploring. We are encountering magic from folklore and legend, and even imagery from tales of Swords and Sorcery. It seems that Dr. Who is taking us far beyond his usual parameters, and way beyond the bounds of tea time TV…!

The 'Leela' season – Season 15 on TV – is one of my very favourite suites of *Doctor Who* stories. It begins in Gothic pastiche mode and incorporates all kinds of wild science fiction comic strip tropes from the then-current Star Wars. A blend of all kinds of influences is produced, with occasional hints of Greek myths poking through, and touches of contemporary satire. All of this is acted with huge flamboyance against a backdrop of slightly cheap-looking sets and costumes. The Annual published in 1978 to commemorate such an unforgettable season has a similar mix of influences and styles – and a robust confidence in its own story-telling and stark, dramatic artwork. It has a tonal and moral seriousness that the TV show was starting to eschew. The Annuals are still tacitly in touch with TV – but are going their own way, rather brilliantly, in this case.

I wonder if 1979 proves to be a high-point for the series?

The Stories

FAMINE ON PLANET X

A cosmic storm and a lack of Essence of Vallo in the Actualising filter have conspired to knock the Tardis off course. Before they land the Doctor sees both Leela's and his own skeleton shining through their flesh. When they wake his space charts tell him they have arrived in a region called 'X.' Here, they meet 'three-legged octopoids' known as the Children of Rha, who are starving and wary of the new arrivals. Ogg and his fellows communicate through 'living hieroglyphics' formed by fleshy strands stretched across their horns. They can only repeat the Doctor's words, not understand them. He brings them fresh fruit and water from the Tardis. Attacked by laser beams shot by Octopoid adults, our heroes retreat into the Tardis, unwittingly taking Ogg with them.

The Doctor sits Ogg upon his knee and, using the lost language of Apstle, they discuss the history of Planet X. It's a terrible tale of famine, sacrifice and more octopoids. But the Doctor knows what to do. He takes seed samples gathered from the planet Lars and, braving laser fire from the more hostile creatures, lobs them into the orange desert sand. Almost instantly giant plants erupt from the dry soil, bearing fat red fruits. While the adults are preoccupied with this sudden bounty, the Doctor frees the children who were due to be sacrificed. He sees to it that Planet X will have a secure future, and there'll be no further religious persecution.

THE PLANET OF DUST

An intergalactic distress signal has brought the Doctor and Leela to an arid world. The scanner shows the skull of a gigantic, flesh-eating cow. They are drawn into a chamber filled with a multitude of plants, and presided over by a massive, horned creature on a throne. He's so big his legs are as wide as motorways. He's Beshi the Larkal and he talks in a shrill voice. He explains that he and his dead colleague crash-landed here a year ago, and their ship sank deep into the dust, from which depths it has been transmitting an SOS. Beshi has been living off the leaves of the plants who share his seclusion, and now – seemingly out of gratitude – he has hatched a plan to give them sentience and mobility. However, he needs tissues from a warm-blooded being. He carries the Doctor and Leela off to his laboratory. The Doctor is given the chance to repair Beshi's ship, to prevent his messing about with genetically modified plant-life, and Leela is kept hostage.

151

The ship has been sabotaged. The Doctor learns this by communicating telepathically with the local plants. A giant, gossipy, purple pansy tells him that Beshi and his shipmate were fighting over a woman. Beshi is stuck here because the Stellaprime – a vital ship component – was hidden by his rival, whom Beshi subsequently killed. The pansy and his friends find the component, fix the ship, and save Leela from having her genes spliced. Presumably Beshi gets to zoom off in his ship in another peaceful resolution to a sticky situation. The already-sentient-thank-you-very-much-plants ask the Doctor and Leela to stick around for a bit, but they head off to the Tardis. They're parched, and it takes seven cups of tea before they feel properly themselves again.

TERROR ON TANTALOGUS

Tantalogus in Galaxy 5 feels like the kind of place that they ought to visit more often, Leela opines. Plump and melodious-voiced alien creatures pop out and deliver a warm welcome. They see glades in the sunshine and visit some immaculate dwelling units. Akhemi their tour guide shows them galleries and dance halls, but the Doctor is becoming suspicious about why they have been brought here. Left alone in Akhemi's house, the Doctor soon finds a hidden room filled by what appear to be inanimate dummies built in the shape of many different alien species.

They are discovered and Akhemi starts filling them in the truth about his people – they brought the Tardis here on purpose. They want the Doctor for his mind and they want Leela as breeding stock! It all comes out that what the deeply-religious Tantalogans actually worship is the death of others..! They themselves are the living dead, and a more chilling set of excuses for heinous behaviour I've never heard in a *Doctor Who* story. We're getting very dark tales here in 1979.

They were sent here in the first place to be plant food. The original settler Tantalog learned to tap into the forces of lightning, magnetism and brain waves in order to ensure his vampiric folk's survival. They just need a regular supply of bodies and brains. In the middle of all this fiendish exposition the Doctor seizes the moment, lashes out with his foot and grabs his enemy's weapon. The plant life, ultimately, turns on the vampires – the lashing branches and the twisting grass – and so the Doctor and Leela can escape this nasty little fable.

THE POWER *(Picture story)*

The planet Shem is the site of terrible infighting between tribes on the occasion of the coronation of the Princess Azula. A lot of backstory is presented in the very first frame, and we are pitched into a tale that stretches the boundaries of a *Doctor Who* adventure. This is an epic, with its roots in the long-established history of tribal leaders and a strange, unseen force that unites them all. Not by any accident are we hearing echoes of Star Wars here. In the late Seventies all science fiction stories were aspiring to the condition of latter-day legends.

During what should be the coronation, the leader of the Monashem is engaging in a brutal battle with the leader of the Pagashem. It is into this rough melee that the Tardis suddenly arrives, bringing with it latecomers to the party. At least this time the Doctor has actually been invited, but his noisy arrival enables Zig to kill Orga, and the Princess to escape. The Doctor emerges blithely – in his best suit and tie, no less – wondering what all the fuss is about. He finds that Zig is announcing himself the new supreme leader of the world.

What's more, the rather ungrateful Zig is going to put the Doctor on trial, for letting the Princess escape. He reasons that the Tardis' ability to arrive out of nowhere proves the Doctor has access to the fabled 'Power', and if he doesn't relinquish its secrets, Leela will be fed to the Porgs, which turn out to be huge, ravenous pig creatures. There is one standing in the crowd behind the table Leela's strapped to, apparently waiting to start eating her. It looks frankly terrifying. There is something extremely compelling and convincing about the very beautiful photo realism of this comic strip. It has an absurd logic to it: ravenous beasts stand around in crowds, and princesses look like snow monkeys.

The Doctor's 'trial' involves being thrown into a pit, and confronted by hideous beasts with lots of muscles and scarlet eyes. In the nick of time he remembers the anti-gravity belt he bought for the Princess as a coronation gift. He flies out of the pit – awkwardly getting the hang of the thing – but then Zig, it turns out, has wings, and a large sword. A battle ensues in mid-air, with Dr. Who almost getting choked, but it is interrupted by Princess Azula, who emerges from hiding with her monkey guard, intent on saving the Doctor.

Azula has decided that the time has come to disseminate the mysterious Power among her people. Zig wants it to himself, of course, and makes a grab for the book that apparently contains it. The Doctor pelts him with the full force of the anti-grav mechanism and propels the usurper into the pit, to receive the fate he had intended for the Doctor.

Now all that remains is for the coronation to proceed, and for Azula to tell everyone that the secret of the power and the book is all about wisdom, kindness, hope and tolerance. And the story ends on a pretty happy note. But in just a few action-packed pages it has managed to conjure the amazing world of Shem – inhabited by intelligent primates and men with wings: a kind of cross between Mongo from Flash Gordon and Ralph Bakshi's 'Lord of the Rings', and surely one of the most intriguing worlds conjured up in *Doctor Who* in any genre.

FLASHBACK

A three man crew of a beacon ship orbiting the planet Pendor are waiting to be relieved and, when the replacements show up, they aren't alone…!

Later, the Doctor and Leela arrive, having aimed the Tardis at Pendor itself, where the Doctor hoped to be greeted by old friends. They find this cosmic lighthouse curiously empty at first, but soon find the crew alongside a squat redhead in a blue metallic uniform. In a flash the Doctor identifies him as Skeeda, a criminal known for malpractice in the subconscious. The arrogant, diminutive Skeeda is a master hypnotist and the Doctor has to slap Leela when he realises she has succumbed. 'Sorry about that… but you were almost hypnotised by that fat fiend down there.'

Skeeda's plan is simple. He wants the beacon crew to create as much chaos with traffic and weather control as possible, wreaking revenge on his fellow Pendorians. The Doctor manages to create his own hypnotic light beam to bring the crew out of Skeeda's malign control. Tempests and hurricanes have already begun down on the surface. Luckily, the Doctor is able to reverse everything, and to mesmerise Skeeda himself into becoming a servant and cook to the lighthouse keepers of Pendor.

EMSONE'S CASTLE (Picture Strip)

The planet Zorka is a strange, fantastic place of reptile-infested swamps and castles containing weird scientific inventions and scheming megalomaniacs. The Doctor and Leela are here investigating the healing properties of a local plant, and are astonished when a living skeleton comes running up, asking for their help. He is Krass, who was invited into a neighbouring castle belonging to the mystic Emsone, who somehow managed to make all of his flesh and clothes disappear. Familiar with the M-Rays that made this possible, the Doctor sets about reversing this process for poor Krass. However, halfway through the recuperation, the Doctor and Leela are brutally attacked by Gurk, Emsone's horned manservant.

When the Doctor wakes he finds that Leela has been taken off to Emsone's castle, and – horrifyingly – the restoration of Krass was interrupted halfway through and now he's looking absolutely terrible. He has a hovercar waiting outside and all the way to Emsone's castle the Doctor can feel the mystic's powerful mind reaching out to deter them. At one point they almost crash into the swamp and the hungry maw of a giant lizard. But at last, they batter down the psychic defences of the castle and there the Doctor confronts the elderly Emsone. He learns that the old villain has created a machine – half magic, half mechanical – that will make him extremely rich and powerful. All he needs to complete it is the mind of Dr. Who.

A terrible battle of wills ensues. Emsone clearly has never heard that this is the worst thing any self-respecting cosmic villain can do. The Doctor tricks him by making him believe that the castle falling down is just an illusion created by the Doctor's mind. But actually, the castle *is* falling down because of the ructions from their mental duel. Emsone is squashed under falling masonry: SPLATT.

The story finishes happily with a fully-fleshed and clothed Krass enjoying a mug of tea, made from the mountain herbs that the Doctor and Leela came here to study.

THE CROCODILES FROM THE MIST

Keen to see how life is developing on a world he's been watching since its creation, the Doctor takes the Tardis to somewhere rather depressing and rainy. Playing board games till the weather clears up, it's a little while until they emerge to see hills of dirty ice and what appear to be crocodile-like creatures arranged in a pile. They have harmless teeth and spikes on their tails and sniff the air at the strangers' approach. Creatures somewhere between bats and birds arrive, and the Doctor feels that the space crocodiles are fond of them. Less so, the 'slavering tusker' that then bolts out of nowhere to attack our heroes. A crocodile intercedes to fight the brutal creature.

After the fuss has died down the Doctor returns to the Tardis to get his Mental Image Intensifier to work. It turns out he often uses this sometimes erratic device to communicate with telepathic or recalcitrant aliens. Cheerfully he hooks it up to the snout of one of the space crocodiles. He empathises with images and emotions from the creature, and finds that it is scared of something living in or around a nearby volcano: something that came from the sky. There is a poison in the land itself, the Doctor finds, that is preventing the crocodiles from evolving naturally.

The Doctor and Leela use stilts to walk all the way up the volcano, and at the top they peer down into the crater. Down there is a crashed Areelian spaceship, with engines futilely and dangerously pumping away. The best thing is to lob a bomb down there to blow the ship up, and to reignite the volcano and to basically mess the whole thing up, in order to stop any further radiation leakage. However, an hour's fuse makes the stilt walk back down the volcano slightly hair-raising. The Doctor ends up doing the splits to an almost lethal extent, and Leela saves his life.

Using his image intensifier machine again, the Doctor informs the space crocodiles of what he and Leela have been up to. The creatures are extremely glad, and insist on licking their saviours with their forked tongues to express gratitude. Then they slope off, as the Tardis dematerialises, to lie in a tidy sort of heap, and wait to evolve.

And so ends the Annual from 1979: possibly the strangest and most ambitious and confidently written of all of these books so far. Characterisation of the two leads is spot on, and a range of colourful and memorable allies and villains have made their dramatic exits. Wonderful, utterly exotic worlds have been visited – most notably Shem and Zorka. I have to say, this Annual is

155

probably the best, all in all, that I've read so far on this odyssey back into the oeuvre.

Other Content

SHIPS OF THE SKY

Sometimes the Annuals go a bit mad and print articles on subjects which are simply not true (remember the article on Atlantis in the first Troughton Annual?). This one isn't quite at that level, but two pages are given over to the Skyship, 'a British design, developed to succeed the Zeppelins and other airships', which does feel in the same ballpark. As big as a 14-storey building, weighing 800 tons and capable of speeds of 144 kilometres per hour, the Skyship – obviously – never took flight.

- PUZZLE IT OUT – Crossword.
- JOURNEYS OF DISCOVERY – Pioneer 10 (again!)
- TRICKY CONNECTION – Maze puzzle.
- DRESSED FOR A WALK – The mechanics of the spacesuit.
- GUESSING THE GARZL- Visual puzzle based on a drawing of a tree!
- PRISONERS OF THE PREFUSSIONS – A board game, in which for variety it is suggested players split into two teams (otherwise it is the exact same as every other board game in the Annuals)

Doctor Who Himself

Reassuringly, he's always very much himself, casually arriving on the most outlandish of new worlds. Faced with the bizarre Children of Rha he greets their bravest member: 'Hello, little fellow. Pleased to meet you.' There's always something very kindly and calming about this man who feels at home anywhere. He trusts that everyone is his friend, until they prove otherwise.

During the business of ending famine on Planet X, he resorts to 'crude emotional blackmail', ensuring that the octopoids stop persecuting and sacrificing people, and warning them that the seeds will no longer grow unless they mend their ways. He dislikes these heavy-handed methods, and leaves instructions for his ally Ogg to 'defuse this myth' in future, by mastering the agricultural skills necessary to feed all of X's inhabitants. It's a brief, interesting insight into the Doctor's methods of brokering peace. He isn't averse to leaning heavily on bullies, and exploiting their own dodgy belief systems to get them to do the right thing.

Similarly, when dealing with Beshi inside 'The Planet of Dust' the Doctor rubbishes his plans for horticultural dominance and reminds him that he is a warrior and a barbarian and fiddling around with tissue samples and giving flowers limbs is not worthy of him.

Again he's using his knowledge of the creature in order to manipulate him. The Doctor becomes his 'most persuasive' whenever there is the chance of a peaceful solution to a problem.

This continues a compelling theme that runs through the Fourth Doctor stories of the Annuals – to do with his pacifism and how he turns his intellect upon creating peaceful solutions. Already we are a million miles from the cartoonish explosions of the Third Doctor's years, and it feels as if we are heading towards the forming of a utopian sense of what Dr. Who's role in the universe might be. Not just an explorer or a dilettante, a policeman or an action hero. He's becoming a kind of ambassador for peace and good. He's making the universe a better place – haphazardly. One unwelcoming, hostile, bizarre world after another.

The counter-argument – and rather nasty accusation – comes from Akhemi the Tantalogan, when he accuses Dr. Who of being a dabbler in other people's affairs. 'A useless pontificator, a peddler of invented morals' with an egocentric shell that houses little of substance. Strong stuff! Possibly the sharpest criticism the Doctor has ever received. Sharp because it is spiced with a little truth.

The Doctor is forever being caught on either the horns of a moral dilemma, or those of hideous creatures. In 1979 he is put to the test rather strenuously – physically, mentally and ethically. But on the whole, he is a simple and carefree soul. The type who thinks an anti-gravity belt is a suitable gift for a space princess' coronation.

The 1979 Annual is making me wonder if the Fourth Doctor isn't becoming a little camp. In 'Flashback' the 'fat fiend' Skeeda tries to hypnotise Leela and the Doctor has to slap her in the face to bring her round. When she observes ruefully that she's very glad they're on the same side, the Doctor replies airily: 'My dear, it's the only place to be.' He murmurs this. He's being dry and witty, and he's striding about in some dreadful metal spaceship, in the middle of an adventure.

I always felt this Doctor had something very camp about him. A blithe, knowing camp, not specifically gay. Just a strange kind of otherness that allows him to be flippant and silly when those in his company would least expect it. Or to be dark, melancholic, even depressive, when everyone else is being cheery. He inhabits his moods in a very dramatic, flamboyant way, relishing every moment of the performance.

Describing the relativity of time and space, and the experience of subjective time to Leela, he rather charmingly tells her that an hour might be ages to a child waiting for his mother buying Christmas presents. But it will seem much quicker to people trying to escape an exploding volcano on stilts. In this one comparison he links the absurdly dangerous predicament within the story to the idea of a child at Christmastime: that is, the likely reader of the tale.

Monsters and Villains

The Octopoids of Planet X are prepared to sacrifice their Children for a decent meal. Beshi the Larkal is a formidable horned being, frustrated at being on a world where he's 'breathing dust with a row of old cabbages.' He wants to give all the plants sentience and mobility, and wants tissue samples from his visitors to help achieve this strange aim.

The Tantalogans are hideous beings living in a perfect world. The Doctor is right to be entirely suspicious of them. They breed other species in order to gain sustenance from their sacrificial deaths. They have a weird sense of ecology. To farm or fish would harm their living world, but to sacrifice visitors apparently pleases it no end. Akhemi is scathing about Earth people, and how they spend thousands of years in bloody skirmishes, all within six feet of their planet's surface.

The various warring factions of the planet Shem are weirdly convincing and multifarious, Simian types and winged warlords inhabiting a Medieval-looking fantasy world. Skeeda of Pendor is a flame-haired dwarf with an inferiority complex, who wants to bring about havoc to public transport and the weather. Emsone the elderly mystic is a terrific enemy for the Fourth Doctor, drawing him into a splendidly Gothic world where science and 'the black arts' have the lines between them blurred.

Curious Companions?

Leela is this year's companion and she's in character straight away: disturbed by the erratic flight path of the Tardis, she clutches her dagger and behaves like a trapped animal. During long voyages aboard the Tardis she longs for sunshine and stiff breezes. She is bright, though. She recognises a universal sign for peace transmitted by the fleshy horns of Ogg. She remembers it as something her mother taught her as a child. Strange, these Annuals are often accused of getting the companions very wrong, and yet I've often found – in revisiting them – that their characters come up quite distinctively, and sometimes reveal odd little nuggets of backstory that actually fit. I love this tiny flashback to the infant Leela and her mother.

Elsewhere Leela's speech becomes a little formal – she describes a new planet as 'first rate' – which makes me wonder if she's aping the Doctor's vernacular, or whether it's just a mistake. In the picture strip 'The Power', however, she utters the line that, to me, is a perfect example of Leela reacting to rhetoric of which she approves. When Princess Azula talks about tolerance and learning, and everyone in their fancy headgear and clutching their swords is shouting their approval, Leela just goes: 'Fine talk.' And she's right. She's pithy to the core. And, what's more, it seems she's starting to wear jeans.

It's almost as if, in this alternate, loopy timeline of the Annuals, the Doctor is having more success than his TV counterpart, in educating Leela and teaching her to be an appreciative citizen of the universe. And also to dress a little more casually than the usual chamois leather bikini.

She can beat the Doctor at draughts – and he sulks when she does. It has to be said that they seem fonder of each other in the Neuronic Nightmare universe than they ever did in Season 15 on TV. It is Leela who saves his life in the exploding swamp, as they try to make their escape on stilts.

Fiendish Wheezes

Getting the crops to grow by a) sacrificing your young or b) giving the crops arms and legs are both bad ideas, whichever world you live on. Akhemi the Tantalogan admits that he breeds living alien creatures and milks their brains. Skeeda of Pendor has a good plan to hypnotise the lighthouse keepers who control the weather of his homeworld, and it would have worked too, if the Doctor hadn't arrived by chance that very afternoon on the space beacon. Emsone has a fantastic machine to take over the whole universe and all he needs is Dr. Who's brain in the middle of it, connected by these dangling wires, to make the whole thing operational.

TV Feedback

The vision of a world filled with clever, ambulatory plants in 'The Planet of Dust' is close to that of Harrison Chase in TV's 'The Seeds of Doom.' The genetic experiments of Beshi also recall the mad butchery practiced by Mehendri Solon in 'The Brain of Morbius' in that same season.

Inanimate dummies coming to life in 'Terror on Tantalogus' send a shiver of remembered Auton fear through the readership. Skeeda's plan to manipulate the weather control beacon above his homeworld of Pendor reminds us of other mankind-menaced-by-weather-control stories from TV such as 'The Moonbase' and 'The Seeds of Death'. The lighthouse crew in space walking around as if possessed reminds us a little of 'The Horror of Fang Rock.' Emsone and his brutal manservant Gruk in their Gothic castle, eager to get hold of the Doctor's brain, are a clear reminder of Morbius, Solon and Condo on Karn. The mind duel between Emsone and the Doctor is another echo of that TV classic.

Egregious errors

Dr. Who's screwdriver is no longer simply sonic. It's 'cosmic.' I'd prefer to think this is an upgrade, rather than just an error. Imagine the things a cosmic screwdriver might do!

Classic moments

The Planet X's inhabitants planting their new crops in that shape of the sign of peace so that the Doctor and Leela will see it before they leave is quite touching. The Doctor feels miserable when Leela is held hostage by the giant, flesh-eating space cow, Beshi. He despairs of being able to fix the broken spaceship, but a telepathic pansy and his friends introduce themselves and help him out. Only in Doctor Who Annuals does this heady, wonderful stuff ever happen.

In Akhemi's dwelling unit on Tantalogus, Leela notices that the supposed dummies are opening and closing their mouths in mute supplication! In 'The Power' the Doctor is tossed into a pit and menaced by flesh-eating apes with evil eyes. In a flash he opens up the gift he brought from the Princess – and it's an anti-grav belt! He rises like Icarus to the astonishment of the massed hordes of Shem!

Krass having his flesh restored inside the M-Ray machine, watching helplessly as Gurk attacks both Dr. Who and Leela is a wonderfully exciting and scary moment.

What I learned from the Doctor Who Annual 1979

Persecution and sacrifice are both are waste of time, and not at all nice. It's necessary to cultivate your own garden. And, if you do, you might get help at just the right moment from the unlikeliest of sources. Watch out for gigantic space cows in ermine robes. Anyone too smiley and happy and perfect is bound to turn out to be a vampiric fiend. Always buy Princesses anti-grav belts as presents. If all your clothes and flesh are made to disappear by a crazy mystic in a castle, run straight to Dr. Who, who understands how M-Rays work. And never, ever get into a mind duel with him – but you already know that, don't you?

Illustrations

The artwork this year seems to be less abstract and experimental. The pictures are actually **of** things: they seem to depict recognizable characters and situations. The colours are, in places, muddy and grey and brown and blue. In many places the illustrations still look wet and sticky. We are living in a less psychedelic age. This is post-punk Dr. Who and the pictures are a bit more grim.

Sometimes photo references from sources other than *Doctor Who* are used, notably from classic science fiction movies such as 'Village of the Damned', 'The Shape of Things to Come' or recent TV series such as 'Space 1999.' We will never know whether this was a result of creative desperation on the part of the artist, or whether it was a deliberate nod towards the TV show's very self-conscious and witty replication of images and tropes from classic SF and horror cinema.

'The Power' features some of the most beautiful artwork seen so far in the Doctor Who Annual.

Credits

Paul Crompton takes artist credit, and also, apparently, some of the credit for writing this Annual, which may account for the quality and confidence evident in the picture strips especially. Both 'The Power' and 'Emsone's Castle' work as perfectly articulated capsule adventures, exploring worlds and characters with believable pasts and motivations. They also read rather like comic strip adaptations of tales that pre-exist in some other, more elaborate form, giving further credence to the possibility that they are the product of greater investment of time and imaginative energy by a single writer / artist.

The 1980 Annual

It's another year of change for Dr. Who. The slinky know-it-all Time Lady Romana has joined him in the Tardis, as well as the endlessly reliable K9, and the three of them seem to have a mission of sorts. K9 has to remind the Doctor politely of their on-going galactic day-job when he seems to seriously consider settling down on a pleasant and remote world. No mention is made of the Key to Time, however, and there isn't a great deal of urgency about them. They are rather loftily wafting about in the cosmos, visiting places, and fixing things when they feel compelled to, or otherwise leaving well alone.

The three already behave like old friends, with their sniping and in-jokes, but the Doctor seems a little different somehow. He unflinchingly kills the giant ape menacing the locals on Xaboi. His more warlike self is brought to the fore when he is made to take part in war games on Banto: we see him bloodied and wielding a sword. It's the year we discover him being less flippant and taking himself a little more seriously, perhaps. His wilder, crazier, far-flung adventures of recent years are coming to seem excessive. He's drawing in his horns, becoming less utopian in his thinking… he might even be becoming conservative. He's no longer calling himself Dr. Who. He's simply the Doctor, now that it's almost the nineteen eighties.

It's a period of redefining the role of the Doctor and his companions in the cosmos. (At different points both the Doctor and Romana are transformed into shapeless blobs: emblematic of a time of endless flux.) What is their role here? What are they trying to do? On the evidence, they are policing the planets they visit – thwarting renegade, failed Time Lords, toppling violent tyrants. There is a lot less aimless wandering and a certain amount of moral confusion and ethical redefinition going on. Romana's presence as a young, enthusiastic Time Lord seems to be having an effect on the Doctor. He seems torn between his instinct to get involved and fight for justice, and his training to act all high-handedly and coldly put things right, or leave them alone, as he judges fit.

The Scripts

X-RANI AND THE UGLY MUTANTS

Are hideously deformed mutants classed as normal on the planet Xethra? This is what's got the Doctor and Romana pondering as soon as they arrive. The Doctor chucks handfuls of sand at the unfortunate locals in order to scare them off.

163

On this evidence, I don't think Romana – snooty so-and-so that she is – is turning out to be a very good influence on our hero.

Chasing mutants through the wilderness, they soon come to an area where a veiled figure observes a whole lot of the wretched beings engaged in energetic bouts of wrestling. The Doctor addresses the beautiful veiled lady as if they're in a singles bar, and Romana is piqued. This is X-Rani, mistress of the mutants and misfits exiled from Xethra, and she makes the Doctor mutate on the spot, to show him the extent of her powers. She's concerned about food supplies not coming through, and wants to make use of the Tardis. Romana must stay and wear the veil and control the mutants with her beauty.

Ethra is a world that 'exudes perfection'. The foodstuff that X-Rani needs is the lush grass growing freely, bavita. The Doctor watches all the handsome couples strolling about the place, aware that his companion is hatching some kind of plot. To get to see the Controller she turns the Doctor monstrous again, scaring everyone out of the way.

During the battle of Mind Control between X-Rani and the Controller the Doctor realises that the Controller is the victim here. X-Rani was the one doing all the banishing and the bossing about. He sees things are set to rights and is pleased to find out that bavita makes first class tea.

LIGHT FANTASTIC

The planet UX80 – previously known as Culturus – is the next destination for Dr. Who, Romana and K9: an uninhabited, radioactive world where a Gallifreyan native has recently disappeared. On the dark, partly-fluorescent planet, our heroes don protective suits and detect a relatively new Tardis. They are addressed in upper case lettering by the suddenly-living single occupant of UX80, Radik, who is a shape-shifter who can control radiation. He was thrown out of the Gallifreyan Academy for unlawful experiments, and absconded with the intriguing-sounding 'red cone time machine.' (A Tardis disguised as a traffic cone, was my first thought.)

Radik is out for revenge, and when Romana gets hoity-toity about Time Lord exam results he turns her into orange slime, a monkey and finally 'a shapeless mess.' The Doctor is horrified to find Romana gelatinous and 'somehow tacky'. Tentacles of slime reach out for the Doctor while K9 looks on helplessly and is, presumably, shocked. The Doctor manages to save all their lives by concentrating his mental powers very hard and making Radik change from violent orange slime into radio waves.

They tune in the Translator to hear him rant some more at them. (The Translator reminds me of that amazing-sounding *Doctor Who* toy which was then available, and often advertised in *Doctor Who Weekly* – the Tardis Tuner. It was a radio, I believe, with several superfluous space-age knobs and dials. This story is almost product placement for that legendary plaything..!)

Radik seems very bitter about failing his Finals. Turning Romana into orange slime and absorbing the Doctor's brain waves seems a rather nasty alternative to the more conventional Academic Appeals process. Romana turns the sonic screwdriver on him and tunes him into something on a much lower wavelength.

TERROR ON XABOI (Picture strip)

Drawn off course to the extremely snowy world of Xaboi the Doctor and Romana put on some 'warm kit' to have a wander in the tundra. Soon they can hear the screams of primitive life forms rising above the freezing winds. They find a cavern filled with people of 'a very early evolutionary type' whose speech consists chiefly of 'RUARRL!' and 'GRUND!'

They are the prisoner of a hideous, giant, apelike beast. When it sleeps, the Doctor slips out to get to the Tardis. He intends to bring back something called the 'stun-sensor' and set the humanoids free. When he returns though, the beast is going mental, and so he's forced to fire a 'destroying charge.' The giant ape lies dead and defeated on the ground and the Doctor and Romana leave the primitive humanoids to evolve by themselves in peace.

RELUCTANT WARRIORS

Our heroes travel to a dazzling city on the planet Banto, to meet an old friend of the Doctor's. Public viewing screens show battles happening in muddy fields, and a voice announces that the Yemites and the Thralls are fighting to the death as an entertainment for the green-skinned populace.

When they arrive at Alix's apartment he isn't very pleased to see them. It turns out that Leondin – who promised the people longer leisure hours and less work – has come to power and become a bit of a dictator. He sprays contending armies with his 'ray of wrath' and gets them fighting on the telly. Arrested for being found in an illegal meeting, the Doctor and Romana are taken to Leondin's palace, where the little man is surrounded by displays of bloody weapons. Romana is taken back to the cells and the Doctor and Alix are transported to the battlefield to take part in the gladiatorial games.

The Doctor resists the anxiety-inducing ray of wrath, and decides that the Thralls are the exact colour of potted meat. Given a sword and a breastplate – which he still wears his scarf over – Dr. Who feels himself succumbing to the effects of the ray of hate. Meanwhile, K9 calmly rescues Romana from her guard, and they hurry to Leondin's control room, where they manage to switch off the ray of wrath for a few crucial seconds. K9 zaps Leondin and the Doctor regains control of his marbles just as he's waving his sword about. He leads an attack on the observing cameras: the real enemy in this game.

THE WEAPON (Picture strip)

Beautiful, rural England – 'Land of tea and toast!' – during an undefined period in the past. While the Doctor goes exploring, Romana relaxes for a second – actually enjoying herself for once. Almost immediately she is picked up by armoured men on horseback, intent on taking her back to their castle. However: the Black Knight and his men appear and a skirmish naturally ensues. They have a terrifying, futuristic weapon, which kills the White Knight. Romana is hustled away by his men.

Meanwhile the Doctor happens upon the castle, thinking it a National Trust property, and is menaced by a Medieval soldier and taken before the king. K9 and Romana are brought in – and everyone is excited that the 'strange metal creature' seems to have the Weapon, too.

When the Black Horsemen attack again, the Weapon kills the White King, but the Black Knight is put out of action by K9. The Doctor exhorts his companions to flee the scene. Romana can't believe he's letting the Black soldiers win. They make their way through misty meadows towards the Tardis and the Doctor becomes rather callous, and then philosophical, about the nature of good and evil, and the forces of darkness.

This is a strange story in terms of the Doctor's stand-point and morality. We've seen him outraged in the past, when primitive beings are given advanced weapons by people from the future. Here, that very thing seems to be happening again, and yet he is content to walk away, knowing that the White soldiers will be wiped out. He refuses to put an end to the situation, to confiscate the weapon, or even take sides. He seems to allude to the eternal struggle between the forces of good and evil, and simply rises above it all – as any old Time Lord would. The anachronistic laser weapon he dismisses as an 'intervention' by the forces of evil. His job was to 'restore the balance', by lending the White side K9's fire power for a moment. (Does this mean the robot dog actually slays the Black Knight?)

As a child I wondered about this for ages, spending a long time thinking about that draughty castle, thoroughly absorbed in the lavish colours of this wonderfully painted strip. My conclusion then, as now, is that the Doctor knows that he has walked into another site of the eternal struggle between the Black and White Guardians. This is a kind of coda to the whole 'Key to Time' saga – and much more lyrical and complex and ambiguous than 'The Armageddon Factor' ever was. In this, the Doctor removes himself safely from the chessboard – and walks away from these people as if they were emblems rather than real flesh and blood, without even looking back. Even at Christmas in 1979 I knew that this was the true, properly fitting end to his yearlong adventure under the auspices of the all-powerful Guardians. Never before and never again was an Annual story related as elegantly to its TV counterpart as this – resolving key themes and tropes in an oddly understated, and wonderfully evocative way.

RETURN OF THE ELECTRIDS

We begin at what seems like the end of a story: with democratically elected Zeebon happy that planet Zed is freed of the 'dreaded Electrids,' and bidding farewell to our Tardis team. But Zuli, Zed's assistant, makes sure they can't

166

leave. He explains that the celebrations were a sham. The Electrids have actually returned, and Zeebon doesn't want the people to know.

They are sent, with K9, on a wild goose chase through underground corridors, looking for burrowing, worm-like Electrids. Romana finds that they are being controlled by the emotionally unstable Zani, a scientist who has bred his very own six-foot long killer worms. He intends to clone them, and himself, like crazy. Naturally, the vast, electrified phalluses turn against their creator: 'I am the only one who cares for you. No, you can't, you mustn't, you... aaagh... aaagh...'

THE SLEEPING GUARDIANS

Randomised coordinates (counting his Jelly Babies; getting his friends to think of a number) brings Dr. Who and the Tardis to a world where they find a deactivated robot army, and a town and a people under siege from blazing rocket ships. The populace enter the chapel and hide underground. An old man called Tallis, 'Keeper of the Ten Thousand' explains that the enemy hails from 'the dark side of the planet.'

Again, this feeling of moving away from the stark, prosaic quality of conventional space opera, and into something more fantastical and nebulous. Evil is a darkness, and a force emanating from unseen quarters. Knights arrive on horseback in armour, wielding swords as well as ray guns. This is a very complicated, mongrelised version of the universe that 1980 paints – and one clearly not unrelated to the worlds conjured by 'The Ribos Operation' or 'The Androids of Tara': a kind of olde worlde / Excaliburish / Merliny thing, summed up best by the Annual's at first odd-seeming cover image: Dr. Who in chain mail armour. But it perfectly fits 1980's sojourn among worlds of wizardry and high romance.

There is a hint of legendary magic in these tales that chimes with ideas from popular children's authors of the time: the sleeping warriors evoke for me Alan Garner's 'The Weirdstone of Brisingamen', and the idea of disembodied dark forces locked in endless struggle with the light has a touch of Susan Cooper's 'The Dark is Rising'. Those books are very strongly connected with myth and folktale and so, I feel, are the stories in the 1980 Annual. *Doctor Who* fiction is coming perilously close to enjoying and flaunting a literariness that we haven't quite seen before. Both 1979 and 1980 have brought a new level of sophistication. Like *Doctor Who* on TV in the Graham Williams era, there is an evident sifting through mythic sources; a rummaging through the possible origins of the Doctor's own story. It's a very exciting time for this unfolding text.

Back to the climax of the tale: the robots downstairs were put there hundreds of years ago, to protect the good folk of Valeria. Tallis is the most recent keeper of the magic key that could reactivate them, but rather embarrassingly, the key is lost.

When the final assault comes, the enemies are revealed as terrifying beasts: lumbering, covered in black plates of armour, their eyes glowing red. The Doctor urges his friends to turn tail and run, though he doesn't like to leave the Valerians to their bloody fates. The Tardis is blocked, the Doctor's hands are bleeding. In desperation he turns to Romana, sounding sardonic as he snaps: 'Surely a graduate like yourself must have some ideas!'

Clever old K9 – after some careful sniffing – manages to locate the crystal key to the great doors. After the dormant army rouses and saves the day, Tallis emerges to thank our heroes. K9 emits a small cough, spurring the Doctor to praise him. The day is saved. But it very nearly wasn't.

Other Content

SPELL OUT A SPACE ALPHABET

Surprise! It's another – increasingly desperate – space alphabet! Amongst the obscure terms used this time are 'H is for Halley Rille' (a canyon on the Moon, visited by astronauts in 1971) and 'Z if for Zulu Time' ('wherever you are in the world, local time is referred to as Zulu Time') But the highlight is perfect in its simplicity – 'Q is for Q!

- PREPARE FOR TAKE-OFF – Article on space flight.
- A TRICKY PROBLEM FOR THE DOCTOR – Maths puzzle.
- THE MOON – Mythical moon feature.
- WHICH IS THE SMALLEST PLANET? – A: Pluto.
- SPACE-WORD PUZZLE – Crossword.
- JOURNEY THROUGH TIME – Board game, somewhat based on Snakes and Ladders.

Doctor Who Himself

Sarah's gone, Leela's gone – and now here's Romana. No mention is made of why the switch in ladies; and no allusion is made to the Key to Time. It's like Dr. Who's just hooked up with another lady-friend and everyone's too polite to mention it. In some pictures she looks a bit like Sarah and others like Leela. In some she even looks a little bit like Mary Tamm. She's very sophisticated and cool and, in her presence, the Doctor is rather different…

I'm wondering if, having got himself an upper class fancy woman, he isn't cleaning up his act. The Eighties are coming. Is he going to be less Bohemian and scruffy and free-thinking? Will Dr. Who be less footloose and fancy-free..?

At the end of their adventure on UX80 the Doctor is even thinking of settling down. He makes a jokey kind of proposal to Romana: 'You, me and the dog?' K9 reminds him they have a job to do, out in the universe, and they josh about it. But surely some part of the Doctor is in deadly earnest here. Could he really be thinking it'd be nice to settle on an empty world with his new companion?

He flicks switches on the console at random, Romana believes – just as he fancies. He's as capricious and childish as ever, but I think he may be changing. When confronting the dictator Leondin he wonders aloud whether there isn't something wrong with people who live only for pleasure. It's never been true of him, but would the Fourth Doctor have been as judgmental as this before – in 1977 or 1978, say?

In 'The Weapon' Dr. Who's first line of dialogue is the most characteristic one he ever gets, as far as I'm concerned: 'Mmm, 20th Century England, land of tea and toast!'

At the end of 'The Sleeping Guardians' the Doctor almost flees the scene of battle. There is nothing he can do. He urges his friends to run to the Tardis. He almost reverts to Time Lord type by refusing to interfere. Only his small robot dog helps him to become heroic once more.

Monsters and Villains

The poor, deformed, wrestling Xethrans! In thrall to the awful X-Rani and seemingly despised by all. Radik the radioactive renegade from Gallifrey seems a nasty piece of work. Like all stolen Tardises, his soon went wonky and he landed in the wrong time and place: 'BUT THEN I BEGAN TO TAKE MY REVENGE ANYWAY, AS PLANNED.'

Leontin of Banto is a rotten ruler who has a 'ray of wrath' to make his people fight bloody battles on TV. Like many wicked leaders of corrupt regimes in late Seventies TV *Doctor Who* he is a little coward in the flesh. The Black Knight with his mysterious laser weapon is frightening, as is the amoral Electrid-breeder, Zani, deep under the surface of Zed.

Some of these enemies seem sent by the ineffable powers of the darkness – the Black Knight and his men, and the monsters from the dark side of Valeria.

Curious Companions?

Romana can put alien beings of all kinds in thrall to her beauty. She's rather disparaging about the Tardis and its status as an antique. Endlessly proud of her academic credentials, Romana is quick to point out that Radik flunked out of the Academy, and never even became a Time Lord. She is the one, however, who has the presence of mind to use the sonic screwdriver to defeat this overbearing bully.

'Really it was a miracle that they ever landed anywhere...' She is quite disparaging about the Doctor's abilities at the helm of his own ship. She snaps at him for his silliness and attention-seeking: 'Is it old age, or are you doing it to annoy me?' Sometimes it's reassuring to hear her behave just like any old assistant: "Look out!' cried Romana. 'The Electrids!"

Christmas 1979 and the 1980 Annual sees K9's debut in the world of the World Distributors' Annuals. A little late, perhaps, but he's very welcome – and very much his own, fussy, smug little self from the off. When the Doctor asks him to verify the old cliché about teaching an old dog new tricks, I can't help feeling a twinge of fondness when K9 says that he can't, being 'a relatively new dog.'

K9 is discovered actually sniffing round a lamp post in 'Reluctant Warriors.' Later, when Romana and the Doctor jokingly dispute over who saved the day, the robot dog diplomatically keeps quiet. These three know each other very well already, it seems.

K9 is the hero of the 1980 Annual. It is he who finds the magic key that saves the world in the final story of this book. Even after Dr. Who has given up hope of rescuing everyone, K9 is dogged.

Fiendish Wheezes

X-Rani and her band of energetically-wrestling mutants are a rum bunch – pretending there's a famine when there isn't, and trying to defeat the queen of the neighbouring planet. Radik's plan for revenge against his Time Lord professors consists of kidnapping travelling Gallifreyans and stealing their minds. Zani of Zed intends to clone himself and his deadly, home-grown, dubiously-shaped Electrids to his heart's content, probably until they overrun the whole world.

TV Feedback

The primitive space tribe encountered by the Doctor and Romana on Xaboï are a reminder of the Tribe of Gum, though they seem to be having an even rougher time.

'The Weapon' has Medieval soldiers with devices from the future, taking unfair advantage over their enemies, just as in 'The Time Warrior.' The Black and White Knights of this story always make me think there's a deliberate echo here of the Black and White Guardians from Season 16 on TV, and that this story is a more localised, even allegorical, version of their more cosmic struggle.

Another echo comes with the crystalline key that unlocks the door that imprisons the warriors in the Annual's final story. It's a lovely version of the Arthurian myth of the army hidden inside the cavern, and again it gives a more palpable and dramatic and epic conclusion to the battle between light and dark. The monstrous, red-eyed beasts attacking from the dark side of the planet Valeria are a much more effective vision of the creatures in thrall to the Black Guardian than anything seen on TV.

Anticipating the Future

Romana defeats failed Time Lord Radik by using the sonic 'as if it were a gun', and in so doing anticipates the current era of TV *Doctor Who* in which Doctors are content to be seen pointing, waving, brandishing and cocking their screwdrivers all over the place as if they were much tougher action heroes than they actually are.

Another glimpse of the future comes with the picture strip 'Terror on Xaboï', when the Doctor and Romana stare out of the glass panels of the Police Box windows at the blizzardy world outside. This was wrong as far as the TV show of the time was concerned, of course, when a cumbersome set of swinging interior doors stood between the ship's inside and the external shell. In the revamped series that began in 2005 the Tardis was equipped with the more straightforwardly quaint double doors that had featured in the second Aaru *Doctor Who* movie, *Daleks: Invasion Earth 2150*. But they are here as well: wooden doors with small glass panes that look out onto each new world the Tardis visits. As a kid I used to love this moment in this strip. I was fascinated by the snow gathering at the corners of the panes, and the faces staring through the glass from the ship's interior dimensions.

I must make mention of two curious moments of prolepsis when it comes to Doctor-ish couture: here, on the final page of the comic strip, 'The Weapon', the Fourth Doctor appears to be wearing the Eighth Doctor's clothes. (And, equally impossibly, in 1976, on the third page of the picture strip, 'The Neuronic Nightmare' he is sporting the Sixth Doctor's outfit.) This is clearly impossible, both in the fiction and outside of it. I'm really not sure what is going on there, in either case. But it seems further evidence to me that the Annuals and their strange illustrations are a-quiver with all kinds of echoes from *Doctor Who* past and future.

Classic moments

The Doctor being transformed into a three-armed mutant, and then into something beyond recognition, by X-Rani on Xethra is a very memorable moment. As is the image of Dr. Who and Romana in her white furry Ribos outfit, trekking across the snows on their way to a rendezvous with a ferocious giant ape. The Doctor and Romana with K9 visiting the bucolic splendour of Medieval England, and the Doctor visiting what he thinks is a National Trust property is a great moment. And then the Doctor walking away from the adventure to play chess is both striking and perplexing. The bloody, epic climax to 'The Sleeping Guardians' brings the whole book to a grand finish.

What I learned from the Doctor Who Annual 1980

Ugliness is never only skin deep. Never say 'NOTHING CAN STOP ME NOW!' to Dr. Who. And never assume you can mess with his brain waves. You already know what happens in mind-bending contests – so why bother?

Can you just walk away? If a situation seems futile, and war inevitable and you can't save anyone's life – is it easier just to remember your Time Lord training and stop yourself getting involved?

The Doctor Who Annual 1980 taught me that it can be all too easy to be swayed by the company you keep. This Romana is too snooty and callow for traipsing around the universe. The Doctor would be better off listening to K9, who always tries his absolute best to save the day. K9 is the Doctor's true conscience, and Romana is the voice of his upbringing. I learned from 1980 that it's very hard to listen to both.

Luckily, Romana proves – fairly shortly after this – that change is possible. It's inevitable.

Illustrations

Paul Crompton's final year working on the Annual brings some of his finest pieces yet. Also, he is responsible – in both 1979 and 1980 – for both writing and illustrating the best of all the Annual picture strips.

'The Weapon' has the most amazing artwork seen in any of the Annuals, finer even than 1979's strip, 'The Power', though it seems contiguous with that miniature epic. Here the artwork always struck me, from childhood, as looking like tiny oil paintings coming to life. Each frame is sumptuous and richly colourful, with each character depicted incredibly vividly and dynamically. Even as a child I could see that someone was going well over the odds to create something special: something well beyond the remit of a piece of cheap tie-in merchandise.

Elsewhere, the drawings are inky and dark. They are full of menace, superbly matching the murkiness and dark complexity of the stories.

The 1981 Annual

At the beginning of the Eighties the clock turns backwards. For the final few years of the nineteen seventies the Doctor Who Annual was becoming stranger, more esoteric and mind-boggling. It was reaching into areas *Doctor Who* had never been before, and the character of the Doctor was actually evolving into something even more interesting: a cosmic anti-hero who isn't necessarily going to save the day, who questions his own perceptions and his place and role in the universe.

When the Eighties begin in earnest it seems that he has put all of his self-doubt behind him. He is presented more like his earlier selves: an eccentric galactic do-gooder, unafraid of villains and their schemes. Unbeatable and unflappable.

This happens just as his TV persona goes the other way. On TV the Fourth Doctor played out his swansong against a backdrop of autumnal hues. He looked woebegone and haunted. His close companions left him one by one. He looked confused by the presence of strangers in his life. he lost all of the jollity and the straightforwardness that had hitherto been his lot.

It's almost as if… his sobriety in the TV timeline means that the inverted dimension of the Annuals sees him automatically brighten up.

The Stories

COLONY OF DEATH

The Doctor, Romana and K9 visit an Earth colony in the 23rd century, only to find it deserted. He finds the leader Garderon, who is perplexed that a stranger has managed to get under the Dome on Paradise 1.

K9 and Romana watch as spaceships from Earth arrive, and ragged humans bring out boxes containing frozen colonists. Set to work as a slave, the Doctor learns that the colonists were lured here by false promises and found themselves in a trap. Garderon is using his duped colonists to mine the world. He's even composing fake letters to send to their loved ones on Earth.

The Doctor breaks into Garderon's home, wakes him up in the night and scares him into giving up. The villain and his men will be frozen and sent back to the congested Earth to face trial.

ALIEN MIND GAMES

The Tardis is taking a tempestuous trip through a region of Anti-Matter. It feels like everyone's being sucked down a whirlpool and destruction is imminent. The Doctor wakes in an unknown region where he is confronted by three translucent pyramid shapes. This is the world of ANTI-SPACE and this is the ONE, addressing him as he floats there, crossly. The intelligence wants to quiz the Doctor about which species in his universe besides the Time Lords have access to time travel, but the Doctor is intent on making some tea.

But there is a TEST to come. The pyramids get straight to the point, asking him straight off the bat: 'What is the SECRET of TIME?' Then he is transported from the Mastermind chair to a rocky world, and the One wants to know all about the Secrets of the Tardis.

This is starting to look a little like a mind-duel and, even though he could be made to explode at any moment, the Doctor surely has the upper hand. He proves this by wandering off and defying his captor to stop him. Then he suggests that the One isn't actually all that he claims to be. This isn't a universe of Anti-Matter at all and the alien intelligence turns out to have been a clapped-out machine that just wanted someone to talk to.

A MIDSUMMER'S NIGHTMARE

En route to Norway for a midnight picnic, the Tardis team find their destination completely dark. Luckily, K9 has a torch fitted into his nose. There is a suspicious orange glow. They track this to an underground lair of some kind. There are Nordic supplicants worshipping a nebulous, glowing shape.

They encounter a scared lad called Sven, whose family has been taken away. Everything points towards devil worship, or some kind of manipulation of Earth myths. The worshippers have luminous dots for eyes… and the Doctor is wondering whether he has invoked the 'wrath of the gods.' When it is suggested that he might be sacrificed, Romana is keen to point out how ancient and not very nubile he is. When they round on the Time Lady instead, the Doctor considers graciously explaining that she's 'past her best', too. A curious battle of wills ensues, interrupted by K9, who shoots his laser at the ceiling, bringing it crashing down around them. All the Norwegians escape.

EVERY DOG HAS HIS DAY *(Picture Strip)*

On the planet Phoenix helpful robots outnumber humans 100 to 1. Romana is perturbed by this – but wait!! What has happened to Romana? She herself looks like a Stepford Wife: like a perfect, doll-faced simulacrum of a *Doctor Who* assistant. Is this just poor characterization, or irony on the artist's behalf? Is it even irony on Romana's part? Given that we know she can 'try on' different 'looks' with a bit of casual regeneration, has she perhaps made herself into a bit of a dolly bird in order to flag up her dissatisfaction with the trad companion role she's been cast in so far. The Doctor, of course, takes absolutely no notice of her hairdo, make-up, outfit, or irony.

Anyhow, they find the Doctor's friend Svenson dead in his laboratory, and warrior robots are running around with guns. The Tardis team make it out to the planet's surface, where they find scientists hiding in caves. (Curiously: there are more Scandinavian names – Svenson, Daneman – just as there were in the previous story.) They explain that deputy controller Daneman reprogrammed the robots so they could take over and create a universe-conquering army.

K9 is sent to be their Trojan horse. Confronting the computer in control of the revolution, he wins the day the way the Doctor would: by persuasion and a swift spot of reprogramming. A robot revolution comes about as a result, with the industrial worker robots turning their mops and brooms on the soldiers. By the time the Doctor and the others return, they find the computer and the human traitor both dead, and K9 on the throne, wrapped in ermine and gold.

THE VOTON TERROR

Romana groans at the idea of their pretending to be delegates at the Inter-Galactic Conference. The Doctor's interested in hearing the famous sub-microscopic privacy debate, as a result of which the study of extremely tiny alien things was forbidden. 147 different species are present in the chamber and it looks like a nightmarish zoo. The Doctor makes a speech about peace and harmony while some unseen person presses a laser weapon into his back.

While K9 follows, the Doctor and Romana are taken off by a hideous and hostile Numese mud-creature who claims to be nothing like what he seems. It's really a single-eyed, tree-stump-like Voton spy, who reveals himself with huge relish. His plan is to explode a bomb in order to create Inter-Galactic warfare.

Rescued by K9, the Doctor hot-foots it back to the conference and causes an uproar by saying outrageous things about the sub-atomic species present. He gets the Vandelanian ambassador to raise his voice two octaves, thus not producing the exact pitch to set off the Voton bomb. Everyone's lives are saved as a result. However, the security guard has already saved the day and the Doctor needn't have bothered.

SWEET FLOWER OF UTHE

While the Tardis fixes its own plumbing, its occupants are sent out to enjoy Uthe 4 for the day. It's a pleasant spot to discuss wild flowers, but they soon find themselves falling down an endless pit. The Doctor explains that the whole planet is a monument to peace: commemorating the disastrous war in the last century, which left no survivors.

However, they are taken prisoner by soldiers and brought before their Supreme Commander. The Doctor has to break the news to them that their

176

planet has been at peace for the past 127 years. Their captors still firmly believe, however, that above their heads is a radioactive wilderness and endless conflict.

The Computer is responsible for keeping the war going. It has spread disinformation to prolong the conflict in order to justify its existence. The people have been fed terrible illusions, including the vision of the world above as a barren wilderness. The Doctor refutes this by getting K9 to present his specimen of the Uthanian Scatterbud that the Doctor asked him to find, right at the start of their adventure.

Above ground again, the Tardis crew are thanked, and hurry swiftly off for their tea.

Other Content

THE DOGON AND THE WHITE DWARF

Another venture into the worlds of pseudo-science and conspiracy theory for the Annuals, as one writer uses the case of the Dogon tribe, from Mali in Africa, who have some scientifically valid beliefs about the Universe, to suggest a visit by ancient astronauts.

- UFO'S – FACT OR FICTION? – One page spread on UFOs.
- V IS FOR – Venus, Vega, Virgo and Van Allen Belts.
- SPACE SATELLITES – A reasonably detailed look at different types of satellites (plus the claim that sometime in the 'not too distant future', everyone will have their own personal television channel – YouTube, anyone?
- SPACE FACTS – The perennial Annual filler favourite, this time as an A to Z.
- SCANNING THE SKIES – Radio telescopes.
- TOMORROW'S TRAVEL – Jetpacks, electric cars and other futuristic modes of transportation.
- THE CENTOVIAN PROBLEM – Puzzle/board game based on the movement of the knight piece in chess.

Doctor Who Himself

He's at his jauntiest, as 1981 begins. Landing on a new world, keen to repair the ship, he urges Romana to hurry – 'all the shops will be closed!' This is a marked difference to the blood-spattered, sword-wielding doom-merchant of

177

1980. Nothing seems to faze him in 1981. Zapped into a universe of Anti-Matter and faced by a disembodied intelligence, he's making silly quips again. He claims to have made a mini-Tardis for the purposes of brewing the perfect cup of tea. This is a Doctor who has given up on the epistemological quandaries, moral and ethical minefields and cosmic game-playing of recent years. He seems to have lightened up considerably.

He gamely sets aside his vanity when Romana tells the devil-worshipping cult intent on sacrificing him exactly how old and decrepit he is. This is a fallible Doctor, pompous and with foibles.

Monsters and Villains

Garderon on Paradise 1 isn't much of a villain. He can hoodwink human beings, but when the Doctor wakes him up in the night he is easily scared into mending his ways. Similarly, the One in the Universe of Anti-Matter is given short shrift by the Doctor, who soon exposes him for what he truly is. The Votons are nasty-looking, evil-minded creatures, looking something like a tree trunk with tentacles – and Scaroth of the Jagaroth.

Curious Companions?

In her new incarnation, Romana is a more muted presence in 1981. She contributes little to the adventure on Paradise 1 beyond complaining about the distances they have to walk. With her recent regeneration, she seems to have slipped into a more traditional female companion role. Having said that, she does help the Doctor fly the Tardis.

We are reminded that her views and knowledge are decidedly un-earth-centric in 'A Midsummer's Nightmare', when she refers to 'William Wotsisname.' In the same breath she also refers – mind-bendingly, fourth-wall-shattering – to Douglas Adams, finding his work funnier and more useful than the Bard's.

K9 is delightfully pettish and indignant at times in 1981. He pretends to growl like a lion, and he 'turns away in disgust' at the Doctor's endless teasing. He gets his moment of glory in 1981, however, when he liberates the tampered-with robots of Phoenix. After the revolution, he is crowned king of the robots.

He's extremely clever and loyal. In 'The Voton Terror' he understands the orders the Doctor gives him, couched as they are in double negatives. He thanks the official for the stimulating chat they've been having, and trundles busily after his master. K9 is ever reliable, producing the flower from Uthe 4 at precisely the right moment to prove that life has returned to the world above.

Fiendish Wheezes

Garderon creates a fake 'paradise', recruiting human colonists who he turns into slaves, in order to mine valuable minerals. In the nineteen eighties, it seems, villainous plans tend to be about financial scams and dodgy dealing. The terror unleashed by the Voton spy simply consists of wanting to blow up a galactic conference in order to start a great big war, out of which the Votons will emerge victorious. Meanwhile, Daneman, the deputy commander of the robot city on Phoenix simply wants to ensure the robots take over and create an army that will conquer the universe. This is a terribly straightforward era. You can almost hear the Doctor sigh with relief at finding some properly banal evil to contend with.

TV Feedback

The Colony of Death is probably on a minor moon at the edge of the solar system: just as the world of the 'The Sun Makers' is. During this period, the Doctor finds that many planets boast rich corporations turning the human populace into drones and slaves, working them until they drop. The slaves' tales in this story also recall 'Destiny of the Daleks.' Sending faked letters back home is reminiscent of the Chameleons in 'The Faceless Ones.'

The strangely purposeless and indecisive Norwegian Satanists in 'A Midsummer's Nightmare' have a similar basement set-up to that seen in 'Image of the Fendahl.' The robot drones being reprogrammed and turning the tables on their masters in 'Every Dog has his Day' is a clear reminder of 'The Robots of Death.' The spectacular array of space delegates at the conference in 'The Voton Terror' takes us back to 'The Curse of Peladon' and even 'The Daleks' Master Plan.' Delegates can easily turn on each other when placed in close confinement, and many must reside in glass containers of their native atmosphere.

The reception that the Doctor and Romana receive from the Supreme Commander in his base underground on Uthe 4 is reminiscent of the Doctor's scenes with Nyder in 'Genesis of the Daleks.'

Egregious errors

Passing through an 'area of Anti-Matter' is – in the *Doctor Who* universe – a bigger deal than the traffic hazard everyone deems it in 'Alien Mind Games.' What threatens the whole universe in TV's 'The Three Doctors' is made to seem like a blustery day.

Classic moments

The Doctor realises that the One who claims to have transported him to a universe of Anti-Matter is a sham. (He ain't no Omega. The Doctor knows what being trapped in a universe of Anti-Matter feels like.) He simply walks away from his raving enemy, because he fancies a stroll.

K9 gets his moment when they visit Phoenix, the world conquered by robot servants. Sent like the Trojan horse into the complex, he gets the warrior guards to stand aside, and invites the supreme robotic intelligence to engage in a nice chat. 'Exciting, isn't it?' says the supreme robotic intelligence.

What I learned from the Doctor Who Annual 1981

"Then tell us who you are, and what you are doing here,' exhorted Romana.' Exhorted! What a verb. What a great word for Romana's rather high-handed quizzing of the young lad they find in the darkness of an underground lair. One of the reasons I came to love *Doctor Who* fiction – in Annuals and Target novelisations – was the vocabulary. These were words to conjure with. 'Exhorted' is so much better than the more prosaic 'asked'. Somehow it lets us see the pique on Romana's face; we can hear the frost in her Time Lady voice.

Illustrations

The whole look of the 1981 has taken a few steps back through time. Rather than its immediate predecessors, the illustrations look more like those in the Annuals of the Pertwee years. We're back in 1974 or 1975. Bold, multi-hued pictures adorn these somewhat more straightforward tales. The picture strip is particularly childish in its execution: a million miles from the sophistication of 'The Weapon' or 'The Power' in recent years. This is much more rudimentary work, aimed at a much younger audience. It's hard to tell if this is a result of orders from the BBC, or simply the result of a change of artist. Whatever the practical reasons, the course of the Doctor Who Annuals has changed again, following several years of gradual, astonishing evolution.

Omnibuses

1981 brought us 'The Five Faces of Doctor Who' on TV, in which old Doctors and their dear, half-familiar, half-forgotten faces got themselves some air-time once again after seven delightfully long years of Tom Baker. Baker had just left the show, and it was time for the audience at home to remember that there had, in fact, been other Doctors previous to his triumphant reign, just as there would be new ones in the future. 'Five Faces' was a tremendously exciting series of repeats, with a new Doctor turning up every week, and a chance for young fans to watch episodes from back in the day (with their parents talking all the way through about how this was proper *Doctor Who*, back from the old days, when it was really, properly frightening and hadn't turned silly yet…)

At much the same time, similarly bridging the gap between Fourth and Fifth Doctors (and for me – even more scarily – Junior and Secondary school) World Distributors published 'Doctor Who: Adventures in Time and Space' which might well be described as a 'bumper volume.' World were delving into their own back pages, and reprinting a number of classic stories from the Doctor Who Annuals of old. Each of the first four Doctors were represented, in this almost two hundred page-long extravaganza. The text stories, picture strips and non-fiction pieces reached back to the very first Annual and, for fans of the time, it was very much like being able to travel back in time yourself – from the earliest, rudimentary artwork from the 1960s, to the psychedelia of the late sixties and early seventies and into the more gloomy, surreal adventures of the nineteen seventies. To a child of the seventies such as myself, it was the darker, recent work that was more familiar, and these earlier phases made for intriguing and exciting comparisons.

It was the first time that all of the Doctors were present in one single book. They were all there on the cover, too – in a montage that had the earlier Doctors circling Tom like ghosts in a mist, looking both grumpy and ethereal – with Davison only just present: wispy in ochre pastels like a tantalising glimpse of the future. Much to my chagrin and – I imagine – that of every other ardent Doctor Who fan of 1981, there was not a single story about the Fifth Doctor in that book.

Material such as the opening article, 'Who's the Doctor?' and features on particular monsters, as well as the stories, 'The Vampires of Crellium' and 'On the Slippery Trail' came from the special 1976 'Typhoo' book, and all in all the choices of reprints made for a somewhat Tom-heavy omnibus, with over half the book originating from the post-1975 era.

In 1986, a WH Smith imprint, Galley Press published a similar 189-page omnibus, 'Doctor Who Special: Journey Through Time.' This was a somewhat updated anthology, bringing in only one story for each of the first three Doctors (though they were well chosen ones: 'Mission for Duh', Death to Mufl' and 'Dead on Arrival' for Doctors One, Two and Three respectively.) Again, the Fourth Doctor was very well represented. Naturally the book took the opportunity to bring in a raft of stories from the Fifth and Sixth Doctors' eras, rounding out the volume very nicely.

The two volumes almost make up a kind of 'Greatest Hits' of the World Distributors Annuals. Since 1986, however, the only place that stories and strips from the Annuals have appeared commercially has been as pdf extras on the 2-Entertain *Doctor Who* DVDs. Surely these must count as some of the most wonderfully generous (albeit strange) extras ever presented on a DVD release for an old TV show..?

However, in actual book form, the Annuals have been for many years missing, out of print, endangered and almost extinct. It's about time, I would say, that there was some lovingly-curated volume or two making these classic adventures available once more.

The 1982 Annual

This is the only Annual to switch Doctors somewhere in the middle. What do we imagine happens here? It depends on whether we think of these stories happening somehow 'in-between' the TV stories, or whether they constitute a whole other, tangential timeline of their own. The first option opens up a whole lot of continuity headaches that some would love to try to solve, explaining inconsistencies, absences and errors. But the second option is, to me, more tantalizing. If this is a separate timeline – a kind of shadow-story compared with what happens on TV in 1981 and 1982, then we have the prospect of one day the Fifth Doctor just turning up mysteriously, and getting on with the job of being Doctor Who. It's gentler and more enigmatic than an actual regeneration story, though it does miss out on the muted and autumnal ringing of the changes that Season 18 achieved. Not that this Annual is without its own unique atmosphere…

The Stories

INTER-GALACTIC CAT

The Doctor, Adric and K9 are travelling towards Earth in 2957 but find themselves somehow drawn instead to a warehouse on a station in deep space. Adric vanishes and the Doctor and K9 discover a CAT – a Composition Adjustment Teleport – which is a toy that messes about with atoms. It is owned by a super computer called Genesis III who speaks in upper case lettering and tells the Doctor that it was he who brought him here, in order to brag about his experiments in miniaturization, and how he's built a whole planet in an atom of carbon. Now he wants the Tardis and the Doctor's brain so that he can master all of time and space.

Adric finds himself on a misty jungle world, where he is soon captured by green-uniformed soldiers who are at war with soldiers in blue. His mention of recently having been on Space Station Alpha piques their interest, and it seems that, to their ears, he's speaking some kind of prophecy. Somehow he is meant to end this long-running war. No sign of that happening just yet, as Blues attack and everyone has to swim for safety, only to be picked up at gunpoint by Reds.

Genesis III reveals to the Doctor that Adric is caught up in the CAT machine, where the perfect inter-galactic army is being created. The Doctor manages to pilot the Tardis into the tiny planet, and back through the accelerated ages, to rescue Adric as he's being put on trial by the people of Red City. Next follows a contest of knowledge and the Doctor conquers the machine by tying him up with the absurd logic of the story of 'Puss-in-Boots.'

184

While the machine is tangled up the Doctor pulls its plug and sets about rescuing all the miniature soldiers.

CONUNDRUM

When the Doctor and Adric play chess in the Tardis, pieces start vanishing seemingly of their own accord. Responding to a space distress call, the Tardis materialises inside another Tardis. Worse than that: it has somehow materialised inside *itself*. This could be something to do with them being in that weird place, E-Space.

The Doctor and Adric become separated in the corridors of the Tardis, which are altering and switching about all around them. Everything is in 'a constant state of flux.' The Doctor seems to be chasing himself about the place – convinced that an intruder has made off with his emergency scarf. The mad logic of the story appears to be getting to him. "All right, keep the scarf!" he bellowed after the thief. 'See if I care!"

The eruption of fairy tale logic and *Alice in Wonderland* grumpiness made a huge impression on me, reading this Annual as a child. The frivolity that had been squeezed out of the TV show at the start of the nineteen eighties was still present here – in spots – between the cardboard covers of the Annual.

When the three friends are reunited the Doctor seems to have solved the mystery. He makes a Mobius strip out of paper, demonstrating that its loops actually only consist of one continuous surface, and telling Adric that they are in a place where this same 'contorted logic' has 'run wild'. The space alarm they heard at the beginning was actually their own – sent out by K9 who, thinking about it, has been less than no help in this perplexing adventure.

PLANET OF PARADISE

Elystria looks very different from the last time the Doctor was here, about 150 years ago. Then it was a paradise world inhabited by peaceful humanoids and now it's a bit of a dump. K9 sees off a robot chasing after a ragged man, who is grateful to be rescued. He takes the Doctor and his friends to an underground base, where bedraggled survivors are congregating. To his dismay, the Doctor learns that his old friend Vayla, ruler of this world when he was last here, is apparently responsible for the present situation.

The Doctor declares his intention to put things right. He will set off to penetrate the stronghold of the evil robots, 'discover what evil exists there,' and then he and his friends 'will destroy it.' He asks Sklar – the man they rescued earlier – to accompany them.

This so far rather humourless story is developing into a kind of archetypal tale. It is almost the *Doctor Who* ur-text: a planet of subjugated humans and a stronghold of robots. The Doctor's decision to free the former from the latter, with the help of his friends. It's a little bit stark, so far.

185

Inside the stone stronghold our heroes discover workshops where robots are creating other robots, and the Doctor remembers how Vayla was planning to hand over all menial tasks to his metal creations. But evil has somehow crept in. There is, of course, a robot Supremo – and Vayla himself is looking glazed and defeated and shoved to one side. The Doctor's friends set about creating noise and confusion to discombobulate the deadly robots. A lovely image is conjured – of Adric dancing about the place waving the Doctor's endless scarf, and K9 shouting loudly. (But what is he shouting? What on Earth is he doing to cause the necessary hullaballoo? This is something I would love to have seen on TV.)

I must say, the humanoid inhabitants of this world are all a bit wet. The Doctor rescues Vayla – who goes limp in his arms, and meanwhile, we are told, Sklar is hanging around outside looking terrified. No wonder the robots walked all over them. I can imagine that the Doctor is trying hard not to let his impatience show, which is tactful for him.

Suddenly all the robots stop working and everyone is mystified. Adric has saved the day by pocketing a panel labelled 'The Co-ordination Control.' He seems to be more useful in his Annual adventures than ever he was on TV.

PLAGUE WORLD (Picture Strip)

Publius is a colony world, where a terrible plague has been unleashed. The Doctor, Adric and K9 find a village of thatched cottages all quiet, and a public meeting going on. The rustic peasantry are being dictated to by their leader, Bremar, who sits on her golden throne in her slinky pink gown. She's telling dissidents like Stylo that if they don't like how she does things, then they're free to leave.

Adric causes a kerfuffle, speaking out against Bremar, and a fight breaks out. Kidson the musician (he has a lute on his kitchen table) rescues the Doctor and hides him in his cottage. Kidson fills the Doctor in on Bremar's terrible rise to power. She was only a 'simple technician' in the beginning, but now she's All That.

The Doctor decides that she's got some kind of electronic mind control going on. Kidson takes him flying in his strato-cruiser, and shows him the 'lair of the Druden', who are dreadful green insect people who want to take over the world. They have spread a kind of plague virus among the human beings and Bremar watches, delighted, as they all drop dead. Hanging from shackles (with K9 lying heart-breakingly nearby on his side) Adric listens in as Bremar phones her insect masters and tells them that everything – including the plague-antidote that she is taking – is working out fine.

The Doctor watches the hideous Druden feeding diseased human flesh to their pupating young. It's a horrible image, rendered in Dan Dare cartoon-style. One of the Druden is speaking into an old-fashioned phone to the quisling Bremar, giving her further instructions and looking very pleased with himself.

The Doctor reactivates K9, who zaps Bremar, who can't activate the matter transmitter, which means the Druden can't go to the village, and now the young are hatching too soon, and they'll die. Kidson does the noble thing, using his strato-cruiser to blow the awful insects up. The Doctor runs away and, in a final frame, does one of those quick catch-up things with Adric, explaining how K9 has managed to make enough antidote to save the whole world and now the colony will prosper. In fact, they're harvesting crops as they speak.

It's incredible how much happens – and so quickly! – in this human colony / evil insects / flesh-eating pupae / human traitor / evil queen / space plague story. It's teeming with classic, standard, regulation *Doctor Who* tropes, in a way that the TV show was desperately missing at the time. In a strange reversal of fortunes, it is as if the writer(s) of the Annual this year were more familiar with *Doctor Who* than many of the writers of the TV episodes.

JUST A SMALL PROBLEM

They should be on Xiter in 4095, during daylight hours, but all is dark outside the Tardis. The Doctor reasons that they must be in an underground cavern, but K9 helps him realise the truth: that they have materialised inside the belly of a huge beast. Here they meet a bad-tempered Xiterian, who was swallowed along with four others, who he fears must have been digested by now. When the gastric juices come rumbling after them, everyone runs for the Tardis, which the Doctor manages to rematerialise outside the beast – which they now see is the size of a football field.

He's the giant pet of the emissaries from Pflugon, who got left behind when their mission was over. Somehow the atmosphere of Xiter has made him swell up to tremendous proportions and his owners don't want him back like this. The Doctor has a handy device that shrinks the gigantic wolf to the size of a spider. Adric pops it into a matchbox.

Once they are in flight, taking the creature home to Pflugon, the Doctor realises that his maxi-minimiser is damaged and its effects are wearing off. The Doctor fixes it and Adric bravely volunteers to be a guinea pig. The expanding Pflugon beast is shrunk down to a manageable size once more.

And that's the end of the final Annual story to feature the Fourth Doctor. His very last act is to put a monster in a matchbox and to praise Adric. After such a long and crazy life, and so many adventures and mind-duels and space warps and hideous reunions and terrifying times when he wasn't even sure if he hadn't gone crazy or not. After all those Sinister Sponges and skull-faced Neuronic fiends, he's just going to fade away gently and hang up his woolly scarf. And, when we see him next, he will be quite a different person.

187

THE KEY OF VAGA

The new Doctor and Adric arrive on a hostile world in the Eighth Dimension. Vaga is the most unfriendly place there is, the Doctor announces, and fills in a bit of the terrifying history of the place, explaining how nearly everyone wound up dead. The Vagan scientists invented a craft not unlike the Tardis and so a few people survived. They can be summoned back by using the dimensional Key of Vaga, which the Doctor apparently helped to design, and which he now points out, rather casually.

It seems they've arrived just at the right moment because something odd is happening with the tower that houses the Key. They run towards it, with the Doctor spouting gobbledegook about why he couldn't make a short hop here in the Tardis. Then he comes out with more gibberish as he sets to work with the sonic screwdriver.

Was the Fourth Doctor ever so neurotically garrulous? This new Doctor is nervously unsure of himself in his first adventure.

There are explosions and upheaval and the Doctor spots the enemies of the Vagans – Pyrons – hiding amongst the crags. They are in a spaceship like a shark, stationed between our heroes and the Tardis. The Doctor decides to make a run for it, zig-zagging all the way to draw their fire. He will send the Tardis into another dimension for about an hour. A lot of exploding and swinging about in spaceships happens after that and the Doctor seems to have fixed things by rigging up a force field. Valtar the Vagan – known to the Doctor from two thousand years ago – pops up looking and sounding rather ethereal. He's pleased those pesky Pyrons have perished by their own hand. He wishes everyone peace and then vanishes into silver mist.

It must be pointed out that only the Fifth Doctor's face appears in these very earliest stories. It's as if all the artists had to hand were a couple of publicity stills of the young actor cast as the new Doctor, and were determined to shoehorn him into the last two stories of the book.

However, even though that seems an obvious ploy, and even though this, in itself, is a slightly unsatisfying story, there is, actually, something quite different in the characterization of the Doctor. He comes across as a bit nervous and overly chatty at the start, just as the Fifth Doctor on TV often was. He seems less sure of himself generally, even after he saves the day. We are entering the age of a slightly less heroic Doctor.

PLANET OF FEAR

Thickly forested Ixos-4 brings out the worst in Adric, who doesn't seem very impressed when the Tardis lands there. He's even less impressed when he sees a giant centipede and a colossal slug coating the Tardis with slime. But the Doctor can't see them. What he can see, however, are the giant earwigs that soon grab hold of the pair of them. The earwigs are friendly telepaths, terrified of giant bat creatures who prey on them. The Doctor reasons that the bats are a figment of the earwigs' imagination, just as the slug was Adric's.

I wonder, if at some point, round about now, Dr. Who's memory doesn't start chiming like the Cloister Bell. Does he perhaps start thinking about giant spiders that believe they're being victimised by gigantic birds? Giant spiders who are actually vast bunnies? For, surely, this planet of Ixos-4 is one that forces you to relive repressed memories of adventures you underwent in previous lives? Specifically from the Doctor Who Annual of 1976?

I have no doubt that the Fourth Doctor would cry foul at once. 'Hang on a minute! I've been through this before! This is like that Psychic Jungle all over again…!' But the Fifth Doctor is more polite and reserved than that. He just frowns in consternation and lets the colossal earwigs tell him their woes. When he leads the way back to the Tardis, the Doctor strolls as if he's enjoying a pleasant afternoon in the park, while Adric and the earwigs cower from their worst imaginings.

Soon the Doctor reveals the truth. This whole planet is alive and sensitive to the primal fears of its visitors. Horrible things become real to every living soul who comes to Ixos-4 and now the Doctor must temporarily neutralise the effect, giving the earwigs time to repair their spacecraft. The earwigs are extremely grateful, just as the giant space rabbits were, back in 1976. I can't help thinking that the Doctor is getting kudos for coming up with exactly the same solution here. He's coasting along on past glories and presenting them as something new.

And, just as Sarah Jane asked the Doctor what hideous things had been drawn out of his subconscious in 1976, so Adric asks him here, right at the end of the 1981 Annual. But he's not saying. He shudders slightly and fobs the young Alzarian off.

Yet we long-term followers of the Doctor's Annual adventures can't help wondering if he was besieged by the same horrors his previous self witnessed in the Psychic Jungle, or those that his self before that found inside his own bouffanted head back in 1975.

Other Content

- THE PLANETS – How much do we know about them?
- SECRETS OF THE TARDIS – More 'basics facts' than 'secrets' for anyone likely to be reading the Annual.
- THIS 'N' THAT – The writers aren't even pretending there's much of a link between the facts on these pages now, are they?
- THE BIG BANG THEORY – Short piece on the Big Bang, possibly prompted by the tv story 'Castrovalva' (though that script was not yet public knowledge at the time).

189

- SPACE SHORTHAND- Astronomical symbology.
- STAR GAZING AT THE LONDON PLANETARIUM – A history of, aNd advert for, the Planetarium.
- THE MYSTERIES OF METEORITES – Quite a science heavy analysis of meteorites ('the carboniferous chondite class have been found to include amino acids').
- KEEPING A WATCH ON SPACE- What manmade objects are floating about in space?
- THE DEADLY GRAPEFRUIT – Disappointingly, a discussion of Plutonium.
- COSMIC QUIZ – Quiz.

Doctor Who Himself

The Doctor is at his quirkiest, silliest best at the start of this Annual. He's chirpy and good at answering back to mad super-computers: 'I don't suppose some small part of your circuitry makes tea, does it – conquering the universe can be a tiring business…' He defeats the super-computer Genesis III by using fairy tale logic and his imagination. His foes come a cropper because his mastery of whimsy unsettles them. He is like the Mad Hatter set free at large upon the universe, and quite a lot cheerier than the rather sombre version of the Fourth Doctor that his final year on TV presented.

When the Tardis materialises inside itself the Doctor gets a terrific line: "Look, there's my emergency scarf – in case I lose this one." It's a line much wittier than anything in 'Logopolis', from which the mind-bending imagery is nicked. It's a wonderfully in-character line for the Fourth Doctor – capturing his mock-indignation and off-kilter focus.

For the first and only time that I know of we get a brief glimpse of the Doctor's bedroom, which is compared to 'an untidy child's toy cupboard.'

It almost seems as if the Fourth Doctor has mellowed with age. When Adric is reluctant to explore caverns he is told: 'We needn't stay long if we don't like it here.' It almost sounds as if the most headstrong and heedless Doctor is going soft.

When he turns overnight into his Fifth incarnation, no one mentions it. There is only Adric left who might notice that the Doctor's persona has changed. K9 has mysteriously vanished. The Doctor is younger, and less certain in his actions. He seems to gabble about everything going through his mind during his first story – baffling Adric and the reader with backstory, exposition and various explanations, whereas his earlier self would just have said something flippant and made saving the whole of Dimension Eight look like a doddle.

Monsters and Villains

Genesis III the super-computer, one thousand years in the future – with his big plans and tiny planets. His appalling arrogance means that he submits to a duel of minds with the Doctor which, as we know by now, is always a terrible idea. Bremar the human traitor on 'Plague World' is a worthy foe for the Doctor – subjecting her people to a terrible disease and then feeding them to alien insect babies. The gigantic Pflugon's wolflike pet is an impressive monster, but all it really wants is to eat people.

Curious Companions?

Adric crops up for the first time. The very first story he appears in has him disappear almost at once. His role is the traditional companion's role – to be kidnapped and embroiled in danger, as soon as the Doctor's back is turned. His arrival on the miniature world brings a nice memory of his back story, his brother and his origin on Alzarius, in a rare moment of Annual / TV show continuity overlap.

Adric is a lot more light-hearted and content in this Annual than he is on TV: 'Every day spent with the Doctor held surprises in store.' He's brave, too: 'I am dispensable', he tells the Doctor. 'Even if I perish (in testing out the maxi-minimiser machine) you will be able to land the ship safely.' However, when the new Doctor turns up – younger, more hesitant and less boastful – Adric starts getting a bit cheeky. He moans about the new planets they visit, pulling a face at how they smell and how boringly leafy they are.

K9 is his calm, sanguine self, right from the off. Except when his sensors are detecting danger approaching, when he becomes more urgent and shrill. What a fantastic ability that is! What a very convenient method of ramping up spurious tension – it always works a treat!

He doesn't like spending too long travelling inside the Tardis, feeling the need for solid ground, just as Earth dogs do when they've been cooped up inside their masters' cars. He's generally present in these stories in order to provide information, and he always has a perfect get-out clause when he doesn't know the answers: 'Insufficient data to analyse situation.' This is his response when faced with anything outré or surreal, and he's on steadier ground when the story is more prosaic.

Occasionally, though, he oversteps the mark on the information-giving front, explaining to the Doctor what the universe consists of and what atoms are, but at this point the Doctor appears to be in a good enough mood not to care about being patronised by a tin dog. They're old friends and, what's more, every moment with K9 counts, since he is due to exit this Annual somewhere in the middle, with no explanation at all. He just trundles off into a separate universe…

Fiendish Wheezes

The super computer Genesis III has created miniaturised worlds in order to breed an army of super soldiers that will take over the universe for him. Bremar of 'Plague World' has been collaborating with her insect over-lords to get rid of all of her fellow colonists.

1982 isn't a great year for villainous masterplans. A lot of time is taken up by witless armies of robots, insects, invisible viruses, giant dogs and telepathic planets that make your worst fears manifest.

TV Feedback

Some effort has gone into aligning the annual stories and illustrations with the TV show. Right from the start of the first story – with its mentions of the Doctor's yo-yo, the hat stand in the console room, and the accurate depiction of both Adric and K9, we are in a universe more closely related to TV *Doctor Who* than the late Seventies' Annuals ever were.

The stories in this book sometimes echo environments, themes and tropes from the current TV show, almost as if they were responding sensitively to the imaginative ripples sent out from one tangential timeline to another or, perhaps more realistically, the artists and writers were provided with a set of reference stills from the recent TV show. I prefer to believe the former explanation, though. This is a timeline that contains curious echoes of Season 18 – with its florid jungle worlds, Tardis corridors turned inside out into endless loops and medieval villages on alien planets.

'Conundrum' very obviously echoes TV's 'Logopolis' with the image of the Tardis' Police Box shell materializing inside the Tardis itself. The Doctor tries to explain the oddity by blaming it on their still being in E-Space. This is news to the reader. Is this whole Annual set inside E-Space, or just this story? It's like the Neuronic Nightmare of 1976 all over again: we are in a messed-up universe where anything can happen, and there's apparently very little chance of escape.

'Planet of Paradise' simplifies things nicely again, with a straightforward tale of a world of robots who have revolted against their human masters. The juxtaposition of stone castles with futuristic robots might well have been lifted from the relatively recent TV story, 'The Androids of Tara.' 'I have seen this happen before,' says the Doctor sagely. 'Creator taken over by created.' His encounters with echoes of the Frankenstein myth have occurred quite frequently during the Fourth Doctor's lifetime. We quite often see Creators being attacked by their Creations – from 'Robot' to 'The Brain of Morbius' to the Doctor himself being on the receiving end of grief from his unwanted offspring in 'The Face of Evil'.

Anticipating the Future

There are reverse echoes here of TV's 'Forest of the Dead', with the Doctor separated from his companion, who is living out some virtual reality life, not knowing how they got there.

In 'Conundrum' the warped interior dimensions of the Tardis corridors, looping round each other, and the repeated iterations of the Doctor and his companions are quite clearly repeated in the Matt Smith era on TV: 'The Doctor's Wife', 'Journey to the Centre of the TARDIS' and 'The Name of the Doctor'. Each of them are toying – to a greater or lesser degree – with imagery from this story, which in turn is a reflection of 'Logopolis.' The echoes of *Doctor Who* imagery from story to story sometimes work like a hall of fairground mirrors. It's hard to figure out: unconscious homage, deliberate leitmotif, postmodern sampling or an outright steal..?

Egregious errors

There are questions all the way through this Annual about which universe we are in. 'Conundrum' places us quite firmly inside E-Space, as per much of Season 18 on TV. E-Space being that 'mysterious region in which time and space are slightly green.' Elsewhere, the Doctor is talking about old friends on planets they visit. And Adric is erroneously aware of the same galactic history as the Doctor. Obviously Adric originates from a different universe to the Doctor, but the mistake raises intriguing possibilities. Could E-Space contain alternate versions of worlds from ordinary space? Is it somehow parallel to the universe *Doctor Who* normally takes place in? Is E-Space actually the universe of the Annuals?

Alternate universes are usually the best way of covering up, explaining or burying egregious errors.

Classic moments

The Doctor explaining the story of Puss-in-Boots to the megalomaniacal CAT computer that TALKS IN CAPITAL LETTERS ALL THE TIME. The Doctor chasing after a reflection of himself through the illogical Möbius strip of the Tardis corridors. The spectacle of K9 distracting the deadly robots of Elystria by piping loads of noise down his metal nose like a party blower.

The kerfuffle caused on 'Plague World' when Adric speaks out against Bremar the tyrant is a very entertaining moment: 'SEIZE THEM AND THEIR METAL DEVIL!' being one of my favourite lines from the Annuals.

The Doctor blithely refusing to acknowledge his most primal fears as they manifest themselves around him is another classic moment. We've seen it before and we'll see it again. He can be very tight-lipped about what it is he's most afraid of. It's one of his most beguiling mysteries, and we feel sure that one day we will find out the truth. What is he endlessly running away from?

What I learned from the Doctor Who Annual 1982

If completely surreal things happen to you – such as being whizzed onto a planet no bigger than a mote of dust, or finding yourself in a world turned inside out and getting chased by a doppelganger – don't fret. It's because you're in a region of space-time where the laws of physics don't work in the way that you're used to. It's not you going mad, or losing your grip. It's just the way things are round here. You'll soon get the hang of it.

When you've got an old friend who's in charge of a whole planet and he explains that he's going to create an army of robots to do all the dirty work? Just warn him first what's likely to happen.

In the Doctor Who Annuals, if you regenerate and suddenly appear as a completely different person, old friends, companions and enemies are much too tactful to mention it.

Illustrations

Glenn Rix illustrates the Annuals of the Davison years, 1981 – 1984 inclusive.

Just as this Annual tides us over from the era of the Fourth to the Fifth Doctors, some kind of change is coming to the illustrations. Some stories – such as 'Planet of Paradise' – have the same kind of smudgy obscurity as the stories of the late Seventies. They appear to be happening in the same badly-lit, rather grotesque universe. But elsewhere those heavily-inked swirls are becoming a little lighter. It is becoming possible to see what's actually happening in the pictures. In some pictures the style becomes more cartoonish and child-friendly. The picture strip, 'Plague World' is very happily unsophisticated, looking very much like something out of the 1960s. There is a deliberate, gradual evolution from the murkiness and complexity of recent years into something much more suitable for young children. Christmas 1981 was the end of an era in more ways than one.

The 1983 Annual

There's an extra liveliness to these adventures for the new Doctor at the start of the nineteen eighties. The writer has discovered short, declarative sentences and the exclamation mark: 'The Doctor knew what he had to do. He was going outside!' There is something very endearing about the straightforward, unabashed pep of it all, and the spirited way the text bounces along. The book even has a flavour of the Boy's Own tales belonging to the era that the Fifth Doctor's outfit evoked.

The Stories

DANGER DOWN BELOW

The Doctor has come to Aronassus 49 in response to a call from an old friend, High Minister Threll of the Prime City Triumvirate. Tegan's slowing him down as they trek across a blazing desert. They find the populace starving because an alien being is taking all their food. The Doctor has found one of the deadly tennis balls with which the alien menace is defending itself. Before the Doctor can help there is a violent revolution, and the Doctor, Tegan and Threll are surprised to find themselves helped by one of the alien balls.

In a cavern beneath the city they are confronted by a tentacled, amoeba-like creature that the Doctor recognises as a Migrator from Andromeda. Solitary and voracious, they're only supposed to take up residence on empty worlds. The Doctor brings the Tardis and sets about the tricky task of squashing the amorphous mother-to-be through the Police Box doors.

THE GOD MACHINE

Out exploring alien pyramids on a stormy night Tegan and Nyssa both go missing. The exasperated Doctor investigates, soon coming across a bunch of once-peaceful locals who have returned to worshipping their god, Vi'Al. Sacrifice is high on their agenda, and so is the offering of priceless jewels. The Doctor is very suspicious and dons a ritualistic gown in order to inveigle himself into the holy of holies.

Deep inside the pyramid the Doctor finds five intergalactic pirates are behind the whole murky business, and he also finds his female companions and several pleased-looking natives, who take their revenge upon the false gods.

THE ARMAGEDDON CHRYSALIS

Voorvolika is an intelligence probing the Doctor and his companions' minds, and draining the Tardis of all power. First Nyssa and then the others are drawn to the Observation Room, which gives an unimpeded view of the Ship's surroundings. The Tardis appears to be engulfed by a sickeningly suckered creature of some kind which, the Doctor realises, is draining the travellers' life energies away.

He takes a drug illegal on most planets in order to pep him up. He slips into a space suit and emerges from the Tardis into the gurgling sliminess of Voorvolika's insides. Dr. Who makes ghastly progress through the vibrating, sticky, jelly-like walls of a Freudian nightmare. The muscular walls contract about him, threatening to crack his protective helmet...

ON THE PLANET ISOPTERUS (Picture Strip)

The Doctor is messing about with a wristwatch that he claims is a kind of 'dream machine' that he has picked up on his 'time travels.' 'Huh?' demands an unhealthy-looking Adric.

Crossly, Tegan agrees to volunteer as a guinea pig, and dreams that she's in a field of lovely flowers (though I remain unconvinced that's what Tegan would choose to make manifest, given a choice of anything at all.)

They land on a planet a little like the Vortis so beloved of the First Doctor and soon are captured and coated in a sticky substance that renders them immobile. Once in the termite mound they are informed by a man with a high forehead that they will be eaten by these mutant insects. Luckily, the Doctor remembers his handy dream-machine and conjures the illusion of lush green forests on the other side of the world, drawing the giant termites away...

THE HAVEN

The Tardis team visit Planet 435 and discover it's a paradise compared to what they were expecting. A very calm, ageless man called Carnak welcomes them to the Haven and they discover a collection of almost fifty thousand cryogenically frozen human beings. A bit of snooping around reveals the fact that, with the help of electronic implants, Carnak is treating the frosty humans as his personal slaves. The only way that the Doctor can avoid the same fate for himself and his friends is to engage in mind-combat with Carnak. Now, as long-term readers of the Annual know, this kind of psychic wrestling match is something that Dr. Who positively looks forward to, and always finds a doddle. Is there, though, a touch of hesitation in the Fifth Doctor in this moment? As the youngest, most seemingly vulnerable of his incarnations goes off to prove his mettle?

THE PENALTY

Struck down by Ponassan fever, the Doctor has been tended to by Nyssa and Tegan for a couple of days. While they have coffee and fret in his Tardis bedroom the Doctor sweats and tosses and has some very strange dreams. For the rest of the story we plunge into his unconscious mind, meeting old friends and enemies – some of whom greet him warmly and others who curse his very name. Then he is racing through highlights of several unseen and rather exciting-sounding adventures. Eventually the fever breaks and he is left to wonder whether such an awful time is the inevitable price for a life as full and exciting as his.

NIGHT FLIGHT TO NOWHERE

Tegan is delighted to be back at Heathrow airport (again) in order to catch up with her friend and fellow air stewardess, Julie. The Doctor isn't quite so keen on a humdrum reunion, and seems almost relieved to uncover a nefarious plot.

He finds that his old enemy the Master is planning to replace a whole planeload of VIPs with sinister robots and eventually to take over the world. Just before the Master can fly the plane through a 'gash' he's created in the fabric of space-time the Doctor manages to pilot the Tardis safely and miraculously aboard. There follow classic scenes of the Master gloating, of mass hallucination and finally a full-out punch-up between the Doctor and Master in the flight cabin as the plane teeters on the brink of a celestial gash.

Other Content

BEHIND THE SCENES AT DOCTOR WHO: VISUAL EFFECTS

Finally, World Distributors think to include some behind the scenes content in the Annuals! And given the restrictions of a one and a half page spread in an Annual aimed at the Christmas market, it's a decent first attempt, with a long interview with designer Simon Macdonald, who discusses special effects on the show in general and on the story 'The Visitation' in particular.

BEHIND THE SCENES AT DOCTOR WHO: THE PRODUCER

No interview this time, but a text heavy two page spread on John Nathan-Turner and the details of his job (plus, oddly, a definition of the word clapperboard).

BEHIND THE SCENES AT DOCTOR WHO: SET DESIGN AND COSTUME

Photos from the set of 'Castrovalva' and quotes from the Set and Costume Designers from that serial round off the three part Behind the Scenes series of articles.

- OUR NEIGHBOURS IN SPACE – The Solar System and nearby stars.
- ENTER PETER DAVISON AS DR WHO – Illustration of the Dr Who's new outfit, designed by Colin Lavers.
- COMING IN TO LAND- What goes on in an air traffic controller tower?
- WHAT IS A LIGHT YEAR? – A demonstration of how that value is calculated.
- A PROBLEM FOR YOU – A surprising puzzle, which isn't really a puzzle – list 15 essential items in order of importance to a spaceman stranded 200 miles from his mother ship. 'There is no 'correct' answer' we are warned...
- THAW FOR 25,000 YEARS – The possibility of life on Mars.
- WILL OUR SUN ALWAYS SHINE? – No, but there's no need for immediate concern, apparently.
- TO THE FAR PLANETS – How do probes manage to travel to the likes of Jupiter and Saturn?
- BLACK HOLES – What do we know about them?

Doctor Who Himself

He's 'ever-eager', and disappointed when his companions want to have a rest or complain about the hectic pace of things. He has respect for all life forms and loathes violence of any kind. A little bit too trusting at times, the Doctor takes for granted that the Tardis databanks are correct when they declare a planet's inhabitants docile and peaceful. At the same time, he's a little cynical about planet 435 seeming to be a paradise. He's expecting it to show its true, sinister face at any moment.

It's pleasing to note that the Doctor still goes around with a handy piece of wire in his pocket, for the purpose of springing open locks and handcuffs. He has a habit of leaving adventures half-done. He will have to return one day to save the universe from a full-grown Voorvolika, and hopes that one day the dome-headed humanoids of the termite world will be able to return home. At these moments the Doctor conveniently forgets he has a time machine and could, if he wanted, nip forward to sort things out this very moment.

The Fifth Doctor is slightly sickly. Tegan and Nyssa have to carry him in 'The Haven' and 'The Penalty' begins with him being poorly again, just as he often was on TV. The latter story sees him confronting his subconscious fears, just as he did in those earlier Annual stories, most notably in 1975. The Doctor on this occasion is wrestling with the spectres of old friends who turn against him, and of some of his more exciting (unseen) adventures in the past. While the Fourth and Third Doctors faced fears relevant to those earlier personalities, this Doctor confronts his terror of failing in the role he has inherited. His nightmares are not – as the Third Doctor's were – to do with a hubristic and arrogant alter ego, but rather about failing to save his friends and companions. Again, the Doctor is nicely characterised: the Annual stories seem to get each of the individual Doctors 'right' (apart from, of course, the Second, who was never quite 'right' on the A4 page.)

Monsters and Villains

The Migrators are hungry blobs with tentacles that float through space looking for unpopulated planets where they can reproduce. They don't have much to say for themselves. Voorvolika is another slimy organic mass, inside of which the Tardis materialises, forcing the Doctor into a hideously sticky adventure. Carnak with his fifty thousand frozen slaves is a formidable foe but he is as nothing beside the towering genius that is the Master, who makes his first, triumphant appearance in the Doctor Who Annual since 1974.

Curious Companions?

Tegan is moaning and rubbing her feet in the very first page of the 1983 Annual. In moments of danger she wishes she never blundered aboard the Tardis and met the Doctor. When we are told that Tegan 'fell moaning' to the floor it's not always clear whether she is falling and groaning involuntarily, or falling and continuing to raise loud objections to her current situation.

Nyssa often gets left out of adventures. In the affair of the 'Danger Down Below' she is startled to find the horrible body of a Migrator squishing into the console room unannounced, and pressing her up against the wall. Her latent psychic abilities lead her to be the first affected by the telepathic approaches of Voorvolika.

Adric makes a startling appearance in the picture strip, 'On the Planet Isopterus,' just after the reader has come to assume that the stories in the 1983 Annual all occur after his onscreen death in 'Earthshock.' However, here he is, slightly smaller than life and looking somewhat unhealthily jaundiced.

Fiendish Wheezes

A giant pupating creature in space absorbs passing specks of matter in order to sustain itself. An old-ish man prolongs his life by having fifty thousand zombified slaves wait on him hand and foot. The Master has thought up a splendid and non-convoluted plan for taking over the world.

TV Feedback

The Fifth Doctor concentrating very hard and then going limp and lying or falling down is a very familiar image from TV *Doctor Who* of this era. He was forever passing out and leaving his companions to get on with things. Nyssa and Tegan have to wheel him about in 'The Haven' just as they did in his TV debut, 'Castrovalva.'

The Doctor's fever dreams in 'The Penalty' are clearly influenced by the sequence of vintage clips presented during 'Logopolis'. They also anticipate similar moments in 'Mawdryn Undead' and 'The Caves of Androzani.' Rather pleasingly, the flashback moments in 'The Penalty' are to specifically Annual-ish monsters and aliens, and the companions alluded to – Jamie, the Brigadier, Leela and Romana – are those who made significant appearances in the Annuals. On TV in the early Eighties *Doctor Who* was revelling in and recycling its own past. It's quite charming to find the Annual doing much the same. How much more exciting though, would it have been to gain glimpses of the Sinister Sponge, the Mind Extractors and the Fishmen of Kandalinga?

'Night Flight to Nowhere' echoes the abducted passengers and duplicates from TV's 'The Faceless Ones.' It also shares some locations and ideas with the much more recent, poor, lamentable 'Time-Flight' and, quite fittingly, pisses on it from 30,000 feet.

Classic moments

The Doctor produces something that looks like a tennis ball and tells his friend Threll that this is what is killing all his people. Investigating the hideous

201

sticky interior of Voorvolika, the Doctor feels the tunnel walls start to contract and press in all around him in a very scary and classic moment.

The Doctor's nightmare in 'The Penalty' is one long classic moment. Similarly, 'Night Flight to Nowhere' scintillates with great moments, not least the dust-up between the Doctor and Master. I'm also rather fond of the scene in the Heathrow departures lounge in which Tegan is shouting after her friend Julie. She's waving, shouting 'You hoo!' and the Doctor is groaning. But Julie walks straight past, with a robot-like impassive expression on her face. Thinking of this story, I'm tempted to wonder whether Julie Harris isn't just *pretending* to be one of the Master's mind-robbed slaves in order to avoid having to catch up with the irrepressible Tegan Jovanka.

What I learned from the Doctor Who Annual 1983

Watch out for tennis balls, false gods and anything in the process of pupating.

Illustrations

The Glenn Rix drawings have a very distinctive style. They are cartoon-like with shading that looks a little like contour lines on a map. This sometimes has the effect of making the characters' clothes look very wrinkled.

The K9 Annual

The *Doctor Who* spin-off pilot 'K9 and Company' from December 1981 is still one of my favourite TV episodes of anything, ever, and I watch it on Christmas Eve, every single year. Everything about it is absolutely perfect, as well as being hilariously duff.

Each year it summons up the exact same sensation of excitement and intrigue and the sheer wonder of seeing Elisabeth Sladen return to the role of Sarah Jane Smith. There there's the bliss of K9 perching nonchalantly on a dry stone wall in the title sequence. Every iota of this festive special is marvellous: the shonky, hi-NRG theme tune (I bought the single at the Blackpool *Doctor Who* Exhibition in October 1982, I loved it that much); the encroaching atmosphere of Christmassy dread brought on by Satanists lurking around a quaint old village. I even loved the fact that Sarah Jane Smith seemed so narky and cross throughout the whole episode. And then there's the fabulous Juno Baker – unctuous and condescending in her red satin nightgown, wafting a glass of sherry about.

Of course, as we know there was no series. Not yet. Not ever, really, in this particular form. Many years later there was, of course, *The Sarah Jane Adventures*, which is a kind of descendent of 'A Girl's Best Friend', but it isn't quite the same. Similarly with the Australian-produced *K9* series. Neither have the sheer awkwardness of this lovely pilot show – this strange cross between 'A Ghost Story for Christmas' and 'Treasure Hunt' with Anneka Rice.

There was no series but there was, however, a repeat during Christmas 1982 and also that year, that miraculous thing: a World Distributors' Annual. A K9 Annual, continuing his adventures with Sarah Jane and dorky Brendon in the village of Moreton Harwood. These six short stories were surely how a series would have played out? The set of associations triggered by a simple perusal of the titles on the contents page is enough to send the young imagination whirring. Sarah and K9's further adventures would obviously have been concerned with Hounds and Shrouds, Monsters, Horror Hotels, Curses and exotically-named menaces. Supernatural mystery would have been our heroes' ideal genre, much more than alien invasions. It was something I knew deep down and was delighted to find the unexpected tie-in Annual corroborating.

My copy still has pressed in its endpapers – like an Edwardian lady diarist would preserve wildflowers, perhaps – the blue party hat that came out of a cracker over Boxing Day lunch at my Big Nanna's. I'd taken my K9 Annual with me to read in the car, up and down the A1 on that forty mile drive. We were allowed to take only one present with us to this family gathering – and were supposed to make sure it was a fancy one, for showing off purposes, we were told. But I didn't care about that showing off stuff. I took my K9 Annual and even had it with me at the dinner table as my Big Nanna – a school dinner lady by profession – served up an amazing feast.

Somehow – like special Annuals tend to – the book absorbed some of the particular atmosphere of Christmas 1982, when I was thirteen. Really, the last Christmas of childhood, I guess. Mine, anyway.

I still read a story from this book every year, very near midnight on most Christmas Eves. Like Victorian patriarchs used to read Dickens to their assembled family: I sit up in bed and revisit the earthly adventures of a star-born dog.

The Stories

POWERSTONE
More occult shenanigans at Moreton Harwood! A robed skeleton is found beneath Aunt Lavinia's manor house and Professor Clay from the nearby university is on hand to tell Sarah Jane all about the wicked cult that used to gather there over four hundred years ago. A collapsing cave killed them all and robbed their modern day counterparts of the 'powerstone' they need to carry out their undoubtedly nasty rituals. Sarah is almost killed in a ditch, and there's a late night race back home in her Mini Metro, just in time to save Aunt Lavinia and Brendon from devil-worshippers and members of the local press.

THE SHROUD OF AZAROTH
Twenty years ago the demise of the last of the De'Ath family supposedly meant the end of the Cult of Azaroth. Now director George Spielberg is in the process of making a film based on their funny goings-on: bedevilled by accidents and even a death. Sarah and K9 are on hand to investigate and are disturbed and threatened in the night, and almost flattened by a heavy lighting rig. A fake lead actor in a devilish goat mask is running about the empty house in swirls of dry ice and there's a splendidly dramatic finish with murdered scriptwriters and sudden revelations and deadly revenge.

HOUND OF HELL
More Satanists! Sarah Jane, Brendan and K9 are hiding out at Druid's Ring just before Midsummer's Eve, watching hooded figures gather to prepare for their 'night of evil.' Sarah busies herself taking photos and realises that the cultists

are building something from branches and stones. An effigy of a dog! A Wicker Hound..! When they are spotted, Team K9 only just manage to escape with their lives. Even so, K9 is badly damaged by gunfire. Brendan tinkers with him overnight and is content to take the credit when K9 trundles off early next morning by himself. He was sounding slightly strange and there's a chance he might have lost his memory and be confused and dangerous as a result.

Sarah winds up on the Satanists' slab on Midsummer's Eve to find that K9 himself has taken pride of place as their object of worship, Ragok. The only way she can save herself is to remind K9 of who he truly is..!

THE MONSTER OF LOCH CRAG

Sarah Jane is holidaying in the Scottish Highlands with her old friend Susan Hamilton. She's waiting in the pub with a couple of drinks, ready for a night of gossip about old times. (What old times, we wonder? Sarah spent much of the late Seventies travelling into deep space with Dr. Who. Worse than deep space: she spent much of 1976 in the Neuronic Nightmare Zone. Is Susan already aware of all this stuff? It strikes me that Sarah Jane might once – on an Earthbound stopover – have introduced Susan to her eccentric, space-faring friend and something dreadful occurred. Has Susan learned to live with that, or did the Doctor have to selectively erase her memory of some bizarre adventure they all shared circa 1977? And, come to that, what does Susan think about Sarah running about the countryside with a robot dog, chasing devil-worshippers?)

Sarah receives a spooky phone call from Susan, and hurries out into the fog around Loch Crag to investigate. It's not long before Sarah's attacked searching Susan's ransacked hotel room and she's involved in a mystery to do with smuggling, monsters, disappearances and the Laird's golden locket.

The story ends with a lovely scene in the hotel bar, and everyone discussing the end of the adventure (which came all in a rush) in much the same way as the pilot episode also finished, with sherry and exposition all round.

HORROR HOTEL

Melissa Lord does not want to take over High Priestess duties for the Satanic coven from her father, hotelier James Lord. Sarah Jane's Mini Metro has broken down and she winds up at the Crag Cliff Hotel (another hotel quite close to Loch Crag perhaps? Is this Sarah and K9 setting off on their journey home from the previous adventure?) Melissa confides in Sarah and her metal pal that she is being forced to become 'part of an evil which she abhorred!' When everything seems hopeless, can K9 cope with his own injuries, a flight of stone steps, and a horde of ruthless cultists?

THE CURSE OF KANBO-ALA

'The defilers will die!' A couple of Indian gentlemen are keeping close tabs on Sarah Jane and friends as they board the train to London. They are taking the archaeological treasures of their deceased relative, Africana Smith, up to London so that they can be put on display and astonish all and sundry. They are marked out as unwitting victims of the revenge of someone called Kanbo-Ala. Their first hint of this comes with the voodoo dolls they find stuck to their sleeper doors. Then Aunt Lavinia goes into convulsions after dinner and Brendan is dragged off by one of the men who poisoned her. K9 is there – naturally – in the nick of time to prevent Brendan being thrown out onto the rails. Meanwhile Sarah learns everything she needs to know about the evil sect of Kanbo-Ala from Africana Smith's diary… and readies herself for a final confrontation in the luggage car..!

Other Content

- INTRODUCING K9
- MEET SARAH JANE SMITH
- CAN YOU FOLLOW INSTRUCTIONS? – A joke disguised as a puzzle.
- THE SHAPE OF TV TO COME – A look at the new cable television services.
- PROFESSOR RUBIK'S CUBE – What it says, two pages on the popular kids' toy, complete with photos of a couple of football players trying their hands at the cube. A misjudgement of their core audience, I suspect!
- TALKING OF TECHNOLOGY – The Annuals still filling space with random technology stuff.
- K9'S QUIZ – Space related questions posed by K9 himself.
- WHAT IS THE SECRET OF THE STANDING STONES? – Europe's Stone Age megaliths examined.
- MYTH OR MONSTER? – The Loch Ness Monster.
- UFOS – IS THIS THE ANSWER? – Is ball lightning the answer to the UFO question?
- ONCE UPON A TIME, THERE WAS A ROBOT... – The history of the robot.
- GHOSTLY GOINGS ON – Some ghostly stories from history.

K9 Himself

He reads road maps beautifully, sitting up in the passenger seat. According to a wistful movie director, K9 would be a smash-hit at the Box Office. He's a dab hand stopping villains in their tracks with his stun beam at exactly the right moment. He's not very good at wading through marshes, but he's incredibly brave: holding his ground against the gun-toting devil worshippers who come after his mistress.

I love the way K9 complains that he's a bit fuzzy because he's still half asleep: 'Confusion regarding present mission due to fact that I was awoken from rest phase and placed into automobile without sufficient explanation or reason.' Good old K9 raises polite passive-aggression into a fine art.

When Sarah's gang are on the train to London and settling into their sleeper compartments, K9 is to be seen apparently 'engrossed in staring out of the window.' There's something very touching about the robot dog being just as mesmerised by the passing scenery as any other travelling dog.

Monsters and Villains

Journalists on local rags and film director's assistants reveal their true craziness and desire for revenge almost every day. Satanist and hotelier James Lord has got his evil shtick down pat. Not only is he happy to brainwash and coerce his daughter Melissa into a life of black magic, his dialogue is solid gold: 'Oh, but she does, Miss Smith. She does.' And: 'It begins.' The followers of 'evil cult' Kanbo-Ala are extremely sinister and seem to hail from some kind of Edwardian era adventure story.

Curious Companions?

The characterization of Sarah Jane continues the TV pilot's beguiling combination of 'intrigued' and 'miffed'. When Professor Clay phones up to suggest a meeting so he can explain the mystery to her she says: 'Well, I don't know. Is it important?'

Throughout the Annual she becomes keener on solving mysteries and getting her nose stuck in. She encounters danger everywhere she goes and is only too grateful that K9 is there to help her out – usually in the most crucial and deadly moments.

Most of her adventures seem to have a supernatural element, but mostly her job as investigator is as debunker. Loch monsters turn out to be submersibles used for criminal ends. Ghosts are faked and cults are worshipping fake gods and doing it just for kicks. There is no sign as yet of Sarah Jane as ufologist and outer space expert, as she was to become in CBBC's 'Sarah Jane Adventures' on TV (surely, along with 'The Tomorrow People' the TV show most crying out for a World Distributors' style Annual?)

Brendan is a useless, clumsy lump. He causes noisy distractions on stake-outs at scenes of satanic goings-on. He's clever, though. He tries to repair the damaged K9, even though he knows the technology hails from far in the future. Brendan thinks mostly of food and burying his nose in computer and science fiction magazines. He even leaves all the deducing up to Sarah Jane: 'Curse? … Dolls on our doors? Aunt Lavinia collapsing? Kanbo-whatever? Sarah Jane, what the devil is going on?'

Aunt Lavinia is full of good sense and won't take any nonsense. She must surely be perplexed by the sheer number of devil worshippers her niece seems to get herself involved with. She is poisoned aboard the sleeper train by the followers of Kanbo-Ala, but still manages to choke out a vital message about the diary.

Fiendish Wheezes

Tobey Gough is a local journalist who also happens to be a keen worshipper of Satan. He knows the vital powerstone is located beneath Aunt Lavinia's house and he pretends to want to write up Sarah Jane for his paper's 'Interesting Neighbours' column. Sarah learns a valuable lesson here about not letting villains in disguise appeal to your vanity. Elsewhere, Lairds dress up submarines as sea monsters for smuggling purposes, High Priests try to bequeath whole cults to their unwilling daughters and Indian devil-worshippers try to exact voodoo-ish revenge on our band of heroes.

TV Feedback

The cowled devil-worshippers of various types in almost all of this Annual's stories are instant reminders of the TV pilot, of course, but this could easily be a feature of the continuing series. As a child I found it quite natural to assume that Sarah and K9 were uncovering a hidden world of ubiquitous Satanic ritual lurking beneath the tweeness of posh people who live in fancy villages. TV *Doctor Who* had already established this as a convention in stories such as 'The Daemons' and 'The Stones of Blood.' The Satanists jumping out from bushes into the middle of the road is a very clear reminder of events in 'A Girl's Best Friend.'

As a reader back in 1982 – and now – I can't help wishing very fervently that just one or two stories could link more directly into the *Doctor Who* universe. Obviously various copyright stipulations, plus the vagaries of good taste would mitigate against the kind of fanwanky suggestions I would make. But a few more alien menaces wouldn't have come amiss, perhaps. Imagine Sarah getting trolled by Zygon replicants? Or the Master turning up on her door? Or UNIT inviting her to their Christmas party and wanting to impound and examine K9? Or, even better, perhaps, the new current Doctor turns up with Tegan and Nyssa to see how Sarah's getting on with her robot chum. Some time after their adventure at Heathrow in the Annual that was published at exactly the same time as this one? For thirty years I've been imagining fan fictions that tie in with this Annual.

There's a lovely moment when Sarah asks for K9 to keep his sensors peeled for telephone boxes on the misty banks of Loch Crag, and her friend starts calculating the likelihood of Dr. Who suddenly arriving in the Tardis. Sadly, Sarah tells him that she's no longer counting on such an intervention. A little later in this story of Lochs and monsters she muses on the creature in Loch Ness – without going into the precise nature of her acquaintanceship with that elusive beast. There is a very nostalgic feeling about having Sarah running about investigating monsters and lairds, just as she did in 'Terror of the Zygons.'

Anticipating the Future

The six stories are clear pointers to where Sarah Jane and K9's adventures could next lead them. These are all quite Scooby-Dooish, in that they involve the debunking and unmasking of villainous human beings and their pretend supernatural escapades. What I long to read about are the encounters that must have ensued, though the Eighties and Nineties and early 2000s, with actual monsters and menaces from beyond the stars. 'The Five Doctors', 'Downtime' and 'Interference' are only tantalizing glimpses. When we properly see Sarah and K9 again much later, they have been up to all sorts of amazing things and the K9 Annual of 1983 has them at the start of that amazing series of untold adventures.

209

Classic moments

A scary and dramatic moment occurs in the marsh, when K9 actually gets hit by Satanist gunfire. Despite his heaviness Sarah Jane picks him up and runs with him back to her Mini Metro.

One of my own favourite moments is when Sarah Jane gets up in the morning and remembers with a heavy heart the damage her robot friend sustained the night before. But when she goes downstairs to breakfast she is told by her Aunt that he has recovered and already left. He's 'gone off on his own devices.' I love the image of him trundling off down country lanes, intent on sorting the mystery out by himself. But then there's a note of discord. He was brusque with Aunt Lavinia and not sounding like himself at all.

K9's sensors indicating a monster in Loch Crag is a classic moment indeed. I can only imagine Sarah's slightly woebegone expression – concern mixed with pique – as she thinks to herself: that's just one more impossible thing to contend with. Later, we get what must be my favourite moment: when the monster knocks her into the water and K9 is left bobbing about in a rowing boat in the middle of the Loch. Or perhaps my favourite moment is the tussle between the Indian gentleman and Brendan in the open doorway of the speeding sleeper train, with the rails flashing by at a nightmarish rate and K9 once again trundling to the rescue with his stun beam at the ready.

What I learned from the K9 Annual 1983

Even after leave-takings, hope-raisings, revivals and cancellations – there are always more adventures to be had and mysteries to be solved.

Illustrations

Charmingly, the illustrations throughout this Annual are reminiscent of artwork in British girls' comics of the era, such as *Bunty* and *Jinty* and the wonderfully Gothic *Misty*. My favourite pictures include Sarah emerging from her Mini Metro after a prang during a rainstorm, and poor K9 lying helplessly on his side in the grassy verge. I also love the image in 'The Monster of Loch Crag' of Sarah Jane letting her metal friend lead her through the curling green mist.

The 1984 Annual

These stories are simple, but there is nothing undercooked or shapeless about them. They are pleasing little parables about learning to live in peace and harmony in a variety of locations in space and time. The Doctor is a force for good and his companions are all-too human – easily scared or imperilled, but with flashes of brilliant insight. Each story has its own wonderfully distinct atmosphere and tale to tell. In many ways, a touch of this simplicity is precisely what the TV show of the time could well have done with. *Doctor Who* on TV in the early Eighties had many charming features, but succinct, concise story-telling making complete and satisfying sense was not one of them.

The Stories

THE OXAQUA INCIDENT

At first it seems as if Ghum of the Theigs is the villain of the piece. He's pretty unprepossessing with his pointed head and his eyeballs out on stalks. The Doctor is trying to talk him out of destroying the power source of his enemies, the Basks. But it's Obedeee of the Basks who ends up being the real villain, chasing the Doctor and his friends into a lethal sandstorm in order to bump them off. Ghum proves his true friendship in the end and saves the day with his extremely pointed head.

WINTER ON MESIQUE

Arriving on a frozen world, the Doctor declares his intention to find an old friend, Sellot, who rules here. He finds the people of this planet barricaded in against a hard winter, and menaced by an exploding population of coypu and also a race of carnivorous Abominable Snowmen who have come down from the mountains. One of the Sasquatches is taken prisoner and the Tardis team go to look where it sits doleful and starving in its cell. Tegan realises that these creatures could be fed the rampant rodents, thus solving two problems in one. The Doctor is keen to broker peace on Mesique, and is delighted to announce the Yeti's pregnancy.

THE CREATION OF CAMELOT

Tegan and the Doctor are startled to find themselves right in the middle of Arthurian legend, and coming face to face with the impressive king himself in his throne room. There is a delicious twinge of foreboding when Arthur mentions that he has heard the word 'Tardis' before. Tegan realises before anyone else that the king's trusted Merlin must actually be the Master, in one of his cunning disguises. It is he who has ensured that the baby Mordred has survived in order to fulfil his eventual regicidal destiny, and also he's been encouraging the Saxons to invade. But the Master – though piqued at the Doctor's unexpected presence – is sly as ever. He suggests to King Arthur that Dr. Who is the evil-doer after all..! The Doctor has his work cut out, putting all the legends back on track.

CLASS 4 RENEGADE

On Melphis in the 23rd Century, the Doctor and his friends are cornered by a three-headed space pilot who has lost his robot. The Doctor agrees to help – possibly out of pity after hearing DaSamPete's tale of being reassembled from broken bits of three bodies by aliens who had never seen a human being before. So off the Tardis trio goes in a Hovva-Hoppa to a Robo-Mart looking for a cheap Class 4. It's all getting a bit *Star Wars* at this point, and the Doctor realises that he and his friends have been tricked into doing 'The Brothers'' dirty work for them.

THE VOLCANIS DEAL

An inhospitable world of lava, dust, sulphur and acid is the next destination for the Doctor and Turlough. After lobbing a cricket ball into the far distance they leave pretty sharpish, but experience queer after-effects. The Doctor believes his cricket bat has turned into a venomous snake and Turlough thinks his Time Lord friend has sprouted a second head.

A message about brainwashing draws them to the planet Ilium, where the Doctor is put very briefly on trial for trespassing. When he returns to Turlough he quite calmly explains how criminals of Ilium are brainwashed, given new memories and are sent to Earth – just as the British once sent their own undesirables to Australia. (How I wish Tegan was in this story, just to hear her reaction to this.)

Just as we think there's going to be a twist – there isn't.

THE NEMERTINES

'This might be nasty,' warns the Doctor, as he and his friends help out the Brigadier with a horrible case of worms. They're back in London where the Thames is seething with mutants and the Doctor is working with UNIT again. There's a man with all his bodily fluids drained down by the river and, with the Doctor at the microscope in the UNIT lab, it's just like old times again.

There is an actual dullish diagram about osmosis and semi-permeable membranes and then news that it's all to do with a chemical research plant in Oxford. It's no one's evil scheme – just a nasty leak. When the Brigadier demands to know how these horrid worms are to be got rid of, you can sense him waiting for Dr. Who of old to suggest they blow them all sky-high or to look for a nearby dormant volcano they can violently activate.

The solution turns out to involve a big bag of salt, which is spectacularly messy, and Tegan can't even look.

FUNGUS

All the cats in the UK are going crazy and attacking their owners! The Doctor is called in by a Professor Lloyd to help. As they have tea the Doctor is startled to find the milk tasting a bit mushroomy.

Can't Professor Lloyd taste it too? The two scientists smile at each other. 'We don't all have your advantages, Doctor,' says Lloyd, presumably referring to the Doctor's superior sense of taste. It reads rather as if – in the midst of this feline / fungal disaster – the two men are gently flirting with each other.

It's all down to the pasteurisation process and new tanks in dairies. The Fifth Doctor is unnervingly fast and accurate in solving problems. However, the struggle to make the British population make do with powdered milk for a few days doesn't bring the story to quite the same pitch of dizzying excitement as 'The House That Jack Built' or 'The Sinister Sponge' attained.

At least it turns out to be mushrooms from space behind it all.

Other Content

- ONE DOCTOR – FIVE MEN – A history of the character of the Doctor, to date.
- QUESTIONS OF WHO – a dozen or more Annuals in, and the first quiz based on the television show.
- THE COSTUME DESIGNERS – An interesting and impressively in-depth illustrated look at costume design on the tv show, written by Brenda Apsley. Might well be the high point of Annual features.
- MONSTERS AND ROPES – Snakes and Ladders board game.

Doctor Who Himself

Unlike his previous incarnations, who could stroll across icy tundra or through sweltering jungles in opera capes and woolly scarves, this Doctor feels the extremes of climate like any human being would. He's keen on diplomacy, preferring to get warring aliens to talk to each other. This is again unlike, say, his third self, who would have looked for the nearest volcano, reactivated it, and drowned the lot of them in molten lava.

'All it needs is a little trust and kindness,' the Doctor tells the people of Mesique, in the second story in a row about getting alien races to cooperate and live in harmony. Later he tells Tegan that, although she can't help the things she was taught as a child, she can help the things that she believes as an adult – which is brilliant advice. The Doctor is a little bit more moralizing here in 1984, perhaps, than the freewheeling previous incumbent, but I think I like it. He's the voice of the liberal intellectual bang in the middle of the resolutely anti-intellectual, anti-liberal Thatcher era.

Then he talks about how to separate romantic legend from fact and how, as a time traveller, that's kind of his job. He journeys into the truth from which myths spring up. And so, in one story, he finds himself at the heart of Camelot. This is a newish role for the Doctor but also, in a way, a reconnection with the ideas behind the original TV series. Before *Doctor Who* was a show about space shenanigans and invading aliens, it was about travelling back to investigate what might and might not have been true about Aztecs, Romans and Trojans.

Travel still makes Dr. Who 'inwardly nervous' but 'deliriously happy.'

Monsters and Villains

The disturbing-looking Theigs and Basks of Oxaqua with their eyes-out-on-stalks are pleasingly alien and strange. They, together with pregnant alien sasquatches are precisely the sort of creature that the TV show would have resisted attempting to put on screen in 1983, when it was shying away a little from monsters. In those days aliens most often looked like members of a Top of the Pops dance troupe or a New Romantic band.

The Master is a very welcome presence – especially disguised as The Merlin of Camelot. He's just as wicked and conniving as ever.

Curious Companions?

Tegan is quite subdued at the start of this Annual. She calmly hands out the winter cloaks ready for their adventure on Mesique. When Turlough starts to find their adventure on Melphis amongst the robots and gangsters exciting, Tegan loses patience with him and calls him an imbecile.

When the going gets tough Turlough wants to head straight for the Tardis. The Doctor reminds him that they have a job to do. They have to fight for what's right. Turlough never seems keen on that. Sometimes the Doctor gets fed up with his callous, flippant remarks. Turlough is still finding it hard coming to terms with the Doctor's eccentricity.

Brigadier Lethbridge-Stewart is still head of UNIT and, when the Doctor, Tegan and Turlough turn up for a cuppa, he's pleased to announce that there's nothing very untoward going on in Britain these days. He hasn't seen the Doctor – or appeared in an Annual even fleetingly – since Sarah moodily came back to Earth in 1978.

Fiendish Wheezes

I'm not sure what the Master is up to, dabbling with Arthurian myth – but I like it. Apart from the Master's there are very few schemes of the fiendish kind this year. The three-headed pilot on Melphis has a decent one, getting the Doctor and friends to do his dirty work – but apart from that it's mostly mushrooms and mutated worms and hungry yeti to blame for the year's disruptions.

TV Feedback

The Doctor facing the Master is a medieval castle is reminiscent of 'The King's Demons' on TV that year. 'Class 4 Renegade' features a robot not unlike the definitive Giant Robot, K1. The Doctor's cricket bat suddenly transforming into a deadly snake that wraps itself around his arm is a clear echo of 'Kinda' and 'Snakedance' on TV. The 1984 Annual features another reunion with the Brigadier, just as the TV show did. This one takes place in an earlier time, when he was still running about with UNIT.

Egregious errors

The Doctor's forgotten all about the Tardis' telepathic circuits and their ability to translate languages.

Classic moments

Tegan's realization that the Master is present in Camelot is a fabulous moment. The Brigadier announcing that things on Earth have been quiet since about 1978 – followed immediately by a phone call about a mutated menace in the River Thames – is wonderful.

What I learned from the Doctor Who Annual 1984

Don't slavishly adhere to beliefs handed to you when you were a child. Other worlds have Abominable Snowmen, too. If a man with three heads asks you to look for his robot, better check out he's not a gangster first. If you press a certain button on the control console a hot cup of tea arrives almost instantly. Osmosis apparently works both ways.

Illustrations

The artwork takes on a more dynamic and flamboyant feel in 1984. It's as if the artist lets his / her imagination fly a little more than the previous couple of years, when the artwork felt a little stiff to me. As a kid I was particularly impressed by the Fifth Doctor's winterworld costume variant, with its swirling cape – still with question marks on its high, pointed collars (rather like a 'goody' version of the Master's.)

The illustrations are still quite cartoonlike, reminiscent of the artwork in, for example, that year's *He-Man and the Masters of the Universe* Annual or *Terrahawks*. At times, especially in stories such as 'The Volcanis Deal' the pictures seem to deliberately hark back to the very earliest Annuals.

It's important to remember that the early nineteen eighties saw renewed interest in vintage *Doctor Who* merchandise and even a reprint of some of the early stories in a bumper collectors' volume. Perhaps the echoes were deliberate and a more cartoonlike, naïve style was a purposeful move in the twentieth anniversary year. The worlds of *Doctor Who* were made to seem very exciting and exotic in 1984.

The 1985 Annual

The adventures of 1985 feel like the least heroic that Dr. Who has ever had. He is given missions by mysterious aliens and his own people, and he sets off, quite enthusiastically, and accomplishes his targets with very little fuss. He retrieves special blue stones and keeps the Master talking long enough for the cavalry to arrive. Sometimes he gleefully blows monsters and spaceships up, reviving that unhealthy zeal that the Third Doctor had for atomizing his foes.

The Doctor of 1985 is one who seems to have regained his authority and certainty. He knows at once who his enemies are. He can sense them a mile off, and put a name to them, and he knows that they deserve the punishment they are going to receive for their cosmic crimes. He even feels like he can slap his assistant again, just as the Third Doctor often did, when she started to go hysterical. There is none of the self-doubt that plagued the Doctor of the Annuals of the late nineteen seventies. None of that psychedelic confusion and epistemological quibbling about relative states of being has survived into the bright, dayglo, resolutely straightforward nineteen eighties. This is simple fare.

It also rings rather hollow, like a gaudily-wrapped Easter egg.

The Stories

BATTLE PLANET

Attacked by laser beams, the Doctor and Peri experience the dreadful sensation of having their souls sucked out. They wake up dehydrated in a golden cell, and are soon confronted by small golden beings with talons protruding from their chests. They have been brought to Belstar, for a meeting with the Guardian of the Debans, Ranon, who is a golden lizard with purple spikes round his head.

The Debans are at war with the Siros, who have seized a blue rock containing all the secrets of the planets and put it in the Crypt of Pimo in the Tower of Selsor in the Nomed Zone. Because the Debans can't go there themselves they intend to send the Doctor, with a special ring to bring him back. Consenting to this mission, the Doctor and Peri soon encounter the Siros – who are blue with large silver balls for their heads. They shoot death rays about the place.

The Doctor and Peri jump down into the Nomed Zone and enter a system of caves and soon enough they find the blue rock unguarded. The Doctor pockets it. But then he finds he has lost the magic ring.

217

There is a bit of kerfuffle, and a tussle, and a sharp exit, and the ring is found again. Our heroes are transported back into Ranon's presence. Now the Debans can defeat the Siros. The Doctor and Peri are escorted back to the Tardis and that's it. There's no reversal, no twist, nothing. The Doctor and Peri were sent on an errand and it went smoothly.

DAY OF THE DRAGON

The Doctor and Peri find a Colonel Latham burned to a cinder in his drawing room. Nothing else is damaged. The maid Sarah goes on about a dragon in the cellar and she faints at the sight of the burned Colonel. Harper the butler is nervous. The Doctor goes down to examine the wine cellar, where he finds and pockets a large green scale.

Now we learn that three hundred years ago the Doctor 'tangled with' Qualar, the Grand Master of fire, who sometimes took the form of a dragon, and other times that of living fire itself. At the end of that adventure Qualar was 'given' the planet Zaron.

The Doctor leaps quite quickly to the conclusion that Qualar has arrived here on Earth, and is setting fire to colonels. As the duo head back to the Tardis they note that it's getting warmer and, nearby, a tree goes up in flames. The Doctor calls his reptilian enemy out into the open. A whole family of dragons appear and the Doctor gets singed.

Qualar appears in his true form, which is a seven foot high mass of pulsating grey matter. He's absolutely sick of the dead planet Zaron, and has come to Earth for victims and secrets. The Tardis is surrounded by flames. The Doctor dashes to Colonel Latham's laboratory. Will they be able find a way to defeat the dragon in the Colonel's files? No.

They hear the crashes and bangs of the approaching Qualar family. The Doctor turns on all the gas taps in the laboratory and sets it alight. Qualar and his family expire in a huge explosion.

THE REAL HEREWARD

Following the Battle of Hastings a bunch of Saxon outlaws are hiding out in East Anglia. The fugitives visit an old man they can trust. In his cottage they encounter strangers who claim to be lost in the marsh – the Doctor and Peri. As they eat bread and cheese together, it becomes apparent that the leader of the fugitives is King Harold, who has survived the Battle of Hastings.

Norman soldiers are encroaching outside, approaching the cottage. The Doctor produces a toy robot which wanders out and lights up and scares them off. Gaining the king's gratitude, the Doctor asks him to change his plans, and not to march on London. Live on here as the legendary Hereward the Wake, he suggests, and inspire people to carry on under the Normans.

THE DEADLY WEED

Visiting the Planet Kyros, the Doctor and Peri find that the elderly Time Lord Vama is pleased to see them, but he's got a lot on his hands pacifying warring aliens. While he's busy, our heroes go off to look at the purple lake, which they find disappointingly messy with black weed. They watch a small animal nibble the weed and are horrified when it convulses, dies and turns into bronze.

When they mention this to Vama they learn that the same thing happened to experts sent to examine the site of a recently-crashed comet down south. The deadly black weed seems to be on the move.

Peri is attacked by a robot, which also knocks Vama senseless before the Doctor can manage to freeze it. When he regains consciousness Vama recognises the robot as the transformed expert, Neltar. The weed from the comet must have come from the planet Jerimi, realises the Doctor. He's been there. It's a world of robots who reproduce by using black weed to subsume organic beings and turn them into robots.

An army of robots is attacking right now. The guard who brings the warning seems almost embarrassed to announce: 'Vama, an army of... of... well, robots seems to be advancing on us!'

Everyone is armed with vaporisers and they start exterminating things at once. Bits of weed are flying about, contaminating the Imperial Guards. The text is rather tepid at this point: 'The process was horrendous to watch.' The only way forward is to set off a huge explosion putting paid to both androids and their nasty vegetation. Once everything is sorted, the Doctor expresses an interest in coming back another day, to check that the place stays peaceful.

VORTON'S REVENGE

The Tardis has been dragged to a dead planet rather violently. Has there been a catastrophe here? They are soon confronted by four little men in cloaks and helmets, each with one claw protruding from their chests, each clutching a laser gun.

They are taken into a cave and discover a whole lot of these little men. It's starting to seem a lot like the first story in this Annual. In that the Debans only had one claw, coming out of their chests, too. It almost makes me wonder whether this lot aren't just the Debans in disguise, in hastily-donned helmets and cloaks, determined to get the Doctor and Peri to run another dangerous errand for them.

However, it turns out that this is the planet Exclon and the leader is Vorton and he knows the Doctor well. The Doctor remembers that Vorton and his people were aggressive towards their neighbouring worlds and so they were 'condemned' by the Time Lords, who 'devastated' their planet for them.

Vorton's people have built a spaceship and intend taking violent revenge upon Gallifrey. They'll use the Doctor by getting him to pretend they're after a peace treaty. The caves are vibrating as they test out the space-worthiness of

219

their vessel, and a rock fall allows the Doctor and Peri to escape. Vorton shows them his ship and the Doctor is very impressed.

The spaceship explodes for no very good reason. The Time Lords of Gallifrey are safe. Vorton and his colleagues are squashed and / or exploded.

THE TIME SAVERS

The Doctor – who is forever desirous of a holiday (this time the golden beaches of Palaran are what he has in mind) – ends up, rather piqued, in the bright pink council chamber of his Time Lord superiors. You might think he would ask them what the devil they were thinking of, devastating Vorton's world, but he doesn't even mention it. Instead, he is informed that he is to be given a mission. Someone on Earth in 1996 is meddling with time and he will have to sort it out.

The Tardis materialises outside Cambridge and the Tardis duo get directions from a tramp who smells of methylated spirits. Soon after that they see two men with yellowish skin, wearing the uniform of the Ipsilon Foundation of 300 years in the future. At the Arthur Jeffries research building there are further mysterious appearances by ghosts from the future. The Doctor and Peri sneak inside, see the Ipsilon men again, and are captured by guards.

When they are taken to see Professor Thomas he believes they are the ghosts. The Doctor introduces himself as a psychic investigator. It doesn't take long for him to learn that Professor Thomas is building a time machine and he is being helped by the Master, who quickly reveals himself.

It turns out that the Master has been trapped on Earth by the Doctor, who stole the 'time-matter adjustment valve' from his Tardis. Professor Thomas listens to all the Time Lord banter without comment. Perhaps the Master has already filled him in with the backstory? Just as the Time Machine looks about complete the men from the Ipsilon Foundation manifest themselves completely and explain that Professor Thomas's machine will turn out to work. But it will also cause no end of problems and disaster in the future. So they have come back in time to destroy it. Professor Thomas is very understanding and promptly hands over his notes. The Master escapes and the machine is destroyed. The men from the future blink out of existence.

The Doctor and Peri return to the Tardis, and the Doctor realises he didn't actually do very much in this adventure. Though perhaps he delayed the Master with chatter, long enough to allow the Ipsilon Foundation men to get there. Still, it's not that impressive. It makes the reader wonder what the Time Lords were so het up about.

THE MYSTERY OF THE RINGS

The Tardis slips back twenty-odd years to an autumn in the late Seventies, and a quaint village. The shop owner from whom the Doctor tries to buy a screwdriver is wary of strangers. Young folk are coming to the town and going off to see the standing stones on King's Hill. There is talk of the stones coming to life at night, and of lights and noises.

The Doctor and Peri investigate and almost before they even begin he has guessed that there are aliens at work. It's probably the Valiark. This has happened before. They probably want to colonise the Earth.

The aliens are wraithlike beings inside the circle, but they can't leave its bounds yet, or adopt their actual forms, for reasons to do with electromagnetic force and not wanting to scare away the young people they are trying to subjugate.

The Doctor hatches a plan. If he can get one of the Valiark to step out and break the magnetic ring, they will all lose their power. So he taunts them from the undergrowth. The villagers become cross at his interference. Peri joins in, distracting the creatures as they reveal their gargoyle-like true selves. The locals are shocked out of their collective trance, and the Valiark fade out of existence.

The story – and the 1985 Annual – comes to an end with the Doctor congratulating himself on his intellect and the fact that he saved Peri's life by slapping her. She tries to hit him back.

The reader is left thinking what a *useless* pair they are.

Other Content

- DOCTOR WHO: THE (SET) DESIGNERS – Written by Brenda Apsley.
- DOCTOR WHO: SPECIAL EFFECTS – Written by Brenda Apsley.

Doctor Who Himself

The Sixth Doctor dresses like a clown. It's even more apparent in these Annual stories that he's traipsing about the omniverse looking a fool. He is, though, full of urgency. He is glad of being given a mission to accomplish. He also seems indestructible, zooming about the place and falling down holes.

He keeps pocketing things. The pockets on that multi-coloured coat seem to be as capacious any of the Doctors' outdoor jackets. Before embarking on the adventure of 'The Time Savers' he stuffs his pockets with chocolate bars, because he doesn't imagine there'll be time to stop for a proper meal.

He quite casually abandons reasoned argument and peaceful solutions and is quite prepared to blow Qualar and his dragon family into blazing smithereens.

His reaction to such carnage is curious. It makes him hungry for a well-done steak. He generally seems pleased when there's been a large explosion at the end of a story.

He's quite rude and abrupt with people, telling Peri off for not knowing her British History. Both King Harold and Peri are told by him not to be silly.

Monsters and Villains

Both the reptilian Debans and the sphere-headed Siros are quite impressive aliens at first glance. Qualar and his family of dragons seem quite formidable too. The robots of Jerimi who reproduce by using black weed are even more impressive again. I have a sneaking fondness for the Valiark, who first look like bright wraiths dancing in the stone circle, and soon turn into cartoonish gargoyles.

The Master makes a pitiful attempt at villainy this year.

Curious Companions?

Peri spends much of her time wailing. 'Trust us to get involved in a war!' is one of the first things she says in 1985. She is always a little cynical and gloomy about her fortunes. Sometimes, though, she is as game and brave as any of Dr. Who's previous assistants. She's quite okay about jumping down the pit into the Nomed Zone.

Both the Doctor and Peri seem weirdly unemotional and untouched by the things that happen around them. The Doctor smiles with amusement only moments after Colonel Latham has spontaneously combusted.

Peri is mostly concerned with immediate dangers. She's expecting at any moment to be burned or crushed by a dragon. She shrieks and wants to run away all the time. She can also be quite brutally business-like, as when she announces she's sure they can quickly find a way to immobilise Qualar.

Sometimes Peri can be refreshingly straightforward and blunt. In 'The Real Hereward' when all the men are muttering about secret identities, she bursts out: 'So you're King Harold?'

Mostly she is written as an archetypal companion. "Aaaah,' screamed Peri. 'What's happening?" At least Sarah Jane Smith had her sarcasm to make her stand out a bit. Jo was always keen to piece together clues and to try to be useful. Peri really does nothing at all.

In the final story she whinges that the Tardis has done nothing but malfunction since she came aboard. Is it trying to tell her something?

Fiendish Wheezes

The Debans send the Doctor on an errand to fetch a crystal so they can save their world. The fire-breathing dragon Qalar has come to Earth looking for victims to frazzle. The Master gets involved with an attractive Cambridge Professor and wants him to build a Time Machine, even if it does mean the eventual end of the world. The Valiark draw humans to a stone circle and want to take over their minds. Motivations are pretty straightforward in 1985.

In 'The Real Hereward' the only wheeze is the Doctor's. He persuades King Harold not to renew his fight with the Normans. The Doctor carefully puts history back on track. For once he is actually dissuading the people he meets from starting a revolution.

TV Feedback

There's an echo of the early First Doctor historical adventures in the Doctor's keenness to set human history back to rights in 'The Real Hereward.'

As on TV at the time, the Sixth Doctor is given some awful, tortuous lines to speak. 'We'd better try and find out why we are here – and, indeed, where 'here' is!' The kind of dialogue unsure writers use to fill up time. The Doctor and Peri burble as witlessly here as they ever did on TV.

Another good echo of the contemporaneous show is the Tardis being dragged to a mysterious location. This was forever happening on TV in the Eighties. Everyone would grab hold of the console and the picture would go wobbly.

The Time Lords appear in their customary robes and mention is made of the Panopticon. The Master is trapped on Earth, just as he claimed to be back in the 1973 Annual. Nowadays he blames the Doctor, and this raises in my mind the intriguing possibility of an unseen period in which the Master is exiled to the then present day England. Perhaps working for an evil version of UNIT?

'Day of the Daleks' is clearly evoked by 'The Time Savers', in which ghosts from the future come back to prevent disastrous time experiments in the

223

present. 'The Mystery of the Rings' brings to mind 'The Stones of Blood', as does the idea that the number of stones seems to somehow vary at different times.

Anticipating the Future

The Doctor trying to buy a new screwdriver in the little village in 'The Mystery of the Rings' comes as a surprise – reminding us that we are in the scant few years when the Doctor found himself unable to sonic everything in sight with his all-too-handy multi-purpose gadget.

Egregious errors

In 'Vorton's Revenge' we learn that the Time Lords devastated the planet Exclon in order to teach its aggressive inhabitants a lesson. There's an idea in this Annual that the Time Lords of Gallifrey act like heavy-handed galactic policemen.

In the following story, 'The Time Savers', the Time Lords summon the Doctor to Gallifrey in order to send him on one of their missions. No mention is made of that fact that the last time the TV Doctor had anything to do with the Time Lords, he was running away from his elected role as President. Everyone avoids the subject here.

Classic moments

None to speak of. These stories are essentially damp squibs, in almost all cases. Anyone who starts plotting a fiendish caper or a wicked scheme is pretty soon blown into smithereens. Previous Annuals had stories that ended up being disappointing or unsatisfying, but they usually had something interesting or strange or memorable about them.

Though I do like the idea and the conjured-up image of Qualar the dragon mooching about in Colonel Latham's wine cellar immediately before burning the colonel to a crisp.

224

What I learned from the Doctor Who Annual 1985

Absolutely nothing.

Illustrations

Mel Powell was the artist for the Colin Baker Annuals.

The artwork reprises the style of some of the Annuals during the Pertwee era, or even earlier 1960s examples. It is cartoonish and bright, seemingly quite deliberate in evoking a slightly old-fashioned, retro feel. Perhaps, like the TV show of the time, the Annual was looking to its own distant past for inspiration and futilely trying to tap into a more innocent era.

The 1986 Annual

We are approaching the end of our Omniversal Odyssey with the mysterious Dr. Who from the World Distributor's Annuals. Is there are conclusion? Is there a reason for our journeying to come to an end? And is there a fitting conclusion to the Annual Doctor's adventures?

'Time Wake', the second story of the 1986 Annual begins with the Doctor and Peri in London, in January 1986. I remember this giving me shivers at the time. They were precisely here, in our time. They had arrived in our exact present – in the post-Christmas, post-New Year, freezing cold beginning of 1986: precisely the time that Annuals were traditionally read by devoted fans such as myself. And by then, of course, I was – technically speaking – far too old for them. I was seventeen and undergoing the (unfortunately impermanent and not-wholly-irreversible) state known as the end of childhood. It was meant to be the end of obsessions with things such as sci-fi TV shows and kids' books at Christmas. *Doctor Who* on TV was on the way out (spring 1985 was when the first blow had been struck across its bows) and – unbeknownst to us readers at home – the Annuals were coming to an end, too.

Since 1975 I'd been reading them in the haze of post-festive days. Forever, that was, to a kid's sense of the passing years. And I knew they had this long history behind them, even deeper than 1975. All the way back to 1965. It was surely impossible for a journey like this to come to an eventual end?

The Stories

THE FELLOWSHIP OF QUAN

The Doctor and Peri materialise on the inhospitable world of Tuven III, where they are almost shot to pieces by defence mechanisms, spied on by robed and cowled figures and buried in sand. Then they are taken before the mysterious, all-knowing 'Sentinel', whose voice is strangely familiar. The Doctor fills in a little of the back-story: these people are the survivors of a race who ruthlessly exploited their own world for its mineral wealth, and they are waiting for their sleeping deity Quan to awake. The Sentinel reveals himself to be the Master, who is in fine gloating form. He has brought the Doctor here to decipher some mysterious inscriptions, allowing him access to the weird, aggressive robot deity known as Quan, whom the Master wants to enslave as part of his ongoing ambition to take over the universe.

TIME WAKE

On a rainy morning in London, the Doctor and Peri are wandering purposefully about with a machine that goes 'beep', looking for time anomalies. A primitive time machine in January 1986 has left a dangerous wake through the vortex, terminating here and starting in 1720. Poking about in the sewers, our heroes find themselves transported into the Eighteenth Century, where they discover a hidden cache of British Prime Ministers. They are androids! They come lurching through the orange mist to attack...

The Doctor manages to lead them to a watery, fizzing, sparking death in the Thames and then he and Peri confront their enemy: the blue and scaly Tasq from Bestonas, who thinks of himself as a Time Engineer. He's been trying to pervert the course of human history just to get himself home. The Doctor ticks him off and offers him a deal...

INTERFACE

The Time Lords have sent the Doctor and Peri to a spooky castle on a storm-lashed world. It seems that this is the location of an Interface between a number of different time zones: a kind of bottle-neck in the time-space vortex. They wander about, experience strange phenomena such as heatless fires and historical figures carousing one minute and then lying dead the next. The Doctor sorts everything out pretty easily with the Tardis, causing the narrowed time streams to dissipate. It all seems like a big fuss over nothing, or a 'Sapphire and Steel' story.

BEAUTY AND THE BEAST

Peri is easily taken in by the paradisal beauty of the next world they visit. She has her head turned by the gorgeous men and is snobbily chuffed to be invited to meet royalty. The Doctor warns her against being stupidly superficial, but she won't listen. When they get the tour of the palace the Doctor starts thinking that this lot are hiding something. Why are they so touchy on the subject of the savages who live in the western hills?

Peri is outraged to find that the beautiful people keep slaves. She isn't keen on talking to one of the Drones, however, because they are so hideous. Underground, the Doctor and Peri meet with the poor, down-trodden, ugly folk and learn that they are plotting revolution. They hear about the pernicious way society here was divided and the unfairness of life since. The Drones want to restore balance and justice.

Amazingly, the Doctor interrupts and says that he can't get involved. He must warn them that his people have expressly forbidden that he get embroiled in changing the course of history on any of the planets he visits. The poor Drones seem to understand, and claim that they only told the Doctor and Peri all this stuff in order to warn them to get away in the Tardis before the trouble started.

Our very unheroic heroes make their escape, leaving the Drones to get on with it by themselves.

RETRIBUTION

In Victorian England the Doctor and Peri find themselves at the home of a Professor Watkins, who has retrieved a silver casket that landed, out of nowhere, on Middle-Hill. The Professor is scornful of the Doctor's assertion that it may contain a space traveller, and is intent on getting the capsule open. The alien escapes and menaces the occupants of the house, while the Doctor and the Professor's assistant, Lawton, take a swift trip in the Tardis, tracing the mother ship above Earth, and finding that it contains thousands of these silent caskets.

The sleeping aliens are awoken by remote control, triggered by the space-suited insectoid on Earth. The Doctor shoots and blasts his way through the massing creatures and gets back aboard the Tardis. Back on Earth he confronts the alien being Chintor, telling him that he has already turned his mother ship round to return from whence it came. Chintor is here for revenge on the people of the Milky Way, for the mess they have made of the Kyle system with all their radioactive waste. The Doctor shoots him dead.

DAVARRK'S EXPERIMENT

An apparently abandoned mansion in 1924 is the Tardis' next destination, where stone cherubs suddenly come to life and dash about the neglected gardens, and fashionable toffs drive up and start to insult the Doctor's dress-sense. Peri is tied to a chair in the attic by a crazy man with a pincer arm and a hoof for one of his feet. Downstairs statues are coming to life and gracefully stalking the Doctor and his new friends. The statues are so strong they can even jump high enough to break through upper windows of the house.

The Doctor confronts Davarrk, Peri's captor, who crash-landed near here in his ship and has been experimenting in order to make himself as strong as one of his androids. He needs all the new arrivals to use as guinea pigs and they must all pop into his machine. He's already got through several poachers and tramps. Susan the flapper puts him out of action for a time, by smashing a vase over his head, and there follows a terrible battle with the android statues. And then Davarrk wakes and makes his way to his machine, intent upon one final transmutation…

THE RADIO WAVES

The final story in all the Doctor Who Annuals places us in present day London, and a mystery that involves brainwashed people taking to the streets and standing menacingly in front of the Houses of Parliament. The Doctor – working with the Metropolitan Police (rather than UNIT – soon works out that someone is employing mass-hypnosis through the medium of the everyday transistor radio.

The interference is emanating from the top of the Post Office Tower and the Doctor suspects that an old adversary is behind it all. Today is the state opening of Parliament and dark deeds are afoot.

The final Annual story unites Dr. Who's past with his future. The Post Office Tower at the heart of a mystery reminds us of 'The War Machines' on TV all those years ago. It also speaks to the far-future of TV *Doctor Who*, which will present us with zombified hordes of Londoners quite regularly in stories such as 'The Christmas Invasion.' The revelation of the Master as the villain behind the wicked scheme is pure nineteen seventies. He wants to destroy the Royal Family and all the politicians, who have succeeded in doing more damage than good to this country, as far as he can see.

In the final story the Master forces the Doctor to look at the state of the nation in 1986.

Neither of them belong here anymore. 1986 isn't even aware that they are still here.

Bearded in his den, the Master concedes defeat. He sees that the Doctor has the greater fire-power. He makes his escape, and dematerialises. Vanishing out of the story forever. The Doctor and Peri and the police have saved the day, and the opening of Parliament goes on, just as it ought. The Queen reads a long, boring speech that she didn't even write for herself. It's a humdrum day, after all, and no one is even aware that the Doctor has saved their lives.

In the final Annual's final story, Dr. Who falls out with his last companion, routs the Master one last time, and saves the people of England yet again.

And no one even notices.

I wonder where he went and what he did after that.

Other Content

- BEHIND THE SCENES AT DOCTOR WHO: MAKE-UP – A long, text heavy interview with make-up artist Dorka Nieradzik, conducted by Brenda Aspley.

Doctor Who Himself

He's sniffy and imperious, bounding from one place to the next and being snitty and arch towards his long-suffering companion. The Doctor's role in the universe is to leap about 'athletically', preventing 'buffoons' from causing 'havoc.' He's not without a mischievous and pithy sort of wit: 'That's the worst fancy dress party I've ever been to!' he exclaims, when attacked by the melty-faced android replicants of every British Prime Minister up to and including Thatcher.

In that same story, 'Time Wake', it seems as if the Doctor is about to take pity on his enemy, Tasq, and return him to his home. Tasq takes just a fraction of a second too long in looking grateful and contrite, and the Doctor turns on him. He sees to it that Tasq dies horribly in the time-space vortex he'd been so rashly interfering with. This Doctor can be ruthless and rather cruel. He has the righteousness of the Third Doctor about him.

Then, in 'Beauty and the Beast' a promising revolution is brewing. Just the kind of thing the Doctor of old would get whole-heartedly stuck into.

But he simply turns on his heel and walks away from it.

What has put the Doctor off? Surely their cause is as good as anyone who he's helped during his long career of rabble-rousing and putting things to rights?

Obviously, it's a story written to a tight deadline and perhaps the larger implications are only something we can see in retrospect. But with this turning away at the end, something profound has happened to Dr. Who. This is even worse than when he was gleefully blowing up aliens and setting off volcanoes. This is him shrugging his shoulders and walking away. This is him behaving as the Time Lords wanted him to, all those years ago. Just as, on TV, the Show was heading towards the self-appraising turning point that was 'The Trial of a Time Lord', so something is shifting in these Annual stories, too. In the next story, 'Retribution', the Doctor picks up a gun and shoots his insectoid alien enemies dead, one after the next, to prevent their wrong-headed attempt at revenge.

It's as if the Doctor is forgetting how to be Dr. Who. And he's doing this just as the world outside – the brash new world of 1986 – is deciding that it doesn't really need to hear from Dr. Who any more.

Monsters and Villains

The Master is making a nuisance of himself once again: fittingly, since he's the most persistent super-villain throughout all of these Annual years. Here, he disguises himself as a kind of high priest of an underground cult, seeking to awake a sleeping god for his own evil purposes. Later, he crops up in London, keen to bring down the Tory Government and the Royal Family.

The Beautiful People in 'Beauty and the Beast' have kept the ugly people downtrodden for years. The hideous Drones look back on a Utopian past when everyone was equal. In true nineteen eighties fashion, it was an equality and freedom to 'make the best' of yourself.

Chintor of the Kyle system is a space-faring insectoid creature intent on revenge for what the people from this 'spiral arm' have done to his world. Davarrk and his stately android statues are a formidable bunch. Just another set of alien beings who have crash-landed on Earth and have set about doing nefarious stuff, almost at once. Why is Earth such a magnet for these inter-stellar traffic accidents?

Curious Companions?

Peri is called upon to weather the Doctor's mercurial moods and to ask the correct questions. In 'Time Wake' I can't believe that she really needs to ask him what a time anomaly is. She's had her fill of them, surely, by now? It's clear she's asking these things simply to pander to the Doctor's need to partially and grumpily explain things.

She seems just as discomforted and mardy as her TV counterpart: history is smelly, Tardises are laughably unreliable. Stories begin with her looking at the scanner with 'disdain.' In 'Beauty and the Beast' she comes across as quite superficial. For once she's cheerful, because the Doctor has brought her to a planet that seems a bit like paradise, with gorgeous angelic men striding about the place. *This* is what it takes to put a smile on her face. Plus, she has the nerve to accuse the Doctor – after he warns her against taking things at face value – of dragging her down and making everything humdrum..! She is 'disgusted' by his scepticism.

In 'The Radio Waves', as he outlines his suspicions and his plans for tackling whoever is hypnotizing the population of London en masse, Peri doesn't look impressed. He turns on her quite coldly: 'You have no faith. You never believe anything I say, and you never trust me.' In the very last Annual story, Peri fails to be any kind of companion to the Doctor in the traditional sense.

231

Fiendish Wheezes

This rather snappy Sixth Doctor is quick on the uptake. When told that the mysterious 'Sentinel' knows 'all' but still requires Dr. Who's help, the Doctor is quick to point out the irony. Those behind fiendish wheezes are forever bigging themselves up.

Tasq of Bestonas is yet another crash-landed alien on Earth, and he uses his time travel technology to nobble all the leaders of Great Britain between 1720 and 1986. He intends to get them to put more research funding in the way of scientists who may be able to help him fix up his spaceship to get home. (It seems an awfully long way round the houses, as plans go. Surely he could have just *applied* for a grant?)

Davarrk is an evil mutant, crash-landed in the 1920s, experimenting on human beings in order to create a beautiful body for himself. It isn't much of a wheeze. He just draws human beings into his mansion and experiments on them.

TV Feedback

The Annuals have a long tradition of taking images from the most recent TV stories and re-using them in new adventures. Here, for example, just as in 'Attack of the Cybermen' the Doctor stalks about London streets with a machine that goes 'beep' and leads his companion into the sewers to investigate something anomalous.

'Warriors' Gate' is evoked in the over-lapping time streams of 'Interface', in which we see carousing soldiers and then cobwebbed wreckage and carnage in the same room.

'Davarrk's Experiment' itself seems to be an unholy fusion of the TV stories 'The Brain of Morbius' and 'Black Orchid.' The nasty stone cherub with the black mouth is a clear echo of Bok, the prancing, infernal gargoyle in TV's 'The Daemons.'

Anticipating the Future

Insectoid beings in a Victorian mansion and laboratory will recur in the TV story, 'Ghost Light.'

The living statues of 'Davarrk's Experiment' prefigure the Weeping Angels.

'The jubilant Doctor kissed Susan...' when she smashes a vase down on the wicked head of Davarrk. His impulsive snog with this 1920s flapper presages a whole 21st Century career of grateful face-eating.

Egregious errors

Lots of the incidental details from *Doctor Who* lore are present and quite correct: Chameleon Circuits, lucky cat lapel badges and Type 40's and so on. And yet the Doctor's character, motivation and behaviour is sometimes breathtakingly wrong. He is vengeful, spiteful and not particularly interested in helping out the weak and down-trodden.

It's hard to tell if this is, in fact, a series of errors, or just unusual fidelity to the then-current TV show, which also featured curious changes that came over the Doctor in his sixth incarnation.

Classic moments

Like the Pied Piper, the Doctor leads replicants of every British Prime Minister through the ramshackle streets of Eighteenth Century London, luring them to their doom in the 'niffy' River Thames. It's a wonderfully *Doctor* Who-ish image.

As is the insectoid alien with a blaster, running about a Victorian mansion, furious at the Doctor for foiling his plans: 'I have good reason to hate the inhabitants of this spiral arm!'

The Doctor turning his back on the poor, down-trodden Drones in 'Beauty and the Beast' is a classic moment, in its own way. It feels like he's betraying them, and also his loyal readership, who have believed implicitly in his heroism all this time. Even in 1977's 'The Traitor', in somewhat similar circumstances, he shed a tear for those he had turned his back on. Here, he simply wants to get away before all the bother starts. Like many in the nineteen eighties, he's looking after number one.

What I learned from the Doctor Who Annual 1986

Never mess with primitive time machines. Only super-advanced races like the Doctor's can have access to them. There are such things as Interfaces in the time-space vortex, where different time periods get tangled up like a ball of yarn. The status quo is something that needs to be maintained.

If you stay in the business of saving the world for too long, everything starts to fall apart. The Doctor loses his bearings. He quarrels with his companion, who he doesn't like much anyway. He starts shooting at people with guns and murdering his enemies. He walks away from the needy and, if he saves the world, it's only to restore the status quo.

In 1986 we learned that Dr. Who as we knew him was out of tune with the world. Worse, he was out of tune with himself.

Super villains and alien monsters go to elaborate lengths to get what they want. They explain all just at the moment of their final gambit and defeat – pausing long enough to outline every stage of their ludicrous plan. You can almost hear the baroque splendour of their schemes (which must have seemed splendid in the confines of their own imagination) all turning to ashes in their mouths. But perhaps that's what being a super villain or an alien fiend is all about: finding the long way round to a solution. Laying elaborate traps, waking up long-sleeping giant robots to do your bidding, or creating amazing replicants to perform bizarre tasks. Perhaps that's the reason they go in for it all, these wicked beings? They celebrate the impractical and extol the illogical. They indulge in arabesques of evil. Any plan of theirs is just a pretext for dressing up, lying in wait, shouting out threats in a booming voice and generally showing off.

We've come a long with Dr. Who and this is what we have learned at the end of it. By trying to save the universe, you're falling into the villains' trap every time. They don't really want to blow up the universe, or even really control it. They just want you to be there, at the end of the story, to listen to their plans and admit that, for a few moments, they almost had you stumped. It's all attention seeking, actually. The chase was the thing, not the getting there.

So, at the very end, we learn that the Omniverse of Dr. Who turns out to be, essentially, a rather benign place. There are many plots and tricks and traps, but we always find that everything turns out to be all right in the end.

That is, if you hold onto who you are, it does. You have to remember who you were at the beginning of this, and who you became. You have to remember your ideals. 1986 is disturbing because we're not sure if the Doctor knows this anymore. We've learned that he has become curiously amoral.

Illustrations

There is something pleasingly retro and naïve about the illustrations in the 1986 Annual. With their blue, scaly-skinned super-villains in preposterous outfits they seem to be harking back to the Annuals of the early nineteen seventies, perhaps.

A New Life

And then...

There was no 1987 Doctor Who Annual.

If there had been another, in the late nineteen eighties, it might have featured Doctor Who, as played on BBC TV by Sylvester McCoy and his companion, Mel Bush, as played by Bonnie Langford. I can't think of a pairing more suited to the garish world of the World Distributors Annuals. Season 24's TV tales of aliens in holiday camps, dragons on ice worlds, famous replicants and giant brains and carnivorous old ladies in tower blocks already sound to me as if they have been drawn out of the Omniverse of the Doctor Who Annual.

But that Omniverse was gone. World Distributors had stopped producing *Doctor Who* stories by then. The style of those astonishing books lived on in later iterations, such as *Doctor Who Magazine*'s five 'Yearbooks' of the nineteen nineties. Then, later again, in the Storybooks, Brilliant Books and (rather spartan) Annuals associated with the revived, post-2005 *Doctor Who* franchise. All of those latter-day books are notable for the keener attention they paid – in their stories and comic strips – to the continuity and tone of the TV show. Never again did those fictions run deliriously and anarchically free in a universe of their own making...

I would be keen to argue that the spirit of *Doctor Who* as created and sustained for over twenty years by Manchester's World Distributors continued instead in a different fictional universe. Again, it was tangentially linked to the TV show and it filled gaps and hiatuses in the life of that show. It was a fictional universe that expanded to fill the hideous void known as The Wilderness Years between 1991 and 2005. I'm talking about the novels, of course. The New Adventures, the Missing Adventures, the Eighth Doctor Adventures, the Past Doctor Adventures, the Telos Novellas. In those stories of the first eight Doctors – mind-bending, infinitely inventive, continuity-busting, anarchic and sometimes downright odd stories – we see the true continuation of the life and soul of the Doctor Who Annuals.

The amorality of the Sixth Doctor and that sense we have in 1986 of him being somehow lost and adrift is just the way the novels begin, five years later with the Seventh Doctor in 1991. And the questions asked by those many original novels are always: who is this man we trust to save the Omniverse? Who does he think he is? What do we even know about him? And where will he take us next?

The Annuals were, for twenty years, the story of how he started off and became that person. And the twenty-odd years that followed, in *Doctor Who* fiction written and read by those, like myself, who had grown up with the Annuals as well as the TV show, were about deconstructing and reconstructing that heroic archetype.

It was all about setting this multi-faceted figure off again onto further – presumably endless – adventures in time and space.

Appendix 1: The Unofficial 1972 Annual

Introduction

Here's something that's seemingly been dropped through a hole in time and space! It comes spinning through the air to land with a hefty thump...!

A brand new hardback annual. Quite large. Very colourful. Bursting at the seams with new material.

A book that never was. A book that never existed back then, and only exists now through the combined efforts of crazily determined and talented enthusiasts.

I have a great deal of respect for fans who create things. I love the fact that some fans ply all of their energy and skills into willing amazing objects into existence. Whether these are fanzines, costumes, audio dramas or finger puppets, *Doctor Who* fans have enjoyed a long and glorious history of making stuff exist for the sheer, joyful sake of it.

There were, of course, a strange couple of gaps in the Annual Years. 1972 was a very conspicuous one. A golden age on TV – the era of what has since been quite cosily called the UNIT family – yet, there was one long ago Christmas that came and went without a multi-coloured tome from World Distributors.

In 2018 Mark Worgan and friends set about putting this right retrospectively with a not-for-profit glossy facsimile hardback that has the feel and look of a book put together in 1972. This very generously-proportioned volume has come winging its way through the Technicolor imbroglio of the time vortex and it has landed smack dab on my desk: providing me with the perfect opportunity to write a new, extra little chapter for this second edition of my guide to the Doctor Who Annuals.

The Stories

FANGS FOR THE MEMORIES

New assistant Jo has turned feral! This shaggy dog's tale sees her infected by an alien werewolf's scratch, and attacking the Doctor and Sergeant Benton at UNIT HQ.

PHANTOMS OF THE MIND

When horrific visions plague the inhabitants of a tower block, UNIT is called in to investigate. Even the Doctor is besieged by phantoms before he discovers the alien at work and jump-starts their UFO for them.

THE LAST UNICORN ON THE RAINBOW BRIDGE

TARDIS repairs lead to the Doctor and Jo being zapped to a dreamlike realm, where Benton appears as a teddy bear and the Master's giant head chases them across a rainbow bridge.

GISMOS

A gallery run by pink-haired twins is displaying all kinds of futuristic items, including what seems to be a replica of the TARDIS console room...

THE LIVING CRYSTAL

A pendant recently bought from Biba by Jo transforms her into an ethereal, angelic being. Along with the similarly affected Corporal Bell and a visiting Swiss professor, she becomes intent on controlling the TARDIS.

POWERWORM (PICTURE STRIP)

The Master has discovered a flatworm imbued with the mysterious power of the Axons. He intends to use it as an alternate source of self-renewable energy.

THE CRAWLING HORROR

Atmospheric tale set on the moors of County Durham, where the old legend of the Lampton Worm has returned to plague the locals. A reclusive rock star making experimental sounds seems to hold all the answers.

THE DEADLY DECIBEL (PICTURE STRIP)

The Doctor has to dash to BBC Television Centre when the Master hypnotises Jo into fronting pop group Dominus, whose live performance during a telethon will enslave all of mankind.

THE GIANT BEES FROM MARS

A trip to local football match is ruined by an attack by giant bees from Mars. The Master's plans are foiled by a football terrace chant.

OVERREACHING DESIRE (PICTURE STRIP)

In a remote town, the Master is giving classes in transcendental meditation! Luring people in through their unspoken desires, he's harnessing the powers of an alien creature called Krr'N, with whom the Doctor engages in a mental fight to the death.

LOOSE ENDS

The Master is apparently living in a suburban house in Dagenham, and can't get anyone to take any notice of his grand schemes for taking over the planet. The Doctor has to explain to him exactly why no one is taking him seriously.

FANTASTIC WORLD

The Doctor and Jo are sent through an interstitial portal to a mining project in another dimension, where it turns out the Master is leeching precious blood from a creature the size of a planet.

SMOKE AND MIRROR-MEN

An adventure that sends the Doctor back through time at three hourly intervals and involves mysterious Mirror-men from another dimension, and one more dastardly plan from the Master.

THE MASTER'S DIAMOND RINGS

Pilfering precious gems from a vault in Geneva is part of the Master's scheme for a time travel experiment that will help him recover his TARDIS.

THE HAUNTING OF HILLSGREEN HOUSE

Investigating apparently ghostly visitations at a stately home, Jo and the Doctor encounter strange Ephenomorphs – aliens drawn to the latent psychic powers of human beings.

KING OF THE MIDNIGHT PLANET

Stumbling into an alternate version of Cornwall, our friends uncover the Master's plot to kidnap locals and breed himself an army of humans to repair his TARDIS, and to build him a Medieval castle while they're about it.

THE NEXXONN MENACE

The Doctor and Jo are transported to an alien ship seemingly composed of water, as it orbits the earth. Here they are met by the servile Bandriini and the Piranha-like Nexxonns, who want to suck up all the salt water from planet Earth.

Other Content

There's a good range of non-fiction and fun pieces on offer here. The book begins with an enthusiastic welcome and a nostalgic look back in the form of Katy Manning's introduction. Elsewhere we get memories from John Levene and Richard Franklin.

There's a classic 'Who's Who' piece – always a staple of the Annuals over the years. This one is an explanation of The Show's history up to 1972, which has the curious effect of making the reader appreciate how relatively little ancient history there actually was to write about at that point.

There is a touching tribute to Annual luminary, the artist Walt Howarth, and various pieces to do with drawing monsters. There are two in-fiction pieces, one presenting Jo's secret diary, and another in which Dr Who himself writes his own 'fun facts' about space.

We get a glimpse of behind-the-scenes monster making, a crossword, some jokes, board games – including one particularly witty take on Snakes and Ladders that utilises some amusingly familiar Pertwee-era story tropes. ("The Neutron Polarity on the Gateway is flowing the wrong way. You know what you must do.' Oh, indeed we do..!)

Doctor Who Himself

The Third Doctor is wonderfully unflappable, even when his assistant grows fur and fangs. 'Oh, good grief,' he mutters and rubs his neck and goes off to find a solution to whatever the problem seems to be. He likes to show off and name-drop, and allude to his travels in space and time. There's a touching regretfulness about the Time Lord, when he reflects that he can help a visiting alien to fix their spaceship, but he can't do the same for his own TARDIS.

He constantly assumes that every opponent is the Master in disguise, and is mostly correct in that. He occasionally attempts to acclimatise himself to British culture, and even consents to attending a local football match to that end. However, he grows tetchier with Earth and its inhabitants as the months of his exile stretch into years.

He gained a D-minus in Trans-Dimensional Theory back on Gallifrey, and this often shows itself when he has to deal with time paradoxes – much to the Master's amusement.

It really feels wonderfully like being back in the world of the Annuals when our hero is frequently and casually referred to as 'Dr Who.'

Monsters and Villains

We've got: werewolves from space, illusion-generating aliens in pearlescent jumpsuits, the giant green disembodied head of the Master, ethereal crystalline beings, the slavering reptilian Mordassi, deadly Martian bees, Krr'N, who wants to live in a dimension filled with desire, the mysterious Mirror-men, and the Kolaak, who revel in destruction for its own sake.

Bragging, the Master tells Captain Yates that the Cybermen, Autons and Axons are mere minnows in the great ocean of the universe. Planet Earth has seen nothing yet, he promises.

Curious Companions

Jo Grant is new to her role as the Doctor's assistant, as an excerpt from her journal presented here makes clear. She's fashionable and prone to saying things are 'groovy' and 'far out.' She has a breezy sense of humour, especially when trapped in a nightmare landscape generated by the TARDIS memory banks. She sees it as her job to cheer up the drab UNIT HQ with her fab daywear. She can't sing, except when the Master hypnotises her.

Jo has a calming influence on the irascible Dr Who. She's brave (flinging herself into other dimensions and various rifts and phenomena when the need arises) and she's slightly psychic, rather like her Aunt Flora, who ran away with the circus. Despite not knowing much science, Jo sometimes sees right through to the truth of things.

Those UNIT stalwarts, Captain Yates and Sergeant Benton are present and correct through this volume. One, slightly fussy and old-fashioned, the other able and willing, but somewhat daft.

But… where is Brigadier Lethbridge-Stewart? His is a serious, noticeable absence throughout these stories. He's either in his office, on the phone, or off in Geneva. I rather suspect that he's caught up in copyright hell.

His being missing does lend all these stories the feeling of their being the slightly more rum adventures that the Doctor and his friends had during 1971. These were the ones that perhaps weren't fully reported at the time..? There's a feeling here that we're seeing the adventures that the mice had while the cat was away…

Fiendish Wheezes

The pink-haired artist Rosemary, who tries to use an alien robot to create a museum of futuristic wonders. Crystalline creatures distributing themselves around the world in the form of junk jewellery, and waiting to conquer the earth. Rock star Titus Innesbrook hand-rearing an alien dragon on milk so he can record its strange other-worldly songs. The Master using psychic warlords, Martian bees, Cornish people and pop groups in order to take over the world. Piranha creatures attempting to suck up planet Earth's salt water in order to power their spaceship.

TV Feedback

There are lots of lovely continuity references here, mostly to Jo's earliest on-screen adventures. With the benefit of hindsight, and perhaps greater knowledge of the show's lore than the writers of the original Annuals had, the allusions come thick and fast: accurately and even with relevance. Lovely, lurid visions of Autons and Nestenes attack Jo when she faces up to her greatest fears, and a surviving sliver of Axos itself makes a return appearance.

What I learned from the Unofficial Dr Who Annual 1972

Venusian lullabies work well in taming the savage beast, as do references to memorable moments from classic TV episodes. What seems like a joyride is often a necessary research trip. It is important to trust the Doctor and to take a leap of faith, even if things look dire (and you're jumping into the open mouth of the Master's giant disembodied head.) Sometimes you just have to go along with what seems like 'obvious shenanigans' in order to find out what's really going on. Not everything that comes from outer space turns out to be evil. Alternate forms of energy are always good, but you need to be careful if the Master's involved. Rock stars always go crazy when they go off to live in the countryside.

TV marathons, football matches and transcendental meditation classes are as full of deadly pitfalls as you always imagined they might be.

If there's a portal somewhere and you jump through it, it's a dead cert that sooner or later, time and space will have no meaning.

Classic Moments

The Doctor realising that underneath her hat and scarf Jo has been transformed into a hairy, ravenous beast. Yates and Benton getting transmogrified into a unicorn and a teddy bear respectively, in a land of candy floss. The Doctor grabbing hold of the Major's toupee, expecting to pull a rubber mask off the Master, and being woefully mistaken. The Master using a flatworm to fuel a power station. The revelation that a rock star has an alien dragon as his musical collaborator.

A lot of the joys of this book involve TV's Dr Who becoming involved in rather ordinary or jarringly British things – the Doctor going to a football match, Jo singing with a band on the telly, or the Master ordering a Chinese takeaway. Many of these vignettes make you wish these stories really had been broadcast back in the day. I really want to see the Master failing to make himself beans on toast because his gas has been cut off. I would love to see the Doctor being scandalised that the butler of Hillsgreen House is wearing jeans...!

Illustrations

They are extravagant and sometimes wonderfully gaudy, just like back in the day. These are artists set upon reminding us of the heyday of these books. The modified photographic stills are particularly effective in lending some atmosphere to the stories. I could have done with a few more bafflingly abstract or irrelevant illustrations, however, just to make me feel like I was reading an Annual of old.

Appendix 2: Interviews

Stanley Freeman

Stanley Freeman is a graphic artist and designer with some fifty years in the business. In early 1964, he created the cover for the first Doctor Who Annual, until now generally credited to Walter Howarth.

"I began [working] at fifteen years old, at a large litho and general printers studio, based in the outer part of Liverpool, serving a five year apprenticeship as a graphic designer. I worked among about a dozen or so highly skilled artists for ten years. We were engaged in mostly food packaging products, which in those days involved a lot of still life illustration, as photography was not always the best way to show the product. I then moved to Manchester at the behest of a friend who recommended me to World Distributors. One of my early jobs was a colour cover and some inside line pics for a paperback: 'How to catch the fish of the week', a *News of the World* publication. Ironic because they were to take over the company about a year or so later! The cover pic was of a perch on a hook (not still life!)

Most Annuals were allotted by the Production Editor and among the countless scores of colour covers I did there must have been some Annuals although I didn't list them at all. My work began with football books, and pop star stuff like 'Meet the Beatles', Elvis specials and various pop culture books. There were design and compilation of 'Keep Busy' puzzle books and others in that genre. There were also scores of full colour covers, plus inside line work for *Tom and Jerry, Bugs Bunny, Yogi Bear, Scooby Doo, Bewitched, Star Trek, Stingray,* and *Nighthawk,* to name a few! Later work included *Rupert Bear, Magic Roundabout, Ewoks, Keypers, Glo-Friends, Sylvanian Families, Nosey Bears,* and *Little Bear* – covers and endpapers and insides in full colour. Clients were World International, Brown Watson, Wm. Collins, Marvel, Holland Enterprises, Opac Quill Ltd, Waddingtons, The Redan Co, and Kibworth Books

I started with World Distributors in 1961, commuting daily from Liverpool after previously doing some part time freelance paste up and 'as you go' editing of Rip Kirby comics for the UK market in the early days. I worked alongside then Editor/ Production Manager, Alan Johnson who allotted the artwork for annuals to an outside agency. I was responsible for the design of most other products which were many and various, under the directive of John Pemberton (the MD), who one day passed me the phone to take a very vague verbal brief from a company rep in London. This chat, about a new programme called *Doctor Who*, consisted of mention of a time machine in the form of a police box, some robots and Menoptera (half butterfly-half man). A photo of William Hartnell to follow in the post.

I must admit my memory is a bit woolly on the sub-cast on the cover. I don't think at that time the Beeb had actually started filming [stories with some of the figures on the cover] and there may have even been a 'chicken or egg situation'. I am certain I invented the Menoptera from the phrase 'half man, half butterfly' in that phone call with nothing else to go on. I never did see the creature later as I didn't have a television. They were all kept vague and small in the artwork without much definition because of lack of info about their looks or function. I've never heard the other names [of the Zarbi and the Voord].

This would be in early 1964, and I spent the next few lunch times looking for pictures of a police box in the back street book shops of the city of Manchester, before putting together largely guesswork annual cover artwork featuring Hartnell's portrait, which was approved and sent for print to meet deadline. No photo refs were supplied except Hartnell. The Daleks were never mentioned [and] I made up the Menoptera's appearance and took the police box from old magazines, plus guesswork. It was a rush job to meet the deadline for the Harrogate Book Fair sales. Not too good really, but it was OK'd and printed.

I also did the cover for the first *Doctor Who Puzzle Fun* book, and even managed to sneak my initials in: SF, just below the waist of the robot.

Shortly after that I was diagnosed with Tuberculosis and treated in Liverpool for a year. During that time Walter Howarth did the inside line pics as the stories became available. He played no part in the cover art of that first annual, though. Walter was still doing Westerns (he did excellent cowboy stuff) – I heard his garage/studio was full of cowboy gear!

Walter was at first slightly apologetic to me because he'd been given the second annual job. I told him not to worry. I didn't think it would last long anyway!

World Distributors was quite a compact outfit. It was city centre, which I liked, in a narrow four or five storey building in Lever Street, just off Piccadilly. The three Pemberton brothers who ran it were, I suppose, what is called 'driven' and reaped their rewards by being driven in Rollers when acquired by *News of The World*. However they were all affable men and treated me well. I enjoyed the challenges of working with them and I also enjoyed my trip in John's Rolls to the Company do! I don't forget they kept my job and paid me too for a good while during my enforced absence. The company in fact had kept my position open and on my return I just got on with each new project as it came, the *Doctor Who* Annual forgotten – for the time being.

Fast forward fifty years, and the *Doctor Who* celebrations on television – and specifically the drama 'An Adventure in Time and Space' – mention that first Annual. I was inspired by that programme to go on line for more information and was shocked to find Walt Howarth credited with my artwork.

I actually got in touch with Walt's old agent, but he told me he didn't care who painted what, and also with the BBC online, but they seemed to think that being over fifty years ago made it irrelevant, whilst at the same time expecting the public to celebrate the fact that it was exactly that old!

Keith Miller

Keith Miller was the founding member of the original Doctor Who Fan Club, and he wrote the first story in the Doctor Who Annual 1975, 'The House that Jack Built'

"I got the very first Annual and it was fab, though I remember being disappointed it seemed to dwell on the Zarbi and not the Daleks. And the stories were bonkers, but that would only get progressively more so as the series went on…

I was a writer from an early age. I wrote for the school magazine a lot. Sci-fi/horror fiction. Lots of stuff with a twist at the end. Dracula finding to his horror (and hunger!) that he had been resurrected into a future of androids – that sort of thing. They were very popular then.

On November 27, 1972 I popped into BBC TV Centre to watch the filming of 'The Three Doctors' (one of the perks of running the *Doctor Who* Fan Club!) During a break, Barry Letts invited me down to the BBC bar with Terry Dicks and the conversation eventually came round to the Doctor Who Annual.

"We like the running stories you do for the club magazine. To be honest, they're better than the stories in the Annual, which border on bloody awful. Why don't you write a couple of stand alone stories and send them to World Distributors? I'll give you a name drop the next time I'm on the phone to them."

248

I dealt with good old Mae Broadley. It was all done by post. Mae was high heid yin at the time. She gave me only one guide-line and that was don't use any of the TV monsters as it would cost them more money!

It was indeed my first commission and I had a bit of trouble trying to get ideas for standalone stories that didn't feature any of the TV monsters. I was very fond of *The Avengers* TV series and one of my favourite stories was an Emma Peel story 'The House That Jack Built' which was just plain weird. So I thought I would do something similar and even used the same title.

So I typed up "House That Jack Built" and another one called "Seeds of Death" – why I couldn't think up an original title, I'll never know.

I was amazed when I got the letter back saying they didn't want "Seeds" as it was either a) too close to a story the Production Office were working on ('Seeds of Doom'?) or b) too close to a story they published previously – I can't remember which, but they wanted "Jack" and enclosed a cheque for nine quid. I was a published author!

I sent them two stories and they sent me a cheque for one of them. That was it!

I thought the illos. were fab. Not photo-realistic, but good representations of who they were supposed to be – and the scenes were close to what I had in my head when I wrote them. The giant chess-board scene was great. And I like to think a young JK Rowling saw that and decided to include a similar scene in the first Harry Potter novel!

I remember getting my author's copy and being really chuffed I was the first story in the book. I loved the illustrations, they were quite well done and (for the annual) quite accurate. I was puzzled to see Jo there, though. I had a letter from Mae saying there was a new girl coming into the show called Sarah Jane, so Jo's name would be changed and Sarah's head transferred onto Jo's body in the illos. But they must've changed their minds. I was working in a bookseller in Edinburgh when the annual hit the shelves. That was a weird experience, selling copies of a book I had partly written – and nobody knew!

There was no reaction at the time, as far as I can remember, other than Sarah Newman (Barry Letts' secretary) being really chuffed one of the stories had gotten picked up and calling me "a clever boy"!

I wrote again in February of 1974 asking if they wanted any more but I got a reply from Mae saying there was uncertainty if the annual was even going to continue, so that was that.

I think it's great to find out years later (thanks to the invention of the inter-web) that the story has its own little fan club, and is noted as introducing the sonic screwdriver into the Annual and being the first instance in *Who* history of a fan crossing over into professional writing duties. Just think, if that had happened now I could be writing the TV series!

I would love to do more *Who* writing! Now that I've retired I can devote myself to it!

Writing took a left turn as I got older and I ended up doing drama scripts, one of which "The Long Road Home" got to the semi-finals of the Radio Times Film and Television Awards in 1984. It was the first adaptation of Richard Matheson's "What Dreams May Come". Since then, I have written two books: "The Official Doctor Who Fan Club Volumes 1 and 2" and have a third in production: "Genesis of the Who Fan."

Ian Berriman in SFX said when reviewing my books about my time with the fan club that when he looked at his bookshelves groaning with *Doctor Who* merchandise, perhaps things were better when there was just me and the annuals! I loved Russell T Davies' time with the show and fell in love with it all over again. I envy the kids today.

I remember reading a review of *Verdigris* in SFX and thinking 'Doctor Who in the style of *The Avengers*! What a brilliant idea!' and rushing out and getting a copy, and then getting a very real sense of déjà-vu as Jo was creeping in through the open window to find a carousel in the middle of a room... ha! I just wondered why an obscure little story tucked away in an ancient kids' annual would inspire anyone to write a book!"

Mike Wild

Mike Wild wrote most of the Doctor Who Annual 1983 and, in the same year, he wrote the whole of the K9 Annual. He was, he says, always a big fan of Doctor Who...

"Big enough to still be cheesed off that I only won second prise in the Walls Ice Cream 'Win A Dalek' competition in the mid-sixties! My memories of the competition are hazy but I remember you had to write/draw some kind of Dalek story but I, would-be writer of six or seven years old, lost out to some other little shi – ahem, some other boy. He got the Dalek; I got a bike. A sodding bike. Yep, I was a fan, and had, and read, all the annuals from an early age.

I was a bit spoiled because I used to get loads of annuals for Christmas, whatever was around at the time – *Fireball, Stingray, Man from U.N.C.L.E.* etc – but the *Who*s were always a staple. In all cases – because as you mention later merchandising was different then – I just thought it was bloody marvellous that here were adventures BEYOND the TV screen. I also remember being amazed that most of these things were published in Manchester. Manchester! Just down the road. Where was this amazing wonder factory? One day, I vowed, I would find it.

I was freelance, but at the same time not really anything, writing-wise. I was a student Registered Mental Nurse. The commission came in a roundabout way. A friend was buying some stock from World and mentioned I was a writer – at that time only of fanzines and one semi-pro gig – and they asked me to send a sample story. Much panic and weeing ensued, but I delivered 'Danger Down Below' a week later. This went through a guy called Paul Hicks, one of their Production Executives, and then up to editorial. Next thing I knew they'd commissioned me to do not only the Doctor Who Annual but K9 as well.

I went to the pub and bought my first proper writer's pint. Then another six. Seriously, I couldn't quite believe it – my first step on the ladder and it was *Doctor Who*!

Once commissioned I was more or less left to my own devices, but the office doors in Great Ducie Street were always open. It was literally a case of 'if in Manchester drop in for a cuppa and a chat'. I was in Manchester a lot.

I remember Brenda Apsley was one of the editors, but it was Mae Broadley I dealt with in the main. Mae was the one who'd given me the ultimate nod. Her title was Editorial & Licensing Director but she was so much more than that – something of a foundation stone of World overall – who'd been with them, I think, right through the golden age Lever Street days, where everyone kind of dibbed in and wrote the stories etc. Lovely lady: office like a sitting room. Editorially, as I said, I was more or less left alone – all that really happened was once the stories were delivered they were sent to John Nathan-Turner for approval. Happy to say he approved them all. The only kind of 'note' I ever got was later on, when, for an annual I ended up not writing, I was given the shooting script for 'Planet of Fire'.

I had two weeks to deliver all the stories for each annual. I certainly went through a lot of screwed up sheets but drafts, no, not really. I suppose you could say any 'changes' suggested by Nathan-Turner constituted a second draft, but as that only ever consisted of editing one line in one story, maybe that doesn't really count.

The first time I saw the art was in my comps. But I liked it. Mind's eyes to paper for the first time. Who wouldn't?

It was, of course, outstanding to see them on the shelves – you know the feeling, first time, Paul.

Zilch reaction from fandom. At least as far as I was aware. Which isn't to say there wasn't something in some fanzine somewhere, but they weren't as accessible as now. I know over the years I've seen the odd piece saying my *Doctor Who* and *K9* are amongst people's fave annuals, which is great, but otherwise no. As for the production office, they wanted me to do the next annual, as did World, with greater usage of TV mythos, but for personal reasons it never happened. Grrrr aargh. Kill me now.

The airport story was problematic because of my use of the Master, or Anthony Ainley's image or something – I can't quite recall. We got special permission to use him as a character, I remember, which set a precedent to what would have been a greater relationship between series and annuals had it continued. For some reason, this never quite gelled after I left, though. But yeah, I did want to bring more of a feel of the TV show to the stories overall, complement them as you say...

'Lively unabashed pep.' Yes, I like [the way you put] that. To be honest, it was just the way I wrote back then! No!! Yes, really!!! I didn't know what I was doing but I had to get there fast!!!

'Danger Down Below' was one of my samples, and I remember I wanted to write something with a bit more physical scale than the TV show. 'The God Machine' was originally a sample *Blake's 7* story for what became the cancelled annual! As for 'Armageddon Chrysalis' I kind of cribbed off myself – a *Star Trek* story I'd written for my own fanzine, *Tal Shaya*. Don't tell anyone. 'Night Flight ...' came about because I wanted to include a story with a more Earthy feel, just for balance, and 'The Penalty' because there was always that vulnerability about Peter Davison's eyes – I wanted to explore what was behind the windows, as it were.

I loved that period on TV. There was a freshness about it above and beyond the simple fact that Tom had gone – not that there was anything wrong with Tom! With "Castrovalva", Bidmead had instigated a series of intelligent, slightly skewed stories which worked perfectly for Davison and co I think. I remember there was a poster at the time – was it in some special? – of the Doc, Tegan and Turlough, arms folded, looking down at camera, and thinking of it, they look like 'The Professionals of Time And Space'. That make any sense?

No one knew – including the BBC – quite what form a possible *K9 & Company* series was going to take when the Annual was green-lit. And of course it was never to be until *The Sarah Jane Adventures*. But I remember there was a feeling that it should have a different tone to *Doctor Who*, whatever that would be. Given pretty much free rein again, I figured that Sarah's interest in the supernatural and occult would have been triggered by "Girl's Best Friend" and went for the Olde England/Hammer-lite feel, albeit it (was) rushed and with, as someone once said, too many men in hoods. I'd love to rewrite it now – or do an entire new collection of stories in that setting, with that team and that vibe.

It was a wonderful and unique opportunity at the time – a still gestating TV series for me to play with, and one whose characters I loved. My sandpit with TV icon toys! I loved the whole domestic tea and crumpets excuse-me-while-I-pop-out-and-slay-a-(sham or otherwise)-demon set up, but I think it also had potential to stray into Kneale / Wyndham / Christopher territory, or Tom stories like "Talons" or "Pyramids". I'd have loved the chance to do more, take it further than the men in hoods, but am very proud of and grateful for what I had. If you'll forgive me, Ms Smith was, for a while, my Sarah-Jane.

I saw some of the CBBC series but not enough to truly draw an opinion of where it was overall. But I enjoyed those I saw and they had Liz in them, so what's not to like?

I was in contact with Peter Darvill-Evans and ALMOST did one of the "Timewyrm" books at the start of New Adventures, but, to be honest, kind of bottled at the thought of doing a full-length novel. By the time I'd got my act together, others were in there. I also wrote a script for the show itself – "Equilibrium" – but then they cancelled the bugger. Yes, I still want to, but only classic *Who* not Moffat's (per)version, I'm afraid. I've tried with both BBC Books and Big Finish. Ignored by former and dismissed by latter. I know you work for them but don't get me started on the elitist, closed-shop attitude of Big Finish ... somewhere on FB is my stand-up row with Nick Briggs about why it does no one good service.

At the same time as *Doctor Who* and *K9* I did the *Space Invaders, Simon & Simon* and *Fame!* Annuals. They'd also by now realised I knew my TV stuff and so I became a kind of unofficial consultant on what future properties they should buy. This was great because it involved trekking down to Manchester

University to watch new U.S. TV shows on this humongous magnetic tape machine – the only one of its kind in the North West. We all went in a minibus – Mae, Brenda, Joyce, Glynis – and took a picnic. Seriously. I didn't do any more annuals but I did a teen romance for them – "Tides Of Love" – under the name Michelle Wild! After World, I moved onto London Editions – their new magazine arm, housed in the same building – and scripted for *Masters Of The Universe*, *She-Ra*, *Bravestarr* and *My Little Pony*. I'm surprised we ever got any work done because we used to get all the new toys to 'sample' on an almost daily basis.

For a few years after World, I did loads of comic and magazine stuff – that which I've mentioned as well as things like *Starblazer*, *'Allo 'Allo!*, *Triffik!* and so forth. Also quiz stuff for magazines and the BBC. Anything that paid, really. Then I decided I wanted to concentrate on fantasy so, between years, I wrote original *ABC Warriors* and *Caballistics Inc* novels. More recently five novels featuring my Kali Hooper character for Abaddon's 'Twilight Of Kerberos' series, starting with 'The Clockwork King Of Orl' are being republished in omnibus form in March 2014. Coming bang up to date I have a 'steampulp' western, '7 Cities Of Old' coming in hardback from Snowbooks in August 2014. Hopefully this'll be the first of a trilogy.

I'm not a fan of new *Doctor Who*, though it has had the occasional outstanding story. 'Girl In The Fireplace' – need I say more? But I can't be doing with the fact everything has to have an arc, be epic, or deify the Doctor to the extent that people almost pray to him. I also cannot be doing with the fact that within these epic arcs the need for things to make sense has been thrown out the window. What's wrong with one-off, well-constructed stories over four episodes? I could go on for hours about everything I think wrong with what has become Moffat's ego-trip – he's been corrupted and infuriates me with his glib dismissal of internal logic and more story threads than you can count – but I won't. As for all the merchandise, well, in one sense it's nice that people can get their hands on everything, but by the same token, if everything's available, nothing's special. I don't just mean the figures etc either. Talking TARDIS litter bin? F--k off. Oh yes, we were most definitely better off when there was less."

John White

John White wrote many of the stories for the 1986 Annual.

"I did something writers are advised not to do! What you must never do. I spent a lot of time writing seven short stories (truly a labour of love) and sent

254

a covering letter with no introduction. The address was Worldwide in Manchester. The letter was fairly bold. I stated that I had read the previous year's annual and could do better. Then I sat at our typewriter (remember them?) and laboriously typed them all. The creative part was a joy and I tapped into various sources of inspiration including Hammer Horror. I wanted more 'serious' stories, having enjoyed the creative resurgence of *Doctor Who* in the late seventies / early eighties, which was crowned by 'The Caves of Androzani' – a landmark in *Who* story telling. The darker tone influenced my stories.

I remember the Annuals, starting in primary school in the book section. There were two Annuals featuring Dr. Who, a World one and the other was something like 'TV Action'. Both had Jon Pertwee on the cover. The Annuals (and other annuals) were a treat. I carried on buying them. I adored the show and such was the lack of material on offer between seasons I was very keen to have the Annuals. Back then they seemed quite expensive, rare treats but then you received them for Christmas. They were presents that were read and re-read and kept very carefully for the occasional read on a rainy day. Even now I see the Doctor Who Annual and I think *'Christmas'*.

It didn't matter what I had for Christmas as a present at some point I had to read the Annual on the big day. They were a heady mix of seriousness, whimsy and just pure entertainment. Considering there were no DVDs, rare repeats and a few books, they were the main way to stay in touch with my favourite show. Jon Pertwee was my earliest memory and his Annuals were just as compelling for me as a small child as he was in *Doctor Who*. The artwork within the Annuals was a constant surprise too. There was something surreal and unnerving about it.

I looked at the previous Annuals' contents. They seemed to be some distance from the *Doctor Who* I knew, being a bit fantastical and perhaps not the show, as I liked it. Children are (or were) underestimated. They are a tough audience; I wanted something more credible from my stories.

I posted my parcel, one copy of (each of the seven) stories to Worldwide (Imagine if they had gone missing in the post!). Months later a letter dropped through on the doormat... and to my absolute joy I received a letter from the editor. It was very short. It thanked me, they had decided to publish five of my stories and enclosed a fee, £75. I still remember the thrill and the excitement of it.

I wrote the following: "The Fellowship of Quan", "Time Wake", "Interface", "Retribution", [and] "Davarrk's Experiment". I did see [another writer's] name online last year but apologies, I've forgotten the other writer's name. Of course, we never met.

Contact with World was really minimal (Apologies the name of the lady in correspondence with me escapes me.) And no trips to Manchester. I suspect finance was tight and my time with them was rather unusual! They had writers, I am sure, for their portfolio of Annuals. I was the new kid on the block. I assume they were working on small margins and short timeframes. It was literally a letter saying 'Thanks, here is your fee.' The process was (typical of me) one based on taking a risk after a lot of work on the stories. There was no brief. Just myself, my imagination, a desire to have something considered and a typewriter.

My approach in hindsight was twofold. Firstly, technically: how many words were in the stories. I counted the length of each story in the previous Annual! Secondly, the tone of the stories. I think [the current TV show manages] both comedy and fantastical stories so well [but that had been] weaker in classic *Who* so I avoided them. In Annuals the stories I loved were more like the episodes I enjoyed on TV. If the Doctor takes the threat seriously so do I as the reader/viewer.

I really enjoyed the creative process. I have a vivid, restless imagination. I know I am a lateral creative thinker… so I tried in my own small way to get these wild ideas into a format that would entertain and make a younger me reading the Annual think 'This is proper *Doctor Who*.' Not a story that made the show seem foolish. It would be appalling to make the stories childish: children enjoy family drama. Successful *Doctor Who* has themes beyond the realm of the fairy tale or [it] makes them special and new. My stories were my usual pageant of my own dark influences from literature and TV. My influences… included *The Secret Garden* and Hammer Horror. I should have patented moving statues and pitched the idea to Steven Moffat. D'oh!

I didn't see any concept art. But that made seeing that Annual with my stories… like a hundred birthdays in one. Seeing someone imagine the characters and express them in art is one of the best moments in my life. It was amazing. Your thoughts and words and someone understanding them, extrapolating the descriptions and themes into a drawing. Amazing to see them even now, for me.

It cannot be easily expressed. Considering the history. The alchemy of a fertile imagination, love of the show, supportive parents and one modest typewriter. A brief response and confirmation followed that they would be published and we had moved to Norwich by the time it was in shops. I saw it on sale in Jarrolds, a large department store. I opened the book as if I did not quite believe it was real! Then I imagined it being opened in Australia and other territories the Distributor had. A once in a lifetime feeling for a fan.

I only remember reading a review in 'The Celestial Toyroom' fanzine and it was a fairly typical one of the time. My aim was to have some more imaginative, darker, serious Who Annual stories but they had to be accessible for eight and nine year olds. Fanzines were aimed more at teens and older, more committed fans and the review gave some mild praise and a fairly cutting summary…I was disappointed…They were missing the point. But in later years I came into contact with people like Jean-Marc Lofficier and I realised the Annuals are for many people a cherished, quirky slice of British life and nostalgia.

I'm pretty sure I had seen very little of Colin Baker when I was writing, as I remember it. Not much more than 'The Twin Dilemma' which was a long time before the Annual was released. But those early stories did shape how I saw the Doctor. The show had (I thought) with Peter Davison been a bit inconsistent – as much as I loved it – and there were still classic episodes. Colin's portrayal was stronger, more difficult and even angry. Very nineteen eighties! I liked the tone of the stories. They were challenging and yes, probably too dark. Colin's portrayal needed to be made more full and appealing. I think it went a little too far in trying to be like William Hartnell, but that was not his fault. He's a great actor.

I think the Doctor isn't bloodthirsty – more backed into a corner and reactive. On TV I would say scenes and ideas at one point went too far, but it was that kind of era. They really are a mini-study of that time in the UK. I deliberately set out to write stories with varied, unique themes like the show. You would watch a season and the stories would have a range, some lighter ('City of Death') some with brooding undertones ('The Masque of Mandragora'.)

Really, Colin's Doctor in the Annual was my forecast, if you like, of how he would portray it based on little viewing time (I'm sure I have that right)… I am pleased with this. I think it's right based on the little information we had. My stories were influenced by the early stories, particularly 'Twin Dilemma' in which he has a regeneration crisis. I assumed it would soften and change and mostly it did, although I think perhaps a little too late. I thought the show had missed an opportunity with him. It could have been so much better. How did we go from 'The Caves of Androzani' – which is a *Who* classic – to the show being at risk, so quickly. It needed new blood in charge and a change of Producer I think. Look at how well that worked in the 'new' show.

I did try and write to Worldwide about the next Annual but the editor explained they would not continue with a 1987 one. I understand that was a contractual difference with the BBC and low sales for 1985.

I did write a manuscript for Virgin in the nineties but it didn't quite make it. They gave honest feedback. I gathered I needed to spend more time on my manuscript (I am a full time manager in the NHS, so it's hard) but in terms of the creative content they really liked it. I think I even spoke to another writer at the suggestion of the editor-in-chief. I'm trying to remember who it was… it may have been Paul Cornell. He was really helpful but time was always against me with such a busy job. That's a regret, as the Virgin novels are classics.

As for the show: yes, I have enjoyed it all of my life, really. I am particularly pleased with its treatment since returning in 2005. It has come of age and finally has a profile long deserved at the BBC.

If the show can keep going as it is, I would like to see it on the big screen as it was – tantalizingly – for the fiftieth Anniversary. I think Russell T Davies is actually a genius. What luck that he is a fan, and then enlisting the group of creative talents as he did to write, which led to Steven Moffat's appointment, which was so clever. I think the show has been raised to a new creative level and I hope it carries on for another fifty years."

Clive Hopwood

Clive Hopwood wrote many of the stories for the 1981 sand 1982 Annuals.

"I've always written from quite an early age. I think I wrote my first novel when I was 11, a time travel story naturally, partly set in the time of the Rome/Carthage wars. At the time I think I was very influenced by writers like Conan Doyle and his Lost World/Professor Challenger series. *Doctor Who* arrived on our screens later that same year and I was blown away from episode one.

My main interest was fiction although I briefly branched out into poetry in my teens (as you do) and then moved very strongly into writing for the stage; first comedy sketches, short plays and then full-length dramas. I've had about 30 plays performed, and working at World meant that I ended up writing over one hundred books, some for very young readers, in all kinds of genre, quite a number of them translated into other languages.

Whatever World's shortcomings may have been, as an employee I found it to be an invaluable apprenticeship and I learned loads (and it paid the bills), simply through having to produce such a high volume of material endlessly and all sorts of varied projects. I certainly learned how to write to deadline and to a specific word count and that definitely sharpened up my skills as a writer. All in all, I am genuinely grateful for the experience although my two stints there – 18 months and 2 years – were about the right length, I didn't want a job for life. The second time I went into freelance writing and arts work permanently, doing commissions, writers' residencies in the community amongst other things and eventually setting up Writers in Prison Network (now Writers in Prison Foundation) which I've run for the last 18 years in between other freelance work including oral storytelling, video and theatre productions.

I think my one regret is probably not getting into writing *Doctor Who* novels during the nineteen nineties when there was the drought of TV material. Other work and the need to pay the bills for sure meant my energies went elsewhere.

I'm currently working on saving Writers in Prison after some devastating governments cuts (don't get me started about the Tories!) and working on a couple of new young adult novels.

I'd applied for a job at World Distributors a year earlier but had lost out to another male writer (Paul Hunter) who had a background that suited him better to the more boy-orientated stuff like soccer annuals. At the time he was the only male writer on the team. My chance came 12 months later when they advertised for another writer/editor and they got in touch to ask me to reapply.

When I started working for them as an editorial assistant in 1979, easily the most exciting thing about the job was that I could get to work on Doctor Who Annuals. I submitted a story as part of my application to World – after the first interview we were set the task of writing a story for an annual which was a toss-up between *Doctor Who* and *Sooty* (no contest!) and a strict time limit of something like 48 hours.

I wrote a story, subsequently published as 'Intergalactic Cat' in the Tom Baker/Peter Davison crossover annual, and delivered it by hand well within schedule and crossed my fingers. I still remember how excited I was to learn that I'd got the job. Up till then I'd worked in theatre and TV and was employed at the time at Contact Theatre, Manchester (more of that later). I was more than happy working in rep theatre but the chance to write almost full-time and to have the opportunity to write *Doctor Who* was like a dream come true.

It was immensely illuminating to work on those annuals. The company specialised in 'licensed' publications, that is producing annuals and other publications related to popular TV series. The remit was to produce around six prose stories (each well around 2-3,000 words to fit into a 5-6 page story), a comic strip story and a selection of non-fiction features, as well as sometimes a board game. This was the standard format of the 64 page annuals of the time.

Naturally they were highly illustrated, with at least one picture per page, and these were the very early days of cheap colour printing. It wasn't long after that whole annuals would be in full colour but the two *Doctor Who* books I worked on (1981 and 1982 annuals) were still in the transitional stage where only a proportion of the pages were full colour, the rest being in what's called 'spot colour'. In other words the page had only one colour other than the black text – blue, green, pink, purple spot colour. The annuals were very much team efforts, though I'd dearly love to have had one all to myself of course!

As writers, after the company had secured a licence, we would be commissioned to produce the book (or books) and the jobs divvied up between the appropriate writers in the editorial department and the artists in the design department. Normally there would be 3-4 writers per book, and 1-2 artists.

There would naturally be certain restrictions with the licence in that obviously you had to keep within the character guidelines – Dr. Who couldn't go in all guns blazing, lobbing nuclear missiles left, right and centre, for example, totally out of character – and also, because of copyright, various regular monsters etc that you couldn't use in the stories although we had to use the companions of the time – Adric, Romana. The job was to come up with stand-alone stories that nevertheless felt like genuine stories.

The BBC provided some sample scripts from the forthcoming series and a selection of photos as a general guide. Bearing in mind that if an annual was being published for a certain Christmas (meaning they'd be released in the shops around September of that year) we'd be writing them sometimes twelve months or so beforehand. The production process included the text, artwork, design layout, proof-reading; meanwhile the production department had sorted out size, quality of paper, identified a printer and binder. It all worked to a very tight and specific schedule which would mean the books would be delivered to the company warehouse in time for launch and distribution in time for the Christmas market. Bear in mind of course that we'd all be working simultaneously on a number of other books at various stages of publication.

The BBC material was fascinating. Not only would you get a sneak preview of an episode from the upcoming series (they too, of course, were working a long time ahead of broadcast) but also they offered a glimpse into the world of writing for the screen. My script experience up that time had been exclusively in the theatre, so to see the difference between stage and screen was very eye-opening.

TV or film works on the principle of moving pictures so what you see on the screen is of prime importance. Dialogue is not exactly a last resort but it should only be included if there isn't a way of conveying the information through an image; pictures first, words second. Thus, on the page, the descriptions of what could be seen through the lens of the camera far outweighed any dialogue which tended to extremely succinct – sometimes only a word or two – interspersed by lots of directions for the cameramen. The specific shots (close up, long shot and so on) would be added later at the shooting script stage but the screenwriters would be very graphic about everything that would be seen on screen. It made it very easy to imagine in your mind's eye.

The key to any script for the screen is to pare it down, pare down until all that is left is what's essential to show the viewer. The scripts therefore tend to be very fast-paced, starting a scene as late possible, finishing as soon as possible. Few scenes last more than a minute or so, some barely more than seconds. Reading TV scripts makes you look at TV rather than simply watching – you see every shot change, watch the speed of the edit, look at the camera angles. Fascinating. I've never watched TV in quite the same way again.

The style and format of the TV scripts fitted Annual writing really well. You had relatively few words in which to get a short story over and because of the highly illustrative nature of the books you had to keep the action humming along anyway so that the artists would have something new to illustrate every page – i.e. every few hundred words. It meant the stories never hung about but cracked on; a bit tricky if you're trying to convey any idea that had any sort of complexity. For the strip story few words and lots of changing pictures obviously goes without saying.

I was really lucky in that I first arrived at World while Tom Baker was still powering on as the Doctor. It was a huge pleasure to write with him in mind. In that first (1981) annual I was lucky enough to write 'Colony of Death', 'Sweet Flower of Uthe' and the strip 'Every Dog Has His Day'. I didn't contribute any of the features.

The second annual (1982) I worked on we were somewhat taken aback when the BBC announced a change of doctor when we'd already written most of the material, so that there had to be a mix of Tom Baker/Peter Davison stories. I contributed 'Intergalactic Cat', 'Conundrum' (my personal favourite) and the

261

strip 'Plague World' – all Tom Baker. I don't recall very much being done to rewrite the final story featuring Peter Davison to reflect the change of Doctor. It was mainly the artists and the design department that had to make last-minute changes. (The weirdest thing about that annual appears to be an unmistakable portrait of Jon Pertwee on the fourth page of 'Just a Small Problem'!)

I was made redundant in the autumn of 1980 (along with half the company) when the recession hit – nothing much changes does it… – so my 18 month stint only included the two *Doctor Who*'s, although I did also get to write for *Blakes 7* and *Sapphire and Steel* annuals, but then that's another story.

By the time I went back to work at World in the late nineteen eighties, *Doctor Who* annuals were sadly no longer on the menu there.

You have to bear in mind that World Distributors at this time worked in what is now quite an old-fashioned way in that our job as 'editorial assistants' meant that we worked in the offices in Central Manchester from 9-5, Mon-Fri – we were all in-house. The job was to write material for books, edit/proof-read them and others, work alongside the design and production teams and see the books from origination through to publication. It's kind of similar to the way that Hollywood Film Companies back in the day used to have blocks of offices full of writers endlessly turning out screenplays for a weekly wage. I think it was Sam Goldwyn who said that if he dropped into the offices and didn't hear the sound of typewriters clattering away he'd demand to know exactly what he was paying the writers for…

This pattern changed a little over the years in that work commissioned outside work and freelance work became more common; I worked on a number of books freelance after I left the company the second time. This is more the norm these days with less staff in-house and all of these directly related more to editorial and production work.

We were paid a wage and anything we wrote belonged exclusively to the company. In other words there were no such thing as royalties, so that no matter how many books were sold, or even if a book was resold to a publisher in another country and republished, the amount writers and artists earned was always limited to their weekly/monthly wage packet. The company made a fortune out of some of the stuff we turned out.

It was also the norm that writers and artists were never credited, except in what were called 'Gift Books', all non-licensed stuff, and not always then. I think the company, being almost solely in the business of creating 'product', found writers and artists an unfortunate, necessary evil. That did start to change a little towards the end of the eighties but there was a feeling that were plenty more writers and artists out there wanting a regular income if we didn't like how it worked.

The offices in Lever Street, just off Piccadilly, were an absolute warren of rooms and staircases, strangely reminiscent of an M.C. Esher drawing. The editorial department was in one building and the design department and production a couple of buildings up the street. If you were taking original artwork from one to the other you had to have it well protected in polythene to protect it from the weather.

I was in a room with the department's secretary, with my own desk and an electric typewriter. The other writers were similarly dispersed around the building which gave us all a little space and peace and quiet to work. We clocked on and clocked off each day for the company to keep track of our hours and make sure we weren't backsliding. Occasionally we'd do additional work on a freelance basis from home. I can't precisely remember the rate of pay but it was something in the region of £8k a year, I think, for a 40 hour week.

This was, of course, largely in an age before computers so we'd type on carbonated paper – top copy and carbon copy. It was also very much still in the time of literal cut and paste – text would be typeset, printed onto film and then cut up and pasted down by hand onto the ready-made layout sheets before going off to the printers. Ancient history eh?

Being a relatively small company we all knew each other and there was a lot of dialogue and meetings between editorial, design, production and sales personnel.

Books would be lined up either through the purchase of a licensed character (sometimes with a number of different formats to produce), the purchase of a book from an overseas publisher (World would buy the UK rights, use the existing artwork and we'd write new copy) or a suggestion from the sales department. Deals were often done at one of the annual major book fairs in Frankfurt or Bologna.

When a book was scheduled for publication the heads of department would allocate the writers/artists for commissioning. The briefs would generally be very short, most of the publications following very tight specifications in terms of word number, pages and so on. Licensed characters would also have certain rules, even down to particular colour pantone numbers to be used. You'd often get to see a 'handbook' from the owners of the copyright, scripts, photos or other notes which laid down their guidelines.

263

Alongside that, and all important, was the production schedule and deadlines for every stage of the publication, which were missed at your peril; obviously we very rarely did because it was a crucial part of the process.

As writers you'd work very closely with the artists in particular. When writing copy for the books, especially those with very specific numbers of pages and numbers of words per page, it would be writer's job to also write artwork notes, detailing the subject matter of the picture on that page. The artist would then interpret that as they wanted, under the guidance of the head of department, but there was a lot creative freedom within the parameters laid out.

It would be fascinating to work alongside the artists and design team creatively, looking (hopefully) to produce the best book you possibly could.

The editorial department was headed up by the managing editor, Mae Broadley, who'd been with the company many years and had worked on one of the earlier Doctor Who Annuals. Under her she had a secretary and then 4-6 writers/editors of which I was one. Among the writers were Brenda Apsley, Pat Posner (who mostly wrote for the very young), Glynis Charlton and Paul Hunter. Later, in the late nineteen eighties, Roy Preston joined the company. I have fond memories of working with all of them, it was a good team.

At that time there were almost no freelancers employed, although occasionally we'd pick up a writer or artist who'd sent stuff in on spec. It was, however, quite rare this happened as we read through what's known as the slush pile. There was the odd series – when we produced a series of teenage novellas, for example, in the late eighties – in which outside writers were commissioned and those of us in-house would work with them as editors to help shape material to the company house style.

I seem to recall there were around four artists working in the design department. The two artists I particularly remember working for and admired greatly were Paul Crompton and Glenn Rix. I worked alongside them on a number of books, including the Doctor Who Annuals. Paul, in particular, had an uncanny ability to recreate very life-like portraits from photos.

Mae was a long-standing member of the company and had written a lot of material herself in earlier days. When I joined she was managing editor, although when I returned to the company in the late eighties she'd retired and Nina Filipek had taken over the job.

Mae was middle-aged (bear in mind I was 27 when I first worked under her), a very conservative dresser with winged glasses, and had settled well into her managerial role, knowing the company inside out. The eighties, however, were a period of colossal change especially in regard to technology and what it could offer and I think she was of a generation that couldn't quite see what enormous changes were coming or how to take full advantage of them. I remember talking to her about the potential for electronic books and interactive stuff for kids (all still a bit sci-fi then) that lay in the future but it was outside both her experience and her imagination, I believe. At sixty-two, I'm conscious that I have very similar difficulties comprehending the concepts that my eighteen year old daughter can see that technology today offers in her future.

As the head of department and part of senior management she wasn't directly involved in the strictly creative side of things, although she did go to the book fairs, attend senior management meetings with sales and others, initiate projects, set out the (often quite basic) guidelines and had the final say on what went forward for publication.

I remember one particular lengthy discussion where I wanted to use the word 'stasis' in a *Doctor Who* story and Mae wouldn't allow it. I did my best to explain that Dr. Who and any self-respecting SF fan would know exactly what it meant in the context of the story but I lost out on that one. I can't recall what I had to use instead but it definitely sounded wrong and the Doctor wouldn't have used it. You win some, you lose some.

It was a reasonable working relationship overall, however, and she wasn't a bad boss at all. Some of the projects we were given to do were a trifle baffling, in that, as writers, we couldn't ever see them selling (some of them certainly didn't) but you had to write the copy anyway even if was like banging your head against a brick wall for a couple of weeks. As a counterbalance, many of the projects were huge fun.

We got to see the artwork at virtually every stage. Writers and artists, at least in my experience, worked really closely together. It was a huge pleasure. Not all the artists could meet the same standards in the quality of their work, of course, and there were some illustrations for stories I wrote that left me less than enthralled. Others, however, I could have died for.

We received almost no feedback at all from anyone. The licensors took their money and ran, and if they ever fed back to the company I don't recall it being passed on unless it was a complaint or a correction needed which we had to sort.

Every now and then there'd be a piece or a review in one of the fanzines which was always good to see because at least you got a steer on whether you were producing stuff that the fans liked, which for me was really important to know. I seem to recall that 'Conundrum' got a good write-up somewhere which made me really happy. Overall, however, I think I was writing in a bit of a vacuum and writing for me as a *Doctor Who* fan, asking myself 'would I enjoy it?' as the ultimate test.

I do wish that I'd had the time to have a crack at writing one of the early original 'new' *Doctor Who* adventures. I did write a synopsis for one but then a couple of other big (and guaranteed income) opportunities arose and practical reality dictated I went with those.

I maintain my strong, lifelong interest in SF. My all-time hero has to be Philip K. Dick whose ideas I thought were mind-bogglingly brilliant from my early twenties. I was also very impressed by the early SF of J.G. Ballard. I've written a few stories over the years but somehow never got round to sending them off to any specialist publishers of magazines or the like. Life and writing has taken me in other directions.

My work for World included over a hundred titles, everything from bath books for babies to teenage romances, from reimagining of pirate and Davy Crockett stories to rewriting the New Testament in 47 sentences for a colouring book (probably my biggest challenge that one!).

What I enjoyed most, I believe, were the short stories inspired by TV shows: *Doctor Who*, *Sapphire & Steel*, *Blakes 7*, *Fame* (the creative arts academy one), *CHIPS* (LAPD motorcycle cops), *What a Mess* (Frank Muir's dog stories). I did hordes of other stuff, all of which I found something to enjoy about the writing challenge, from *Sooty* to *Neighbours* (sold hundreds of thousands), FA Soccer Annual (always a tough one, since you were writing them over a year in advance), daft poetry books for kids (great fun), a Sherlock Holmes anthology for which I wrote all the features (a real pleasure). And loads I've probably done my best to forget about, and are best forgotten.

One of the young adult novels I'm writing currently is a dystopian tale set in the present day, where Germany won the war. I love alternative history narratives, harking back I suppose to Philip K. Dick's starting premise of "What if? My God, what if?"

Over the last 30 years or so I've written a large number of plays, one of which, *Wallgames*, was SF, another *The Dreaming* was an alternative history story combining the genocide of the Tasmanian Aborigines with a near-future totalitarian state in Britain (very Thatcher-plus). Virtually all the stuff I've written has been for community theatre production; I write the annual panto here where I live every year, and help put it on. There have been comedies, political dramas, all sorts.

I've also done a lot of oral storytelling since the early nineties – traditional folk tales, myths and legends – and that often influences what I write. Not all for children you understand; the structure of these centuries-old stories are brilliant for providing skeletons for all kinds of writing. I spent a year collecting oral folklore material from around Flintshire for a book, *The Land of Stories*; I did a Stop Smoking book (not recommended, it didn't stop me); I wrote and edited *Free With Words* about the work of writers in residence in prison which was really satisfying. Indeed, since 1994 I've spent probably the majority of my time working with creative writing in prison and set up the award-winning Writers in Prison Network, now the Writers in Prison Foundation. We're currently suffering rather severely due to 100% cuts by the government to our funding, but we'll soldier on hopefully.

Isn't it brilliant that *Doctor Who* is back on our screens? I can't help but celebrate its return and there's certainly no complaint from me that they now throw shedloads of money at it. I find it doesn't in any way take away from the warm nostalgia and £2/10 sets and monsters made out of old rubber gloves like the early ones. It was always the ideas and the character that grabbed me, I could happily imagine all the bits round the edges for myself.

It's lost none of its quirkiness and off-the-wall humour. The Weeping Angels – what a fantastic creation, and River Song. The new Doctors all have their touches of brilliance and it's remarkable to see how we cope as audiences with each new generation, thinking he'll never be as good as the previous one and somehow they always are in their own way. Overall I think Russell Davies and Steven Moffat have done a great job. It's maybe got a little too complicated at times or headed off in some weird direction but then we had to put up with Jon Pertwee and bloody UNIT for years, so I don't see that modern day fans shouldn't have to cope with their own doldrums from time to time. Can't wait to see what Peter Capaldi makes of it.

My touchstone is my daughter, Keri. Eighteen now, she rapidly became a massive *Doctor Who* fan alongside me (leaves her mum rather bemused) and we'll trade one-liners from the show with each other and crease up like it was a secret language. I've introduced her to lots of the early Doctors as well, although I suspect David Tennant is her own particular favourite. Given she loves it all as much as I ever did, they must be doing something right.

There is, however, something to said for less is more. Back in the day there was, without doubt, not enough; now, I'd probably agree, there's rather more merchandise that a single human can cope with given the million and one ways in which you can now consume Dr Who material. But then we do have a choice, we don't have to see, read, whatever, everything that's out there, we can pick and choose. Let's just be thankful that it is out there and hope that they keep the standards up. Given I've been watching it since Day One I find it a delightful thought that *Doctor Who* will probably be still going strong when I pop my clogs (hopefully not at some key moment when I miss the end of a particularly gripping story) and that my daughter will be able to enthuse her kids with whatever future generations of the Doctor bring.

Appendix 3: Selected Correspondence

1965

A Horrifying Story

"I am returning this story, which was intended for the third <u>Dr. Who Annual</u>. Story Editor [of] Dr. Who, has read it and writes:- ...quite frankly I am horrified. Apart from the fact that it is abominably written, it is so inaccurate in its dealings of the Doctor and more important, the writer clearly has no knowledge at all of how the Tardis works...it is...way below any standard that we would find acceptable"

> \- Memo from Evelyn Thomas to RS Hargreaves, re 'The Terror Flash of Cygnus', 1 December 1965

1966

['Doctor Who and the Invasion From Space' was originally known as 'Diagrams of Power' and the book itself as 'The Doctor Who Colour Story Book'.]

A Higher Standard of Writing

"I would like to put it on record that this story is of a writing standard higher than any of the various stories sent to us for publication permission during my years editorship of the programme"

> \- Donald Tosh to RS Hargreaves, Undated (late December 1965/early January 1966)

Rather Weak Drawings for the 'Invasion'

"I found the cover and inside drawings of Dr. Who rather weak but I take it you are getting the approval of Mr. William Hartnell for these illustrations which are obviously based on his characterisation."

> \- Evelyn Thomas to Mr R Hoye of Visual Features, 4 April 1966
> \-

Boy and girl

"My understanding is that while we can introduce characters of our own invention...we are not allowed to use the boy and girl featured in the television series. Is this correct or can we use their names so long as we do not depict their likenesses in illustration?"

- Mrs Mae Broadley to WS Hargreaves, BBC Publications, 9 November 1966

Space and Time

"The Dr. Who concept is that if the Tardis moves through space it must move through time as well"

- Evelyn Thomas to DP Mendoza of Walter Tuckwell & Associates (World Distributors' legal firm), 18 April 1966

1968

Unlicensed Yeti?

"The latest edition of the 'Dr Who Annual' has recently been brought to our notice. We were surprised to find, both inside the front cover and on the back of the book, pictures of a Yeti.

"Mr Henderson's letter of the 29th July, clearly stated that all negotiations regarding the ownership of Yeti and Quarks had ceased and that the BBC intended to 'drop the matter'. Yey in this publication, we see that the BBC is claiming sole copyright – a statement patently untrue!"

- Mervyn Haisman & Henry Lincoln, to Roy Williams, 28 October 1968

"[The Assistant Head of Copyright] had very lengthy dealings with Haisman and Lincoln with regard to merchandising rights [to the Yeti and Quarks]. These negotiations in no way concerned publication rights...after consultation with Roy Williams and the Dr. Who production team [we] conceded that Haisman and Lincoln owned 25% of the Quarks and almost all of the Yetis. Haisman and Lincoln claimed 65% of the Quarks, and because it was impossible to bridge the gap between the BBC's 25% and their 65%, A.H.Cop wrote on 29th July, specifically within the context of merchandising rights, to say that the BBC was 'dropping the matter'

"There is no doubt therefore that World Distributers must be told that the right of Haisman and Lincoln have been infringed by the publication of The

270

Quarks of which they are part owners and The Yetis of which they are to and intents and purposes complete owners…bearing in mind that the owners claim to own much more of The Quarks than is conceded by the BBC."
- RG Walford, Head of Copyright, to CR Leegood, Publications, 7 November 1968

"TV Comic" Style

"I have now received the scripts and proofs…The producer makes the point that they are strictly "tv comic" style stories and good of their kind but without much connection with the programme apart from the names of the Doctor and his companions.

The particular comments on each script are as follows:

'Dwellers beyond Time': quite wrong for children's annual; a vast amount of metaphysical speculation and almost no physical action; most children would find it boring and incomprehensible. There is a reference to Jamie's 'record player'.

This story also features Victoria as does '1001 Doors'. Would it not be better to use Zoe throughout?

Jamie is strictly non-technical but 'Run the Gauntlet' has Jamie operating the Tardis unaided and 'Grip of Ice' has him operating a space ship.

The producer also felt it a pity that the links between this material and the programme were not stronger."
- From Printed Publicity Editor to Assistant to General Manager, Publications, 29 November 1968

Entirely Wrong

"Mrs Broadley telephoned in response contained in my letter…

1. "Dwellers Beyond Time". Like us, she felt that this story was entirely wrong for the Annual and will not include it.
2. Victoria has been dropped and Zoe is now used throughout.
3. The non-technical Jamie has been dealt with by a small amount of re-writing."
- Record of Telephone Conversation, CP Leegood, Publications, 6 December 1968

A Replacement Story

"I am enclosing a substitute story for the <u>Dr Who Annual</u>, entitled 'The Mystery of the Marie Celeste'. At a glance I would say this is more action-packed and suitable for children."

- Mrs M Broadley, Children's Book Editor, to CR Leegood, Asst to General Manager, Publications, 9 December 1968

1969

Grim Fate

"We have no objection to the story ['The Mystery of the *Marie Celeste*'] but one comment made by the producer of the programme is that he finds the fate of the crew rather grim and wonders whether the ending could be made a little happier.'

- CR Leegood to Mrs Mae Broadley, 9 January 1969

A New Doctor

"We feel that the publishers should be clearly told that Patrick Troughton will not be the Dr. Who at the time the Annual is on sale.

"The new Dr. Who has not yet been cast and it may be a considerable time before this happens."

- Ayton Whitaker, Drama Groups Organiser, to Printed Publicity Editor, 20 January 1969

Unlicensed Cybermen?

"I have in front of me a copy of the DR. WHO annual, and note that the Cyberman is given prominent coverage on the front, back and elsewhere in the volume...

"As you will know, Dr. Kit Pedler, my client, is the creator of this character, and I Should be grateful if you could let me know what proceeds might be expected from this sale, and at the same indicate which part of the agreement between the Corporation and Dr. Pedler constitutes the basis for your giving permission to include the image in the volume."

- Harvey Unna Ltd, Authors Agents, to CR Leegood, 7 February 1969

Which Doctor?

"This letter is to confirm that Mr. M Anglo called on me last week and showed me some of the artwork for the <u>Dr. Who Annual</u>. Although it was not complete it seemed to be perfectly acceptable. I did, however, point out that Mr. Patrick Troughton will no longer be playing Dr. Who when the series returns to the screen towards the end of the year."

> \- Evelyn M Thomas, Printed Publicity Editor, to Mr Johnson, 11 February 1969

In neither look nor dress...

"As long as the publishers are aware...that by the time this book comes out, Patrick Troughton will no longer be in the programme nor necessarily will the new Doctor Who either look like him or be dressed like him."

> \- Peter Bryant to CR Leegood, 14 February 1969

Coming back?

"As you know the present series will end this month. The programme will return to the screen in January, 1970, in colour, and that series of broadcasts will run for twenty-five weeks with one four-part programme followed by three seven-part programmes. As far as we know there will be a further series in the autumn of 1970, though this not yet definite."

> \- CR Leegood to Stafford Permberton, 16 June 1969

The New Doctor

"Enclosed are four photographs of Jon Pertwee and three of Caroline John, his new assistant.

"Also enclosed are four rehearsal scripts covering the first, 'Spearhead from Space', four part serial and seven scripts, "The Silurians", covering the second series of new programmes...

"You will find in the scripts that a special group called UNIT is involved. The format and characters in UNIT are completely owned by the Corporation, and you may use them in the Annual if you wish to do so"

> \- CR Leegood to Stafford Pemberton, 8 October 1969

Trouble

"Every year we seem to get into some sort of trouble about the monster characters that we are, and we are not, allowed to include in the annual and I would appreciate it if you would let have a list of those monsters that are BBC copyright and are available for use."

- Stafford Pemberton to CR Leegood, 20 October 1969

Likenesses, always likenesses

"Mr S Pemberton asked whether I thought it would be in order for them to refer in the text to Dr. Who's Assistant (Caroline John) but to use artists work in portraying her, which would not be recognisable as Caroline John. This thought has been prompted by the need to keep down fees as much as possible."

- Record of Telephone Conversation, CR Leegood and Stafford Pemberton, 27 October 1969

1970

The Doctor's no racist

"'The Cosmic Tug of War' story has arrived on my desk... The Doctor would not say anything as racialist as 'Up the Earth. Down with all Aliens!'"

- Terrance Dicks to General Manager, Publications, 13 January 1970

Dr. Who Annual

"We have, unfortunately, decided that we do not with to proceed with the publication of this annual in 1971 as the sales that we have made this year would not warrant a new edition.

"We would, however, like to produce a further edition of the Crackerjack annual..."

- Stafford Pemberton to Charles Leegood, 21 September 1970

274

Unlicensed Pertwee

"Tony Hayes of Richard Stone, Jon Pertwee's agent, telephoned me yesterday to say that Jon Pertwee has been featured in the "Dr Who Annual" without permission.

"On looking through our papers, I see that I gave you the name of Pertwee's agent on 10th July last in connection with the use of Pertwee's likeness and emphasised the same point in my letter of 8th October last."

- CR Leegood to Stafford Pemberton, 9 December 1970

1971

An assistant named Joe

"The January to June 1972 series will be broadcast weekly on Saturdays at 6.20 p.m. Jon Pertwee will continue to play Dr. Who with Katy Manning as Joe Grant."

- Charles Leegood to Stafford Pemberton, 10 September 1971

The Most Gentle of Reminders

"As requested, I enclose a selection – seven – of transparencies of Dr. Who and his Assistant so that you may select one for use on the cover. These have been obtained from our Photograph Library, who have asked me to quote you £10.50 each for use on the cover of the Annual and to remind you that in addition to this reproduction fee it will, of course, be necessary for you to clear the use of their likenesses with Jon Pertwee and Katy Manning"

- Charles Leegood to Stafford Pemberton, 11 October 1971

Series January/June 1972

"1st 4 programmes – location – on Earth – title "Return of the Daleks"; introduces new monsters – Ogrens [sic]; anthropoid creatures; includes UNIT. Next 4 programmes – location – on another planet – title "The Curse of Peladon". Revival of the Ice Warriors. Introduces two new monsters – Arcturus; has to live in a tank (? of water) and Alpha Sentori [sic]; like a Henry Moore sculpture – a one-eyed head without ears.

Next 6 programmes – location – on Earth – title "The Sea Devils"; 'cousins' of The Silurians; reptilian, but different, come from the bottom of the sea; includes The Master,

Next 6 programmes – location – on another planet – working title "The Emergents" – race of humanoid beings who change appearance.

Next 6 programmes – scripts not yet written – working title "The Time Monster". Programmes will probably include UNIT and The Master."

- *Undated, unsigned memo*

"Further to my memo of 7th September last, World Distributors have now proposed that in addition to the publication of a Dr. who Annual in September, 1972, publication of another Dr. Who book in early (probably January) 1972 which would contain 64 pages of material selected from the Dr. Who Annual which they published in 1970 (96 pages plus cover – copy enclosed? which please return). The initial printing of the book would be 20,000 copies and would sell at a retail price of 20p through Woolworths or other chain stores.

- Charles Leegood to General Manager, Publications, 13 October 1971

Not a lot of money

"I wrote to Jon's agents on the I3th October explaining that the artist felt a new agreement could be sought, incorporating a percentage in this new book which hardly appeared an extravagant request based on the apparent sales of the earlier volume. In subsequent exchanges between Richard Stones and World Distributors, the latter were generous enough to increase the actual payment to Jon from £52 to £70, but insisted they did not provide percentages to artists. Knowing these are granted, I made direct contact with world Distributors who agreed such participations were negotiated with some artists.

"It is very simple – whoever is the relevant party, all we seek for Mr. Pertwee is some financial involvement in the books returns. I know this seems a lot of confusion for ultimately small money in comparison to Mr. Pertwee's actual income, out such a percentage would act as a splendid incentive for him to promote the book."

- John Stanley, Pertwee's PRO to Charles Leegood, Stafford Pemberton and Tony Hayes of Richard Stone, Pertwee's agents, 17 November 1971

Likenesses

"As spoken on the telephone my reactions concern the likenesses shown in the attached art work.

"Of the four individuals shown there is one acceptable likeness to Pertwee on what would seem to be the back cover. I think it important that any representation shown should relate to regular characters.

"I would suggest that the likeness of Katie [sic] Manning, Dr.Who's female colleague, needs considerable improvement."
- Ronald Marsh to Charles Leegood, 23 November 1971

"Katie [sic] Manning does not want to be represented in the Annual and the front cover will be altered accordingly."
- SJT, 8 December 1971

1972

Earthling?

"I enclose galley proofs of seven stories intended for inclusion in the above Annual, which have been submitted by World Distributors for approval."
– Charles Leegood to Terrance Dicks and Barry Letts, 20 January 1972

"Okay by me except a couple of references in the story 'Galactic Gangster', pages 5 & 7, suggest that the Doctor is human."
- Reply from Terrance Dicks.

"Also on P.8 of 'Old Father Saturn', the phraseology suggests that the Doctor is from Earth."
- Reply from Barry Letts

The Nose Shot

"'Thank you for your memo 1st March enclosing photostats of the proposed artwork for the Annual for World Distributors. This seems of a much higher standard than previously and with the exception of the artwork for pages 2 and 3 is quite acceptable.

"The Producer of the programme informs me that the "nose" shot is anathema to Jon Pertwee. This photograph was taken at our very first photo-call and Pictorial Publicity were requested to withdraw it. It would seem as though it has somehow "escaped" the net, but we are most anxious to avoid a rift with Jon Pertwee over this matter.

"Please convey our apologies to World Distributors but we must request that they do not use this particular piece of artwork."
- Ronald Marsh, Head of Serials, to Assistant to General Manager, Publications, 6 March 1972

"Having said that the previous artwork was good, showing very reasonable likenesses of Jon Pertwee, I was sorry to see that the likenesses were rather less good in this new batch of drawings.

"The "nose" shot of Jon Pertwee appears again in illustration number 23, backing the title "WAR IN THE ABYSS", This is such a sensitive point and the cause of continuing debate between ourselves and Pertwee, I regret I must ask you to request the publishers to change this illustration."
- Ronald Marsh, to Assistant to General Manager, Publications, 17 March 1972

Story Plans

"MOST IMPORTANT
Please note that these represent our plans at the moment We are not committed to them and must be able to feel free to change them if we want to.

Doctor Who QQQ 'Frontier in Space'
The Doctor and Jo are involved in the beginnings of a 25th Century Space War between the Empires of Earth and ~~Andromeda~~ Draconia. The ~~Andromedans~~ Draconians are humanoid but alien in feature.

This story is being deliberately planned to use as many of the space-ships and space-exploration vehicles in the 'Thunderbird' store as possible. So there will be quite a lot of model filming.

In addition to the obvious things such as rayguns, we have the Ogrons returning, and the odd Dalek. There will be one strange non-humanoid monster whose form has not yet been decided.

Doctor Who RRR
A story set on the Time-Lords' planet. A science-fantasy with a feeling of great strangeness. It is to be written by the authors of 'Claws of Axos ' and 'The

278

Mutants', so the story will probably make considerable demands on our creativity.

Doctor Who SSS 'Return of the Destination Daleks'
This takes place on a bleak alien planet. Though we probably will make do with our three proper Daleks, a number of smaller or full-sise non-practical models will probably be required. There will probably be strange aliens and/or monsters (SPIRIDONS) in addition to the Daleks.

Doctor Who TTT 'The Amoeboids' Giant Maggots in a Coal Mine
A present day UNIT story. Strange creatures, giant flying macrophages, arrive on earth and start swallowing up people and things. These are space scavengers, come, to clean up poor old polluted earth.

As they are flying monsters (presumably models on film, plus full size giant jelly fish creatures) we hope to co-operate with the RAF and use gyrocopters and a balloon in addition.
I expect that we shall need model shots of the creatures devouring chunks of London etc (cf. Kitten Kong!). Explosions are no doubt to be expected.

There will probably be a strange extra-galactic super-being who has sent the creatures in the first place not necessarily humanoid."
- Barry Letts, 'STORY INTENTIONS FOR THE FUTURE' memo to World Distributors, 13 April 1972

1%

"The short, formal letter which we spoke of upon the telephone this week. It merely serves to confirm that my client – Jon Pertwee is delighted to he involved in a further annual featuring his likeness in the same manner as that within the 1972 addition.

This means a fee due to Mr Pertwee of £100 and additionally a royalty of 1% of the 1973 Annual, over and above 20,000.

It is indeed satisfying that so many copies have so far been sold of the present edition."
- John Stanley, PPO to Mr Pertwee, to Stafford Pemberton, 1 September 1972

Why can't we use the Daleks?

"I do not know why you have not previously been permitted to use the Daleks and can only suggest you make a further approach to Terry Nation."
- Charles Leegood to Mrs Mae Broadley, 12 September 1972

"Further to your memo of the 13th September my Producer and Script Editor have now examined the stories you sent us for comment destined for inclusion in the above [1974] annual. Minor errors and relationships within the text have been corrected.

"I am informed that these stories contain echoes of the television stories: e.g. "The Fathom Trap" has 'sea-dwellers' reminiscent of our 'sea-devils' and "Talons of Terror" has visitors from the future similar to the daleks. My only point in mentioning this is for any possible copyright implications but our opinion is that this has probably not actually been infringed.

"The first story of this group "The Voodoo Doll" is considered to be unpleasant and frightening with little real science fiction interest except for the fact that the villain, on flimsy evidence, is presumed to be an alien. In this connection I think I should point out that considerable protest was aroused by our use of a killer doll in our television story entitled "Terror of the Autons". It is the Producer's opinion which I support that this story should not be included in the annual"
- Ronald Marsh, Head of Serials, Drama & Television to Secretary to Publicity Services Manager, 21 September 1972

Replacement Story

"I enclose one story "The Time Snatch" which World Distributors have submitted for approval to replace the "Voodoo" story on which we commented adversely.

May I please have your approval of the new story or comments on it as soon as conveniently possible."
- Charles Leegood to Terrance Dicks, 6 November 1972

"Fine by us! TWD"
- Response to Leegood from Dicks (marked on memo)

[NB. There is no story called 'The Time Snatch' in the 1974 Annual. The closest is the picture strip, 'The Time Thief', but from context these are unlikely to be the same stories. A story called 'The Time Snatch', featuring the Fourth Doctor and Sarah-Jane Smith appears in the 1977 Annual however.]

1973

"Needlessly Vicious"

"I feel that the expression on Doctor Who's face in the bottom picture of p.38 is needlessly vicious. I hope it can be changed."

- Barry Letts, note on memo from Charles Leegood, 26 January 1973

Likenesses, again!

"The one comment, from the programme side, is that the likenesses are not as good as some that have been seen for the same Annual. Would you please improve if there is time to do so."

- Charles Leegood to W.G Robinson, 16 February 1973

A Sketch Block

"As promised on the telephone I am just confirming my discussion with you, whereby an associate company of ours, Sandle Brothers, would like to proceed with the publication of a sketch pad (I am sending under separate cover a similar sort of product) based on DOCTOR WHO.

"The first print should be 50,000 and the retail selling price will be 15p per copy. We would be prepared to pay you a royalty of 5% on the retail selling price with an advance guarantee of £200, payable 50% on signature of the contract and 50% on publication."

- Stafford Pemberton to Charles Leegood, 15 August 1973

-

"Further to your letter of 15th August and our interim reply of 23rd August, we now have the views of colleagues about the proposed Dr. Who Sketch Block.

"Before further considering the proposal we wish to have some more information. We assume that the Sketch Block would include drawings of the Tardis and characters appearing in the series; please confirm. It is important that the quality of the representations – the drawings themselves – should be of a high standard."

- Charles Leegood to Stafford Pemberton, 14 September 1973

"I am afraid that our colleagues at Sandle Brothers have gone a little cool on the idea of a Dr. Who Sketch Block since I last wrote to you, but obviously I will keep you informed as to whether or not they may decide to go ahead.

"For the record the Sketch Block would, of course, include drawings of Dr. Who plus the Monster in the same way as our own Colouring Book did and they seemed to be satisfactory as far as the standard was concerned, so I don't think there will be any problem with this product."
- Stafford Pemberton to Charles Leegood, 24 September 1973

The 1975 Annual

"These stories are basically okay by us...

"There are several grammatical and stylistic errors, the more obvious of which I have marked in the text.

One story in particular, 'The Coloured Snails', contains several passages which I would consider far too gruesome for children.

"As the stories are described as 'unedited' perhaps the publishers could take care that these points are attended to in the editing."
- Terrance Dicks, memo re the 1975 Annual, 19 November 1973

"We are not now using the story 'The Coloured Snails' in the next edition of the Dr Who Annual; I completely agree that it is too gruesome for children. I must also say that the comments on the text – particularly one of the stories – were completely fair. While waiting for approval, however, I did edit the stories and I am confident you would have no misgivings about the finished results. In future years I think I will edit the text before sending it to you. My reason for sending the unedited text was purely for speed."
- Mrs Mae Broadley, to Charles Leegood, 26 November 1973

1974

Sarah or Jo?

"As I mentioned to you on the telephone, the Programme people are very concerned that throughout much of the artwork, in words as well as pictures, Dr. Who's Assistant is Jo Grant rather than Sarah Jane Smith. As Jo Grant was written out of the series a whole season ago, by the time the book is published she will have left the programme for 15 months."

<blockquote>- Charles Leegood to Mrs Mae Broadley, 25 February 1974</blockquote>

"I am replying to your letter of the 25th February addressed to Mrs Broadley concerning the above.

"I must first of all say that the text was sent for approval to you on the 17th October and all the stories were approved on the 21st November.

"This text included stories written around the characters of both Jo Grant and Sarah Jane Smith, which was the brief we received at the time we were creating the stories.

"On approval of the text the artwork was started and of course, as you know, we have no agreement with the individual actors (because they do not wish it) to draw the specific likeness of the characters, although the artwork may tend to look similar, ie in hairstyle or type of dress, to the character portrayed.

"You can appreciate that it would take a great deal of work to alter the text stories and artwork, and considering the fact that the text stories were approved as early as the 21st November, you on your part did have ample opportunity to make your feelings known before the artwork was started."

<blockquote>- Stafford Pemberton to Charles Leegood, 5 March 1974</blockquote>

Background Notes on Tom

"The Doctor played by Tom Baker is by turns irascible, childish and charming. Hs has a keen sense of humour but his companions don't always share the merriment. Be can be infuriatingly secretive.

He is 748 years old and dresses like the cosmic hoboe he is. Bernard Shaw, Professor Challenger and Sherlock Holmes seem to flicker under the face.... and a mad, mischievous Harpo Marx beams through the face from time to time.

It is a strongly idiosyncratic, chameleon-like characterisation, difficult to summarise.

Currently the Doctor's companion is a young London journalist named Sarah Jane Smith (played by Elisabeth Sladen). She is a level-headed girl with a will of her own and a temperament that enjoys danger. Although slightly built she is physically quite tough. Sarah is an ardent feminist and her views might be expected to conflict occasionally with those of Surgeon Lieutenant Harry Sullivan, K.N., the Doctor's other earth companion

Harry is clean-cut, clean-limbed, right-minded young fellow who can always be relied upon to do the decent thing. He was brought up in India and is just a touch old-fashioned in his ideas.

The Doctor has a great liking for the ingenuous Harry but can't resist the pleasure of gently sending him up every now and again. Harry is played by Ian Marter.

Semi-regulars in the serial are Brigadier Alistair Lethbridge-Stewart (Nicholas Courtney) and Warrant Office Benton (John Levene). They appear in earth stories set in contemporary times. The Brigadier head[s] the British section of UNIT. This is a semi-military outfit formed to investigate sci-fi phenomena. The Brigadier places great faith in bombs and bayonets as a way of dealing with alien threats. Harry is on attachment to UNIT as a medical officer and the Doctor officially holds the position of scientific adviser. When not travelling, he keeps the TARDIS in his laboratory at UNIT's London HQ."

> \- Memo from Philip Hinchcliffe for World Distributors, 23 September 1974

What's in a name? (again!)

"No comment on the literary quality. I can see nothing in these stories which conflicts with the Doctor's established moral code or modus operandi.

However, the writer of the stories obviously knows more about our show than the person who subbed them. I have reiterated, until I'm sick of iterating, that "DOCTOR WHO" is the name of the programme and not the name of its central character.

I think this error was originally perpetrated by our script typists and has been perpetuated by subsequent generations of typists.

Today, I am sorry to say, it has even crept into the end titles but he has never been verbally addressed as 'Who' on the screen."

> \- Robert Holmes to Charles Leegood, 20 December 1974

Competition to World Distributors

"Doctor Who/Top of the Pops

I thought you may he interested to know that we have received offers for the annuals to be published in 1976 in connection with the above titles. As they have been with your company for some tine I felt it only fair to lot you know of this fresh approach.

What I would like to know as soon as possible are the terms you would be prepared to offer for an extension of this years' agreement."

- John Hore, Assistant to the General Mgr, Publications to Alan Fennell, World Distributors, 23 May 1975

A Dutch Annual

"Further to my negotiations with Mr Hans Kalshoven of Mulder and Zoon in Holland, I have indicated to him that we require a royalty of $7\frac{1}{2}\%$ based on a minimum run of 20,000 copies, for which he intends to charge a retail price of 6.95 Guilders. At the moment this works out at around £1 .25."

- Alan Fennell to John Hore, 11 September 1975

1976

Typhoo

"Following your telephone conversation and this letter I have received from Mr Twittey I have pleasure in enclosing a complete specification for the AMAZING WORLD OF DR WHO Book we are preparing for the Typhoo Tea promotion.

"Fifteen thousand units will be ordered on a firm basis by Sales Promotion Triangle and World Distributors will produce a further 10,000 units which will be held in stock in readiness for call off purposes."

- Alan Fennell to RG Hyslop, Sales Promotion Triangle, 30 January 1976

Willy Nilly

"All in all I think this artwork is excellent. The likeness of the Doctor has been captured extremely well. All the more a pity, therefore, that there are some pages markedly inferior where the drawings resemble neither the Doctor nor Sarah nor Harry. I notice this particularly on pages: 9, 15, 27, 34, 37, 40, 47, and 64. Is there any way we can ask for an improvement at this late stage? After all, the public wiilynilly associates this annual with our BBC series"

- Phillip Hinchcliffe to John Hore, 19 February 1976

Oh, God!

"Fans of the programme will remember a character called Salamander from the days of Patrick Troughton, and so it would be a good idea to change the name in the first story.

"I find "Terror on Tantalogus" a bit macabre and don't think even we would include the scene with the severed heads.

"In this same story, Sarah says, 'Oh, my God.' It happens to be our policy not to use this expression in the television programme. I suggest, 'It's horrible,' sobbed Sarah."

- Philip Hinchcliffe, memo to John Horn, I July 1976

1977

Swappable Companions

"For the other two stories in the annual, we are using two which are surplus from last year. We have been through these to change any references to Sarah Jane Smith."

- Glynis Langley, Editorial Assistant (World Distributers) to John Hore, 22 September 1977

Faint Praise

"[These stories] do not of course have anything to do with "Doctor Who" as we know it, but they do not contain anything actually detrimental to the programme."

- Graeme McDonald, Head of Serials, Drama, Television to BBC Head of Exports, Permissions & Rights, 3 October 1977

286

A Happy Doctor

"I think this artwork would, be greatly improved if the artist could portray Torn Baker (the Doctor) smiling a bit more.

[handwritten] P.S He is, after all, a happy Doctor!"
- Graham Williams, to BBC Head of Exports, Permissions & Rights, 6 October 1977

Ruinous Artwork

"Thank you for your letter of 10 October returning our xerox of the cover artwork for the Dr Who Annual 1979. In fact this cover was drawn – and I do assure you, and I am sure you will agree, that it really is a fantastic likeness to Tom Baker – from one of the transparencies we obtained from the BBC Library. The xerox copy does not do full justice to the colour artwork which in this case is really quite fantastic.

"Our Studio Manager, Ron Smethurst, feels that the shot has a lot more character – and therefore more sales impact – than would a smiling 'holiday-type' picture. We really do hope you will approve the cover on these grounds as we very strongly feel that a change in this case would be ruinous."
- Mrs Mae Broadley to John Hore, 13 October 1977

1978

Complaint and Response

"My son received a 'Dr Who Annual 1976' in that year, which was published by World Distributors (Manchester) Ltd and copyrighted by the BBC 1975. Las[t] week, I purchased a book called 'The Amazing World of Dr Who' published by PBS Ltd of Manchester and copyrighted by the BBS in 1976. My complaint and indeed, that of my son, is that four stories which appear in the first book also appear in the second, exact, even down to the illustrations! We both feel the BBC, when selling its copyrights, should ensure they are not repeated so quickly. After all, two books from different publishers practically in the same year and containing identical stories is hardly fair"
- Complaint letter addressed to Mr W McKenna, Chairman of the BBC North-East Advisory Council, 9 January 1978

"Your letter of 9 January, addressed to Mr W McKenna of the BBC, has been passed to me for attention.

"This book was produced at a low cover price, and this price could only be achieved by the re-use of some previously published material, thus cutting down the cost of artwork and reproduction.

"Normally we do not re-use material within a three-year span but in this case there was some difficulty in obtaining some of the later material back from our printers. "

- Reply from Mrs Mae Broadley, 31 January 1978

Beautifully Sexy!

"In confirmation with my telephone call I can find no fault with the art work which I return to you. I should be grateful, however, if in considering the lady who appears on P.3, you would bear in mind that the album and the programme carefully avoid images of such a beautifully sexy nature. Whilst I personally find the picture most attractive, I suggest that it be toned down to preserve the tone of the programme."

- Graham Williams to Head, Permissions and Rights, 21 February 1978

Remember that complaint?

"Just to confirm our conversation, regarding 'The Enemies of Doctor Who'.

"Roger Lewis would be interested in publishing an Annual on this theme, perhaps incorporating material used in the PBS imprint, produced for the Brooke Bond Oxo premium a years ago.

"I believe there was some doubt regarding the material in that book. Did you not receive a complaint that some of the material had appeared in an earlier annual?"

- Christopher Crouch to John Hore, 6 July 1978

Anything but the Time Cube!

"There is just one more point about which we are not quite clear. As the purpose of Romana is to help Dr Who locate the segments of the time cube, do you wish us to mention the cube in our stories? Obviously we cannot have any segments found in our stories as this would conflict with the series. Or would you prefer us to make no mention of the time cube?"

- Glynis Langley to John Hore, 31 July 1978

288

"The question as to the revealing of the Cube of Time depends very largely upon the intended publication date of the Annual"
- Graham Williams to John Hore, 4 August 1978

Ugly Time Lady

"The artwork is hardly representative of 'Romana', whom we have taken such pains to show as an attractive lady."
- Graham Williams, to Head of Serials, 14 September 1978

Too much violence

"The X-Rani story – apart from being generally tasteless and gratuitously nasty, ends with the Doctor deliberately killing X-Rani with a 'hand-laser1' gun. I suppose it's all right, but it bothered me slightly.

"'Reluctant Warriors' is more worrying, since it involves the Doctor and Romana fighting each other, and neither has any positive role to play in solving the story."
- Graham Williams to Head of Exports, Permissions & Rights, 28 September 1978

The Doctor Who Press Out Book

"They seem to have great difficulty with Tom's nose!"
- Anthony Read to Head of Exports, Permissions & Rights, 3 October 1978

1979

Lovely Lalla

"Thank you for your memo re the Doctor Who Annual – I agree with you that the exact likeness of the assistant is to everyone's advantage and I suggest that you contact the incumbent assistant's agent Robin Dalton. I am sure you will find that Lalla Ward, who plays the part of the Doctor's assistant Romana will be amenable and co-operative."
- Graham Williams to Head of Exports, Permissions & Rights, 16 July 1979

1980

Leela or a round faced 16 year old?

"Thank you for the artwork of the 'Doctor Who Annual 1981. On the whole much of this artwork is first-class. There are excellent likenesses of Tom Baker and K9. However Romana's likeness is frankly appalling.

"In some pictures she resembles Leela (Louise Jameson) and in others she looks like a round-faced 16 year old. I am sure something could be done to improve this. I have marked the objectionable likenesses with a red cross and enclose a photograph of Romana (Lalla Ward) so that you can appreciate the problem"

- John Nathan-Turner to John Hore, 11 March 1980

"I am glad the illustrations were so acceptable to everyone this year. As I explained to you on the 'phone, we are not allowed to draw an exact likeness of Romana."

- Mrs Mae Broadley to John Hore, 20 March 1980

Appendix 4: Annual Sales

1965

"John [Permberton] believes he will sell around 70,000 books"
-     Letter of 26 February 1965

1966

Royalty Statement (to 31.12.65)	
Title:	Dr Who Annual
Retail Price	10/6d
Printed run	207,160
Less review, advertising & soiled	2, 072
Sales	**200, 659**

1967

Royalty Statement (to 31.12.66)	
Title:	Dr Who Annual 2
Retail Price:	10/6d
Printed copies	78,524
Less review, advertising & soiled	785
Sales	**64, 992**

1968

Royalty Statement (to 31.12.67)	
Title	Dr Who Annual 3
Retail Price	10/6d
Printed copies	30,200
Less review, advertising & soiled	302
Sales	**22,387**

1969

Royalty Statement (to 31.12.68)	
Title	Dr Who Annual 4
Retail Price	12/6d
Printed copies	24,300
Less review, advertising & soiled	243
Sales	**22,907**

1970

Royalty Statement (to 31.12.69)	
Title	Dr Who Annual 5
Retail Price	12/6d
Printed copies	24,658
Less review, advertising & soiled	247
Sales	**17,868**

1971

Royalty Statement (to 31.12.70)	
Title	Dr Who Annual 6
Retail Price	62.5p
Printed copies	19,330
Less review, advertising & soiled	280
Sales	**14,435**

1974

Royalty Statement (to 31.12.73)	
Title	Dr Who Annual 1974
Retail Price	75p
Printed copies	65,986
Less review, advertising & soiled	990
Sales	**57,995**

1975

Royalty Statement (to 31.12.74)	
Title	Dr Who Annual 1975
Retail Price	90p
Printed copies	75,270
Less review, advertising & soiled	1,129
Sales	**73,817**

1976

Royalty Statement (to 31.12.75)	
Title	Dr Who Annual 1976
Retail Price	£1.00
Printed copies	92,453
Less review, advertising & soiled	1,387
Sales	**90,540**

1977

Royalty Statement (to 31.12.76)	
Title	Dr Who Annual 1977
Retail Price	£1.25
Printed copies	109,138
Less review, advertising & soiled	1,637
Sales	**104, 998**

1978

Royalty Statement (to 31.12.77)	
Title	Dr Who Annual 1978
Retail Price	£1.35
Printed copies	129,954
Less review, advertising & soiled	1,949
Sales	**106,806**

1979

Royalty Statement (to 31.12.78)	
Title	Dr Who Annual 1979
Retail Price	£1.50
Printed copies	118,074
Less review, advertising & soiled	1,771
Sales	**105,590**

1980

Royalty Statement (to 31.12.79)	
Title	Dr Who Annual 1980
Retail Price	£1.75
Printed copies	78, 335
Less Remainder Sales	15, 921
Sales	**62, 414**

World Distributor Doctor Who non-Annual titles

- Dr Who on the Planet Zactus Painting Book (January 1966)
- Travels in Time Painting Book (January 1966)
- Travels in Time Sticker Fun Book January 1966)
- Travels in Space Painting Book (March 1966)
- Travels in Space Sticker Fun Book (March 1966)
- Puzzle Fun No. 1 (May 1966)
- Puzzle Fun No. 2 (May 1966)
- The Dr Who Colouring Book (January 1973)